Remembering

New York State

Richard O. Reisem

Trade Paper Press

Storm clouds loom ominously over Niagara Falls in 1911. Sightseeing bulwarks are visible at the American Falls at lower left, with densely vegetated Goat Island situated above, another observation point that separates the two falls. A steamboat taking visitors toward the Canadian Falls is just visible at center-right. The rising mists are formed by plunging water striking the water and rocks below at great speed and volume.

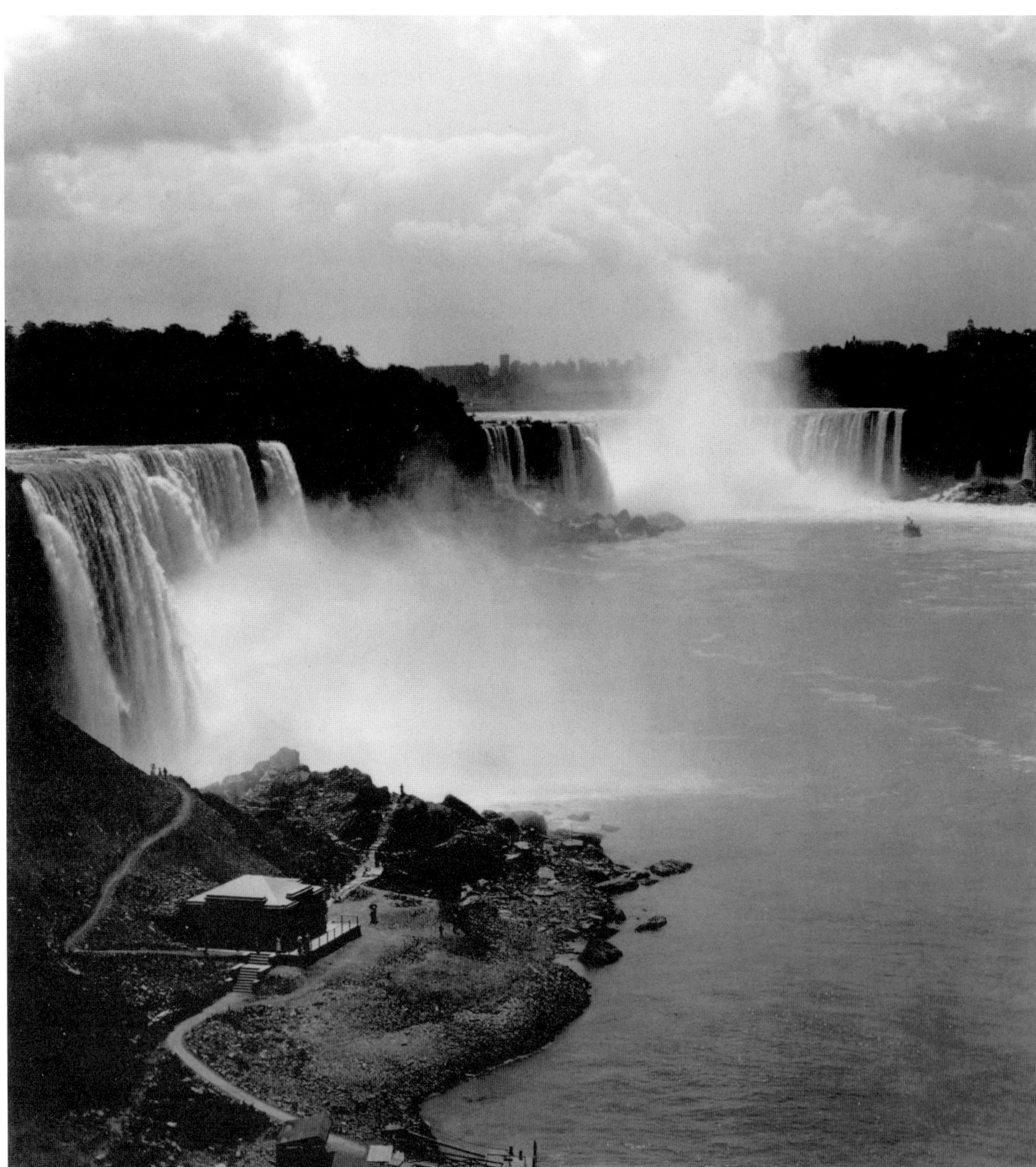

Remembering
New York State

Turner Publishing Company

445 Park Avenue, 9th Floor
New York, NY 10022
Phone: (212)710-4338 Fax: (212)710-4339

200 4th Avenue North • Suite 950
Nashville, Tennessee 37219
(615) 255-2665

Remembering New York State

www.turnerpublishing.com

Library of Congress Control Number: 2010932644

ISBN: 978-1-59652-718-8

Printed in the United States of America

10 11 12 13 14 15 16—0 9 8 7 6 5 4 3 2 1

Contents

Acknowledgments vii

Preface viii

The Empire State
(1850–1880) 1

Age of Extravagance
(1881–1916) 11

Wine, Women, Want, and War
(1917–1930) 101

Notes on the Photographs 132

Frederick Law Olmsted, Sr. (1822–1903), America's preeminent landscape architect, designed many parks and city boulevards, but his most famous is New York City's Central Park, which he created beginning in 1856. This 1904 image shows the lake, near the south end of the 843-acre reserve. To this day, it is a popular place to rent a rowboat. Olmsted's purpose in park design was to provide the illusion of wilderness and peace in the midst of an urban environment.

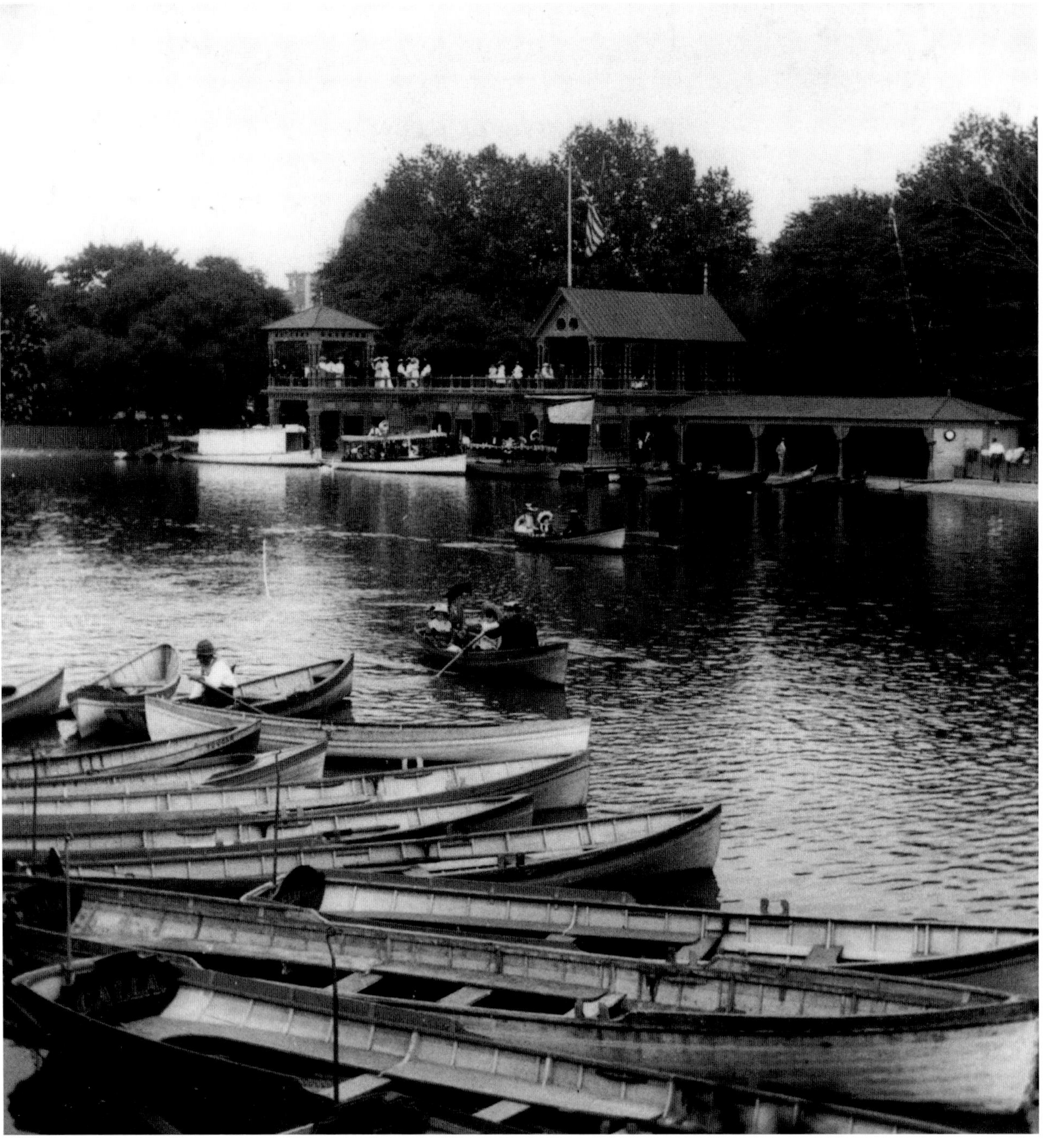

Acknowledgments

This volume, *Remembering New York State,* is the result of the cooperation and efforts of many individuals and organizations. It is with great thanks that we acknowledge the valuable contribution of the following for their generous support:

Library of Congress
National Archives and Records Administration
New York State Archives

We would also like to thank the following individuals for valuable contributions and assistance in making this work possible:

Ralph Amdursky, Tamarack, Florida
Larry Barnes, City Historian, Batavia, New York
Sam Campanaro, Rochester, New York
Susan L. Conklin, Genesee County Historian, Batavia, New York
Grace Good, Chesterfield Town Historian, Keeseville, New York
Josef Johns, Rochester, New York
Sandra Maceyka, Johnstown, New York
Randi Minetor, Rochester, New York
David Minor, Pittsford, New York

With the exception of touching up image imperfections that have accrued with the passage of time and cropping where necessary, no changes have been made. The focus and clarity of many images is limited by the technology and the ability of the photographer at the time they were recorded.

Preface

New York is unique among the thirteen American colonies for having been a colony of two European countries, namely, the Netherlands and England. From 1609 to 1664, it was a Dutch colony called New Netherland. On August 29, 1664, New Netherland became New York. The history of New York, therefore, combines those two quite different cultures, and their impact is still evident today.

In 1609, the famous explorer Henry Hudson sailed from Amsterdam on behalf of the Dutch East India Company, in search of a northwest passage to Asia, which, if found, would be of great benefit to the Dutch trading company. Hudson sailed his ship, the *Half Moon,* up the deep, broad river that would later be named for him, riding the incoming ocean tide. But the tide stopped at a point that is now called Albany. From there on northwest, the river was not navigable.

All was not lost, however. Hudson claimed the river and the surrounding territory for the Netherlands, which set up a manorial system of colonization in America. This system established patroonships, which were giant private estates owned and managed by patroons. One of the first patroonships was that of Kiliaen Van Rensselaer, which covered a staggering more than one million acres. All of the farms, villages, and hamlets that formed in that enormous acreage reported to Van Rensselaer.

By the early 1660s, English colonies in America were seeking to expand their territories, and England's king, Charles II, gave his brother, James, the Duke of York and Albany, a grant to an area that included a good portion of New Netherland. The duke formed an invasion fleet, and the Dutch, with totally inadequate armed forces, surrendered at New Amsterdam. The duke renamed the city, New York.

Dutch ways, however, persisted after the English takeover. Today, Albany, the capital of New York State, still displays more historic Dutch architecture than anywhere else in the country. Dutch words have contributed to American English, including Santa Claus, sleigh, cookie, cole slaw, waffle, poppycock, dumb (for stupid), and many more. Place names to this day also preserve their Dutch originals, like Catskill, Rensselaer, Amsterdam, Rotterdam, and Staatsburg.

Although the Dutch extended their influence to the west along the Mohawk River, the English regarded western expansion seriously. France, with a colony in Canada, looked equally seriously at expansion into New York. A series of wars with the French resulted in a firm British hold of the area now defined as New York State. After the Revolutionary War, a number of people in the new state of New York began to think about increased settlement of New York's heartland with its rich natural resources. The largest obstacles were the coastal mountain ranges and the dense forests beyond, which made travel to the interior difficult.

New York Governor DeWitt Clinton and others proposed a canal through the only relatively easy passageway, the Mohawk River Valley. The river itself was, for the most part, not navigable, but a canal with locks to overcome the changing elevation of the landscape could provide a smooth water highway across the entire state to Lake Erie. The idea of the Erie Canal was born. Without a penny of support from the federal government, which scoffed at the plan, it became totally a state project. No other government project, state or federal, had a more profound influence on our country.

The Erie Canal, built between 1817 and 1825, focused economic growth in New York State rather than in Canada, which bordered the navigable St. Lawrence River and Lake Ontario. The canal overcame prodigious obstacles to become a masterpiece of construction. It created the science of engineering in the U.S., which led to New York's predominance in the Industrial Revolution. And it transformed New York from a wilderness into the agricultural, industrial, commercial, and financial center of the country in the nineteenth century.

The enormous success of the Erie Canal led to the construction of a number of lateral canals—six of them in the first decade after the completion of the Erie and another four soon after. The Champlain and Oswego canals ran northward, and the others ran to the south, connecting vast parts of New York to the Erie Canal. By 1877, the New York canal system, which was the largest in the world, had an impressive 907 miles of canals with 565 locks.

The first U.S. president from New York State was Martin Van Buren. He became the eighth president and served from 1837 through 1841.

By 1850, where this book begins, photography existed, but it was practiced by the very few who learned its complex and cumbersome procedures. Early photographs in this book are daguerreotypes and wet glass-plates created by skilled craftsmen. Then in 1880, George Eastman in Rochester, New York, invented roll film, sheet film, and simple cameras. It is these photographs, made almost exclusively on Kodak film, that fill the following pages. The pictures are presented in chronological order of their being made, even though photos may contain subject material from an earlier time. Our text history of New York State also continues in the chapter introductions and photo captions. It is, as we hope you will find, a fascinating story.

—Richard O. Reisem

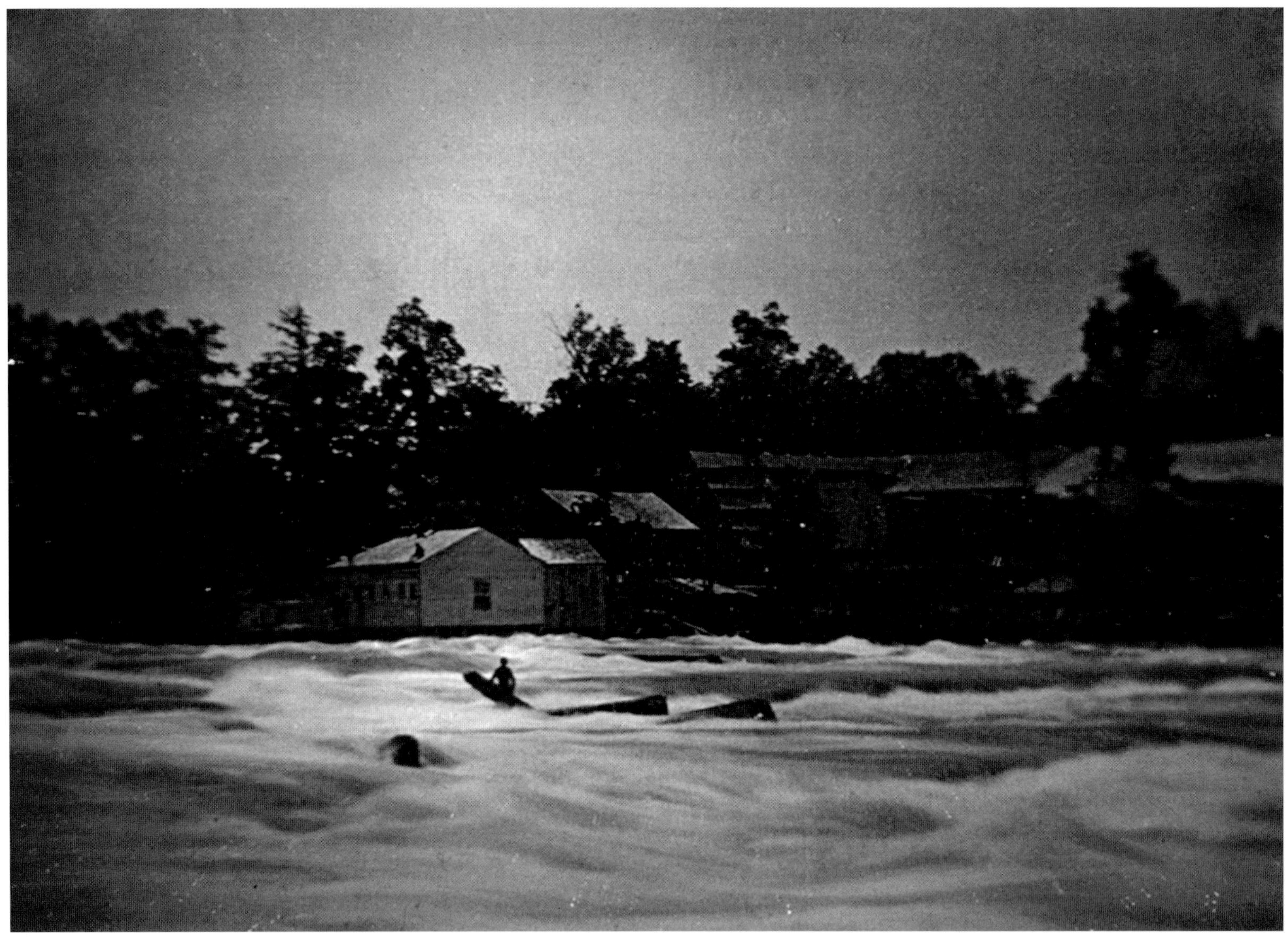

The Niagara River empties water from Lake Erie, moving it over the great falls to Lake Ontario on its way to the Atlantic Ocean. Three men in a boat ventured too close to Niagara Falls, losing control in the 25 m.p.h. current, and crashed into a rock. Two were thrown from the boat and carried over the falls to their deaths. In this 1800s daguerreotype, Joseph Avery managed for 18 horrible hours to cling to a jammed log before losing his grip and being swept over the brink. Today, accidents and suicides average one to two a week during summer months.

The Empire State

(1850–1880)

In 1839, the French painter Louis Daguerre invented the daguerreotype, a silvered copper plate that recorded an image in a camera. Portraits could be made provided the subject could sit still for several seconds. Fredricks' Photographic Temple of Art in New York City offered such a service around 1850 when this daguerreotype was made. In 1851, an Englishman invented the wet-plate process, and in 1884, George Eastman in Rochester invented roll film. Eastman's breakthrough made the story of photography a New York State story from then on.

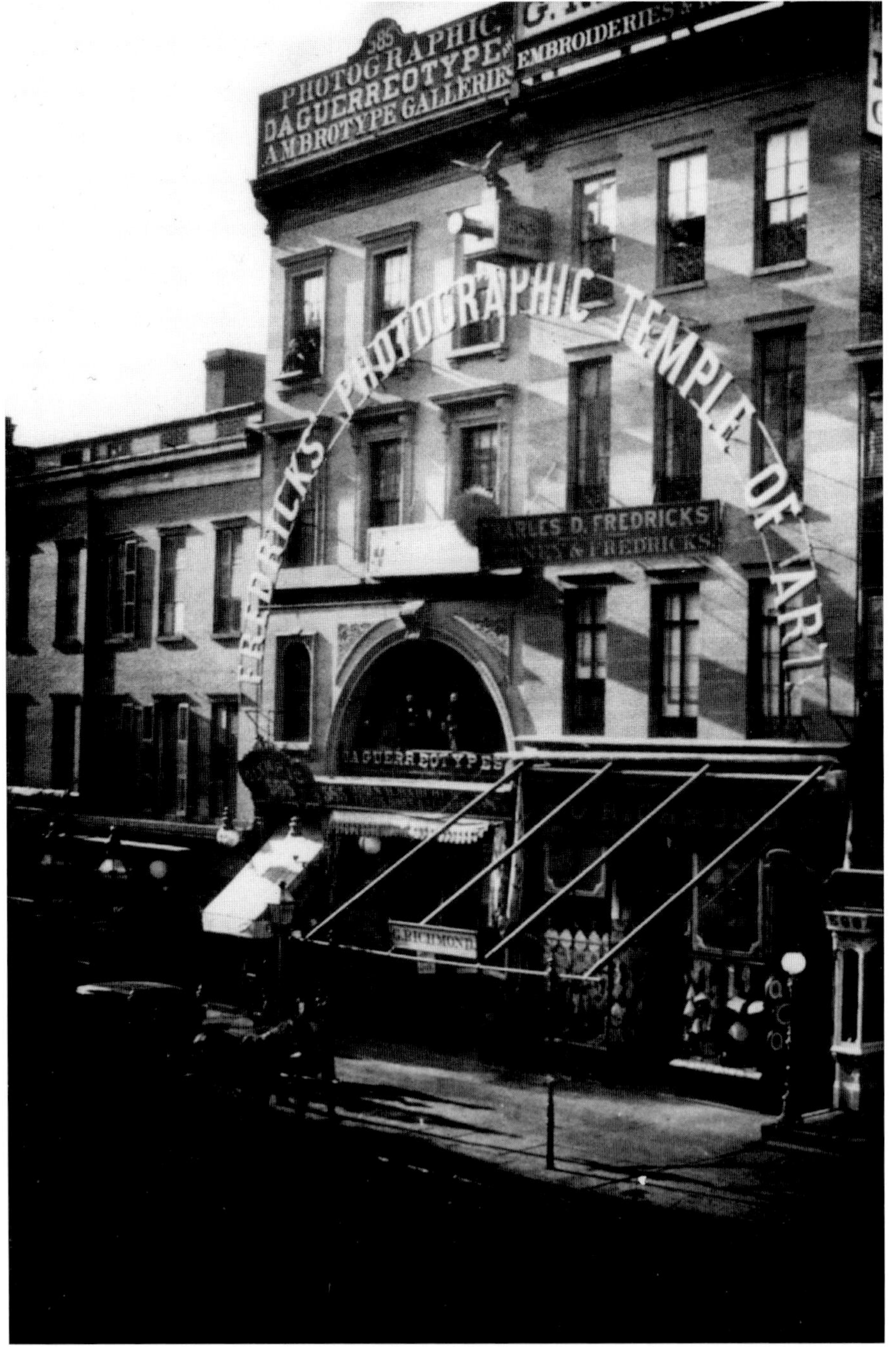

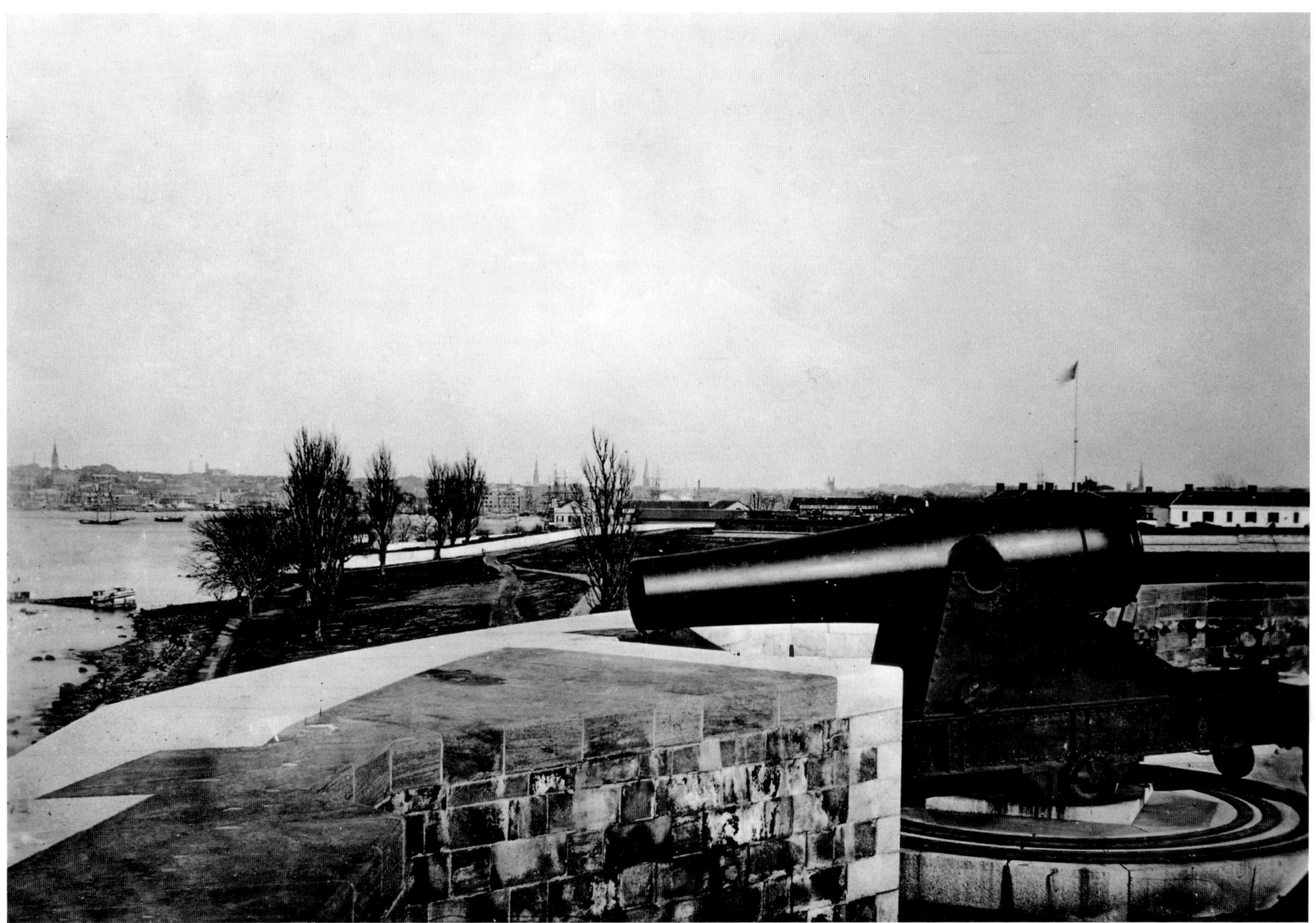

In New York's colonial days, Governors Island, off the tip of Manhattan, was once the home of the British colonial governors. Today, it is the headquarters of the First Army area of the United States Army. Naturally, such headquarters need protection, so there is a fort on the island, which was photographed here by Mathew Brady, the famous photographer of the Civil War.

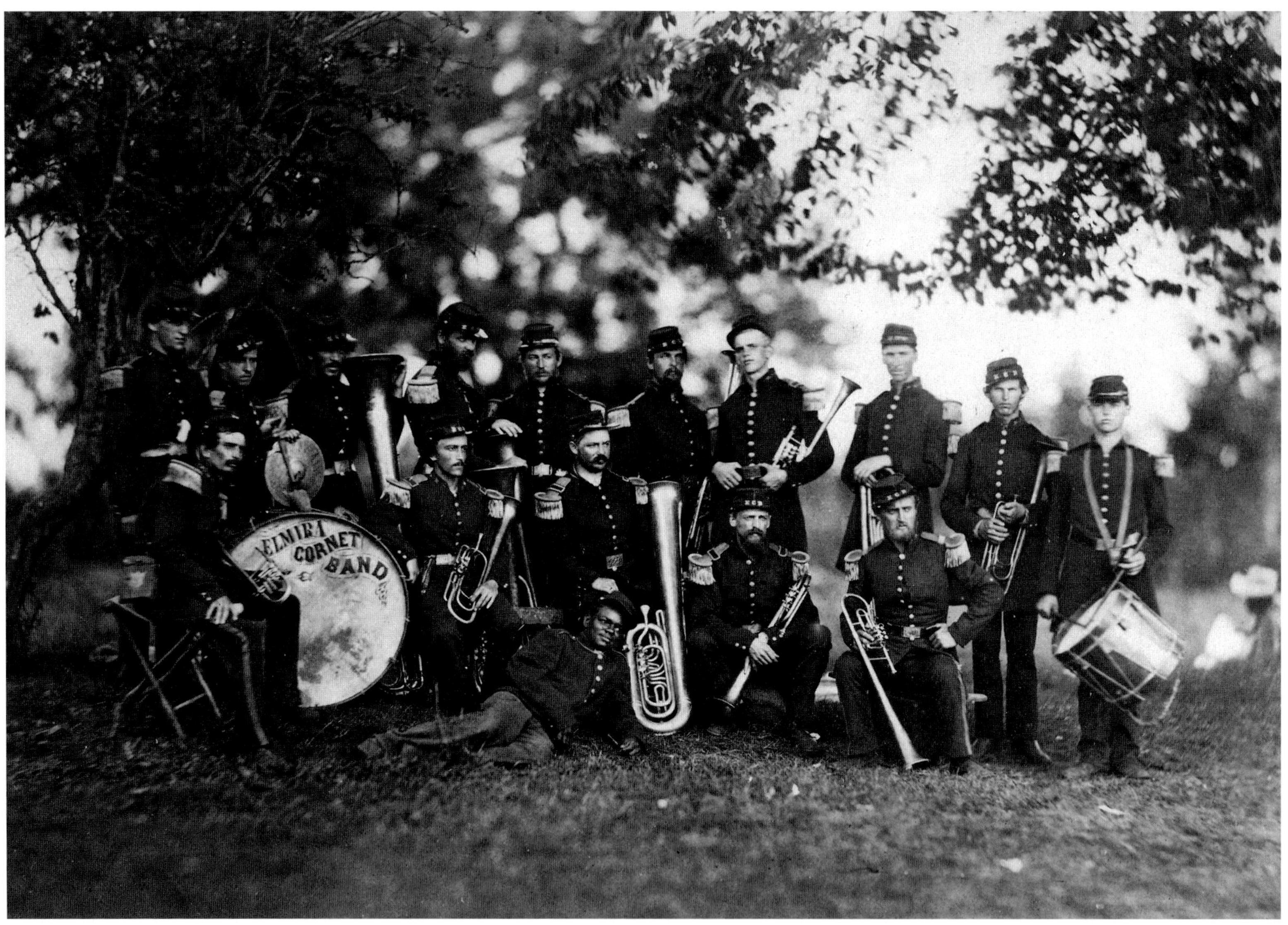

Sixteen young men from Elmira, New York, formed the Band of the Eighth New York State Militia. They were called into service in the Thirty-third Regiment of the New York State Volunteers and posed outside Arlington, Virginia, for a group photo in June 1861, with the U.S. Civil War looming before them. The First Battle of Bull Run would occur nearby just days away on July 21.

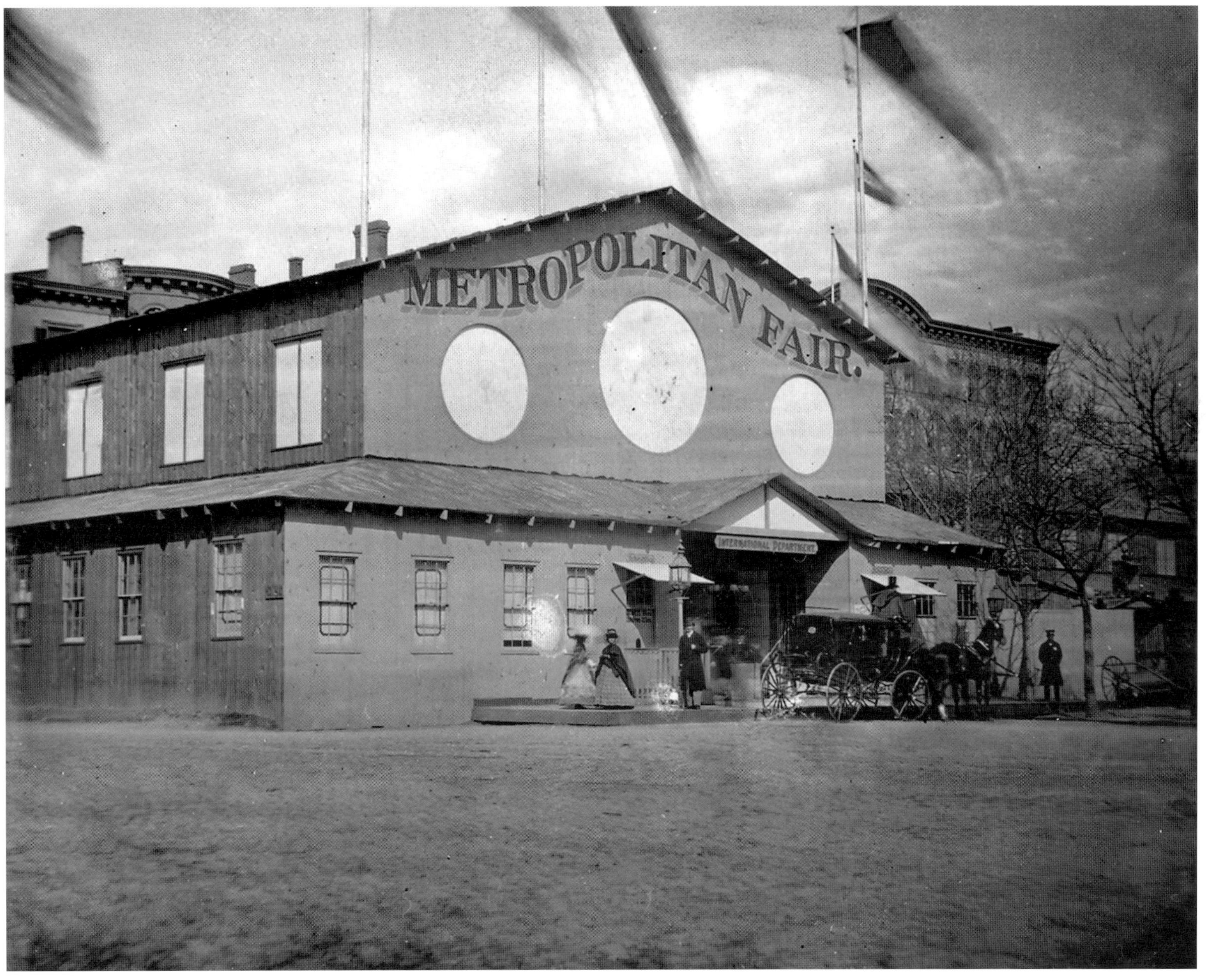

Fairs were popular in the nineteenth century. This photograph of the Metropolitan Fair at a New York location not known is attributed to Mathew Brady. Period dress dates the fair to before the 1870s.

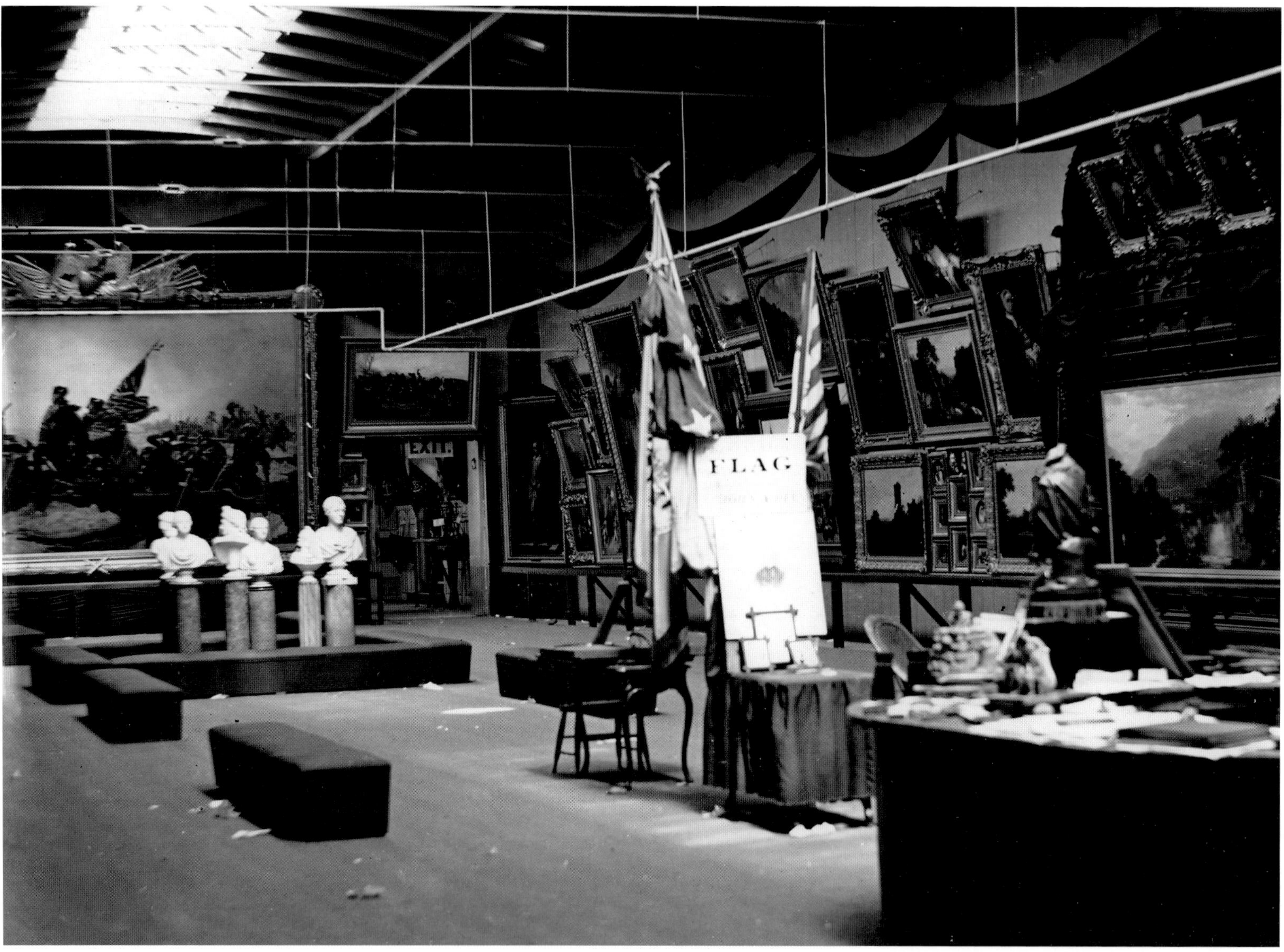

In the nineteenth century, exhibitions of American artwork drew large crowds to view paintings by significant artists and often to buy them as well. There was a customary charge to enter the exhibit. Behind the plaster busts is the famous oil painting *George Washington Crossing the Delaware,* completed in 1850 by the American artist Emanuel Gottlieb Leutze (1816–1868). On view today at the Metropolitan Museum of Art in Manhattan, the painting depicts General Washington leading boatloads of American troops across the Delaware River at dawn to surprise the British forces in the Battle of Trenton on the day after Christmas, 1776.

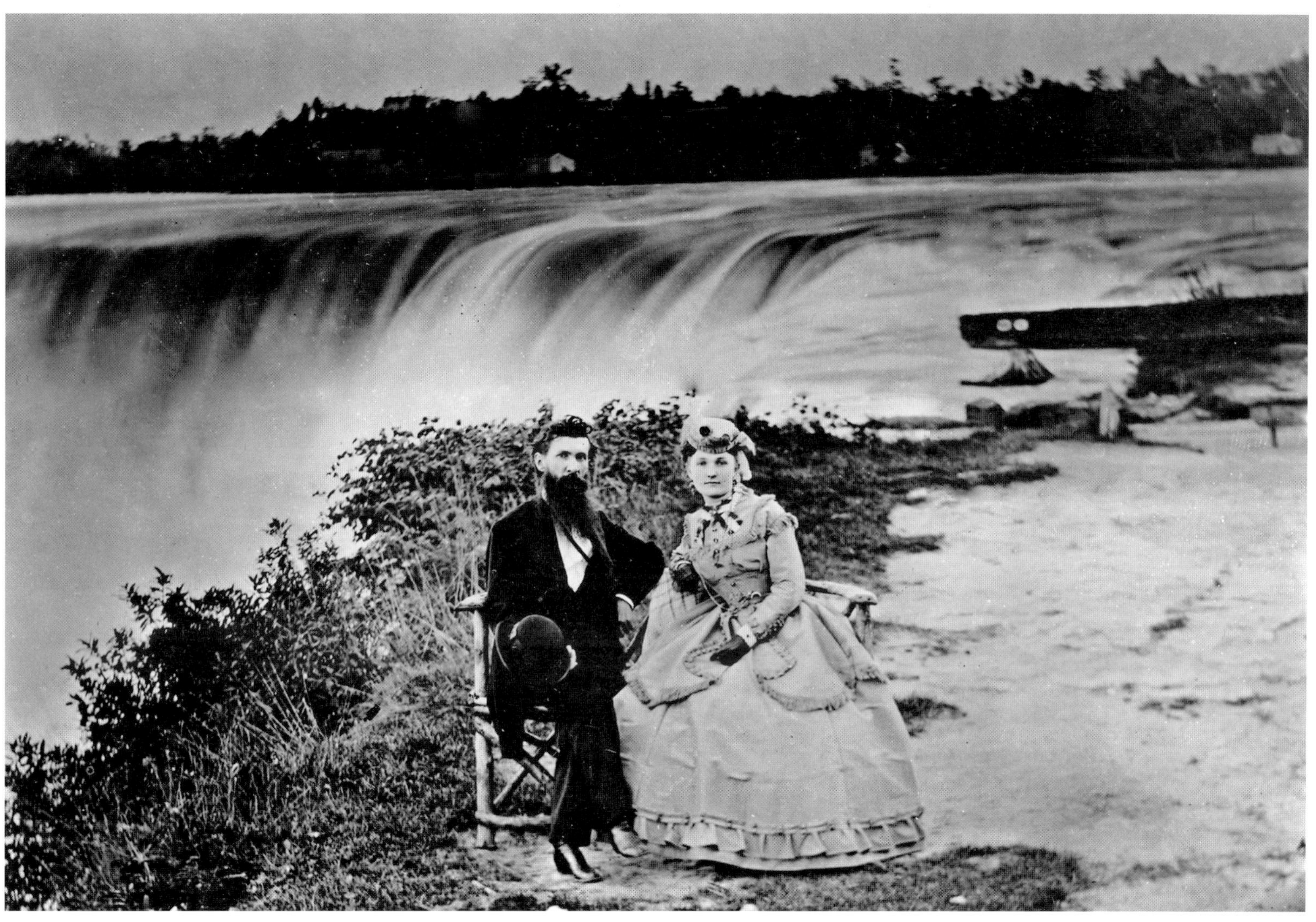

Mathew Brady (1823–1896), who was born near Lake George, in New York State's Adirondacks, operated a portrait studio in New York City. He ventured away from the studio as the need arose, here to Niagara Falls to photograph this Victorian couple at the edge of the impressive cataract. Nearly 45 million gallons of water flow over Niagara Falls every minute. The American Falls shown here are 185 feet high.

Saratoga Springs, New York, was a summer playground for wealthy New Yorkers in the 1870s when this photograph was made. Thousands of visitors enjoyed the mineral springs, the casino gambling, and, of course, the horse races. Saratoga boasted 26,000 hotel rooms—the four largest hotels providing 6,000 of them. The Grand Union Hotel was one of the largest hotels in the 1800s. The rear piazza was covered to protect guests from rain and permit them to enjoy the air and the view across lawn and gardens.

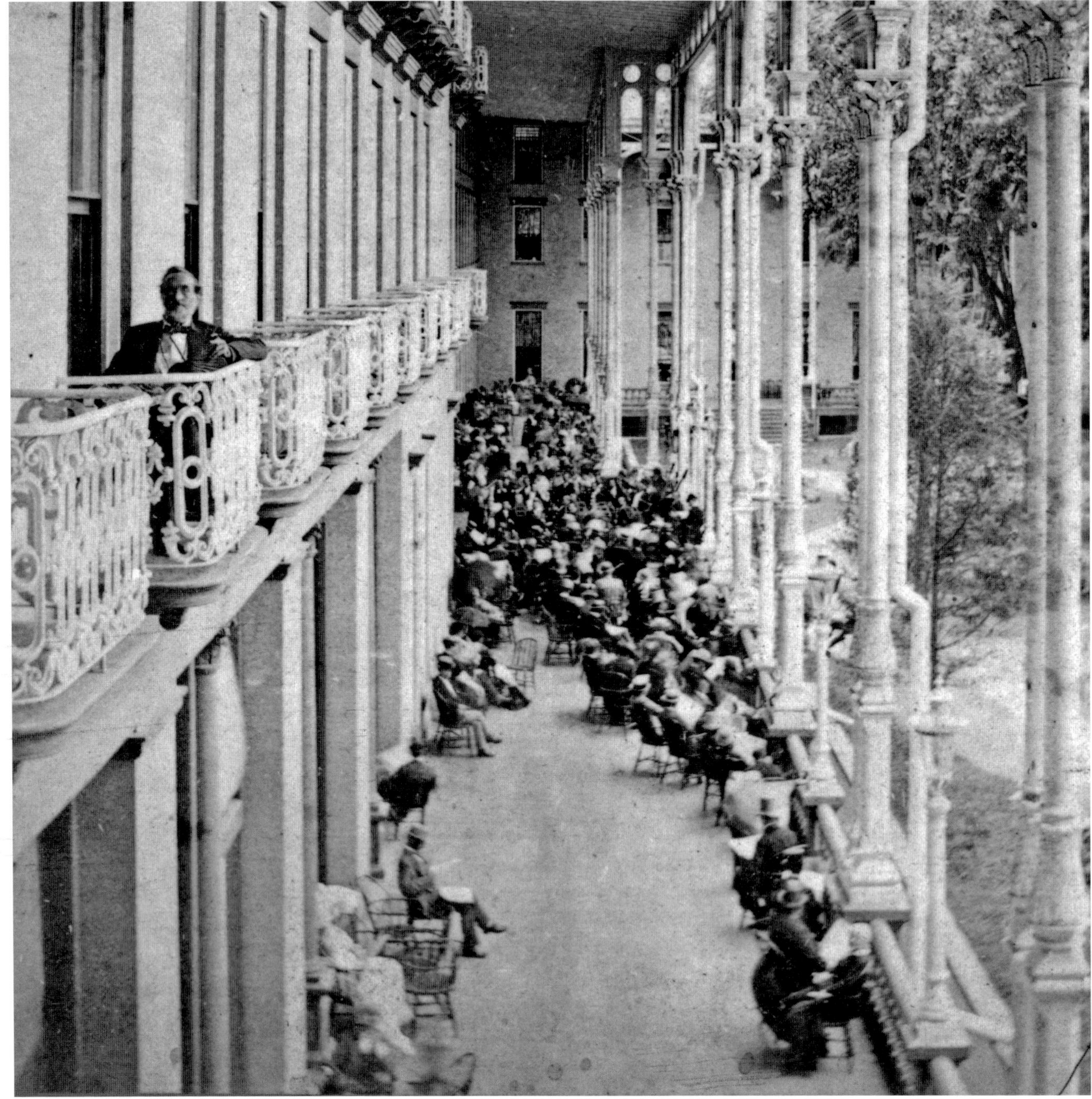

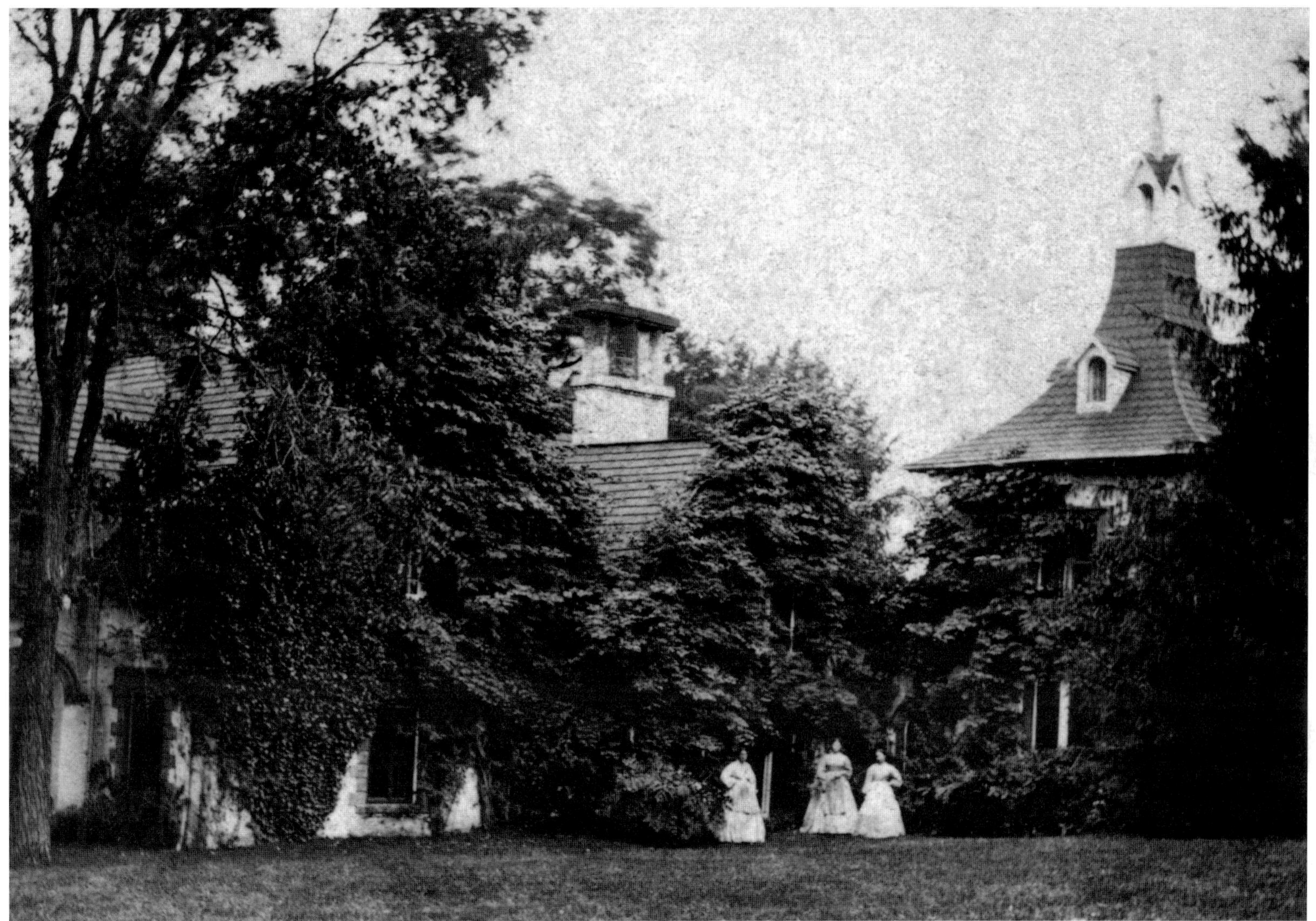

Born in Manhattan (he popularized Gotham as a moniker for New York City), Washington Irving (1783–1859) was the famous author of *Rip Van Winkle, Life and Voyages of Columbus, The Legend of Sleepy Hollow, The Alhambra,* and a five-volume biography of George Washington. He wanted to live in a picturesque cottage and designed, with the help of his friend George Harvey, a Dutch-style cottage called Sunnyside on land that he purchased on the Hudson River near Tarrytown. Although the house was built in 1836, Irving attached ornamental iron numbers announcing a construction date of 1656, as fictional as his stories. Sunnyside still stands and is open to the visiting public.

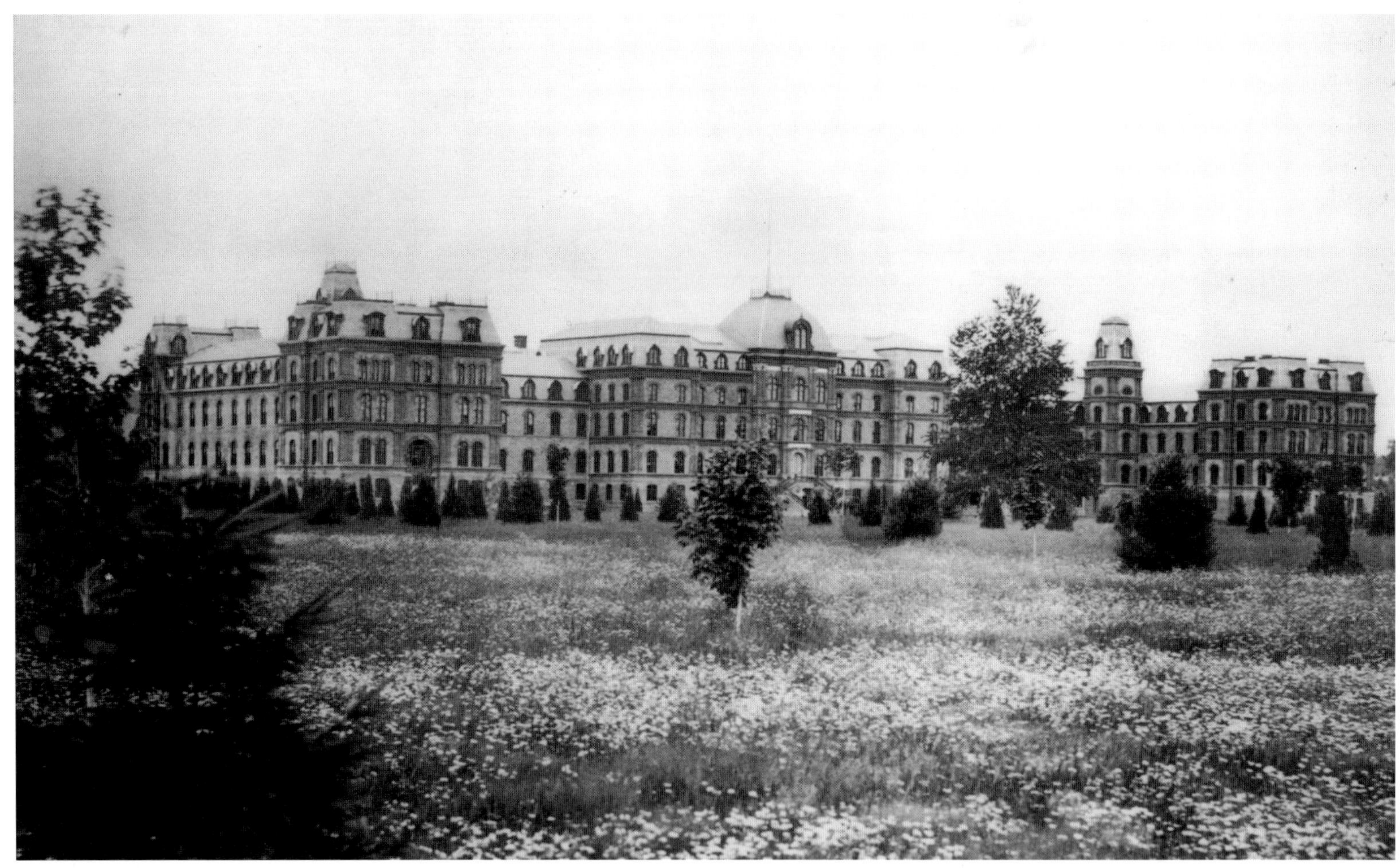

The Main Building at Vassar College, Poughkeepsie, in the Hudson River Valley, is a monumental, five-story Second Empire–style brick building that covers four acres. It was designed by James Renwick, Jr., and completed in 1864. When Vassar opened in 1865, the entire college was housed in this building: living quarters for students and faculty, dining hall, library, art museum, classrooms, offices, and more. Today the building is a National Historic Landmark.

Age of Extravagance

(1881–1916)

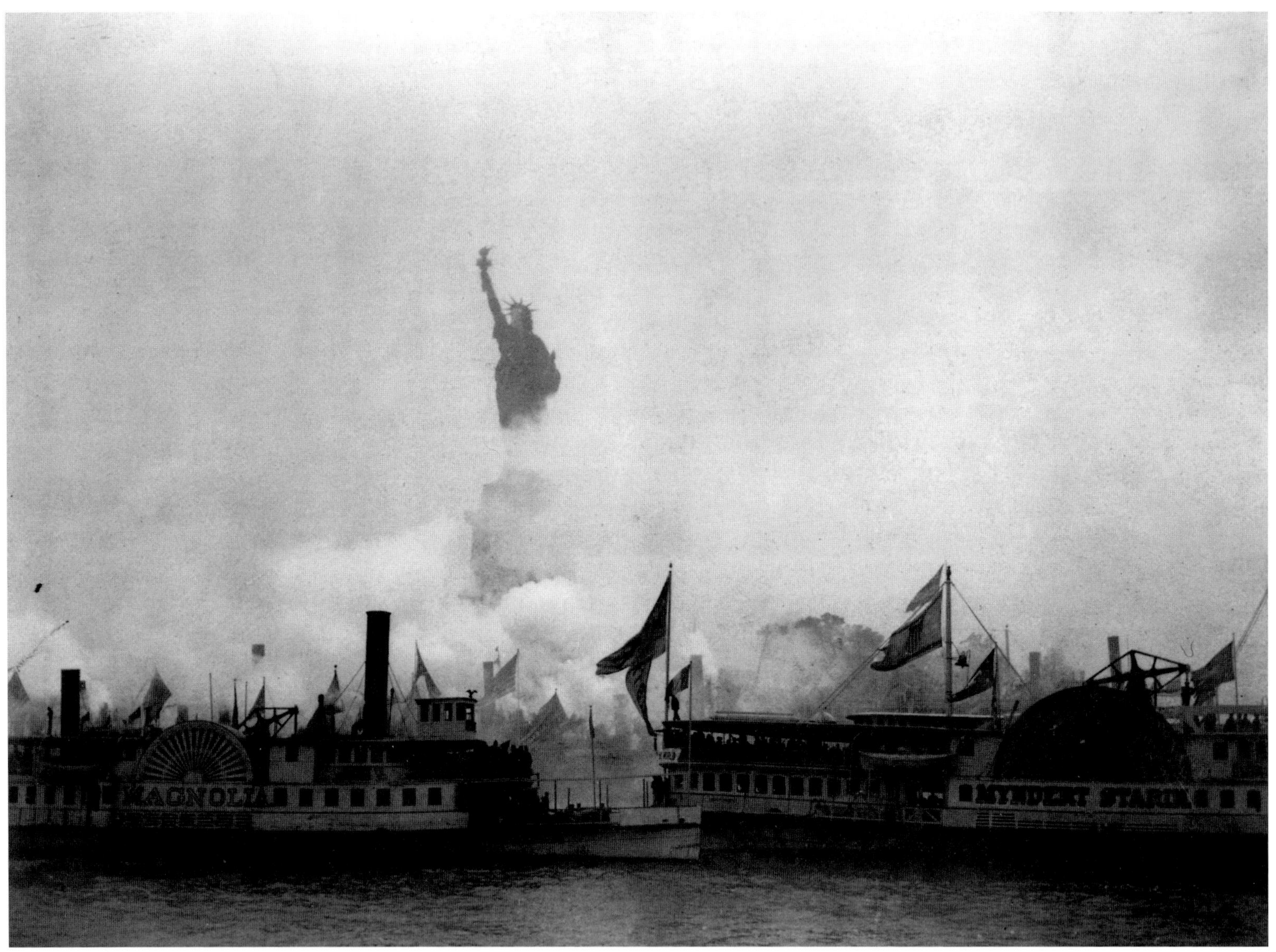

Liberty Enlightening the World, known worldwide as the Statue of Liberty, was erected in the New York City harbor as a gift of friendship from the people of France to the people of the United States. It was created by French sculptor Frederic Auguste Bartholdi. The colossal copper sculpture was inaugurated on October 28, 1886, with a military and naval salute, the smoke from which partially obscures the statue in this image. President Grover Cleveland, a native son of New York State, delivered the inaugural address.

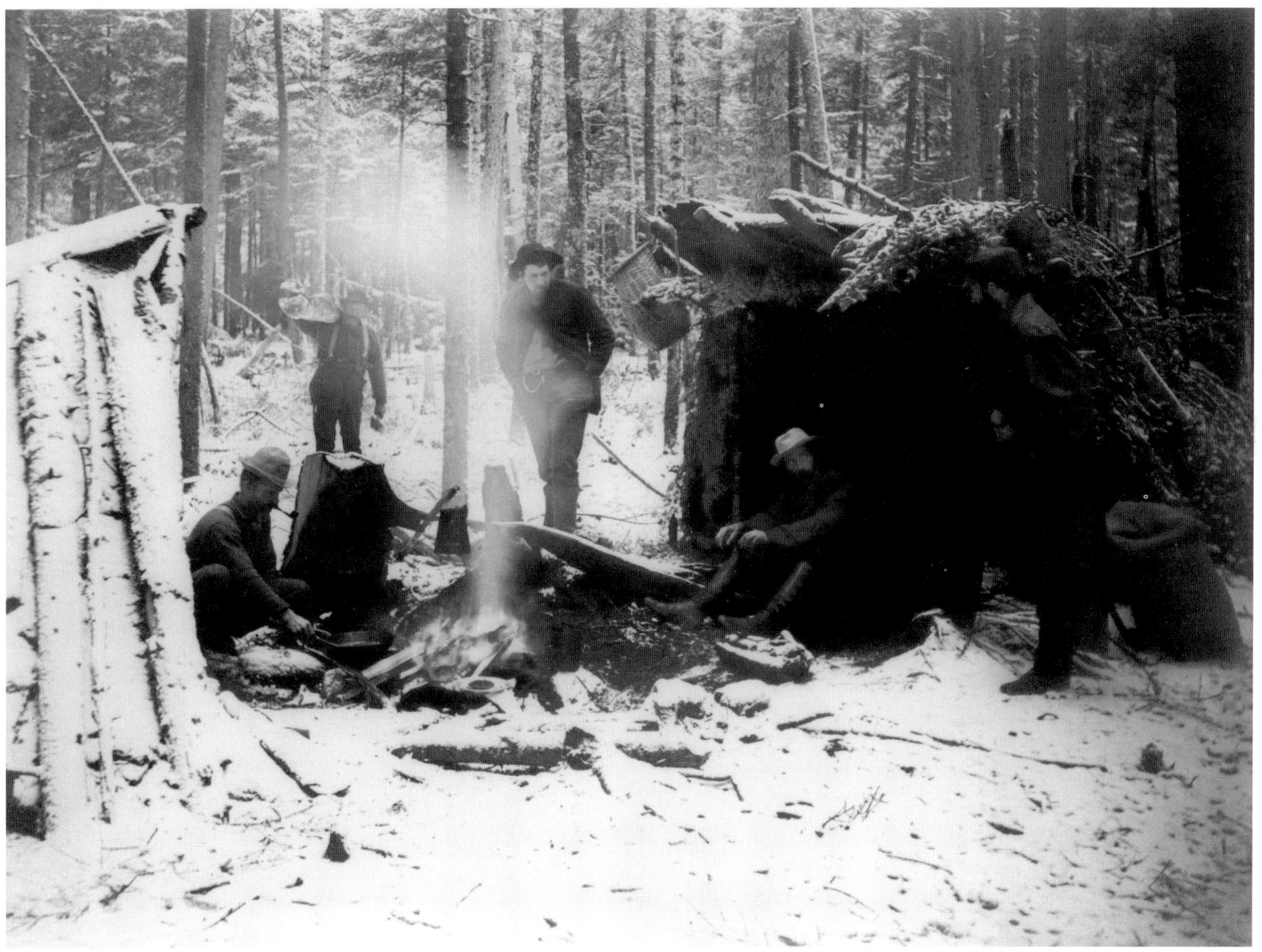

Seneca Ray Stoddard (1844–1917), a largely self-taught artisan, naturalist, writer, and photographer, got his start painting numbers on freight cars. His lobbying efforts to persuade the New York State Assembly to preserve the Adirondacks as a wilderness were influential. Stoddard's two most successful guidebooks, published in the 1870s, introduced thousands of visitors and readers to the sublime qualities of the Adirondack Mountains of upper New York State. This is one of Stoddard's images of winter camping in the region.

Niagara Falls is on record for freezing more than once, although the immense volume of water in play prevents the falls from ever freezing completely. In this image from the late 1800s, fresh snow has covered the buildup of ice on the American Falls. In recent times, a deepening of the American Falls rapids prevents ice from settling there and forming a dam, thereby increasing the discharge of water over the falls, which lessens the chance of freezing.

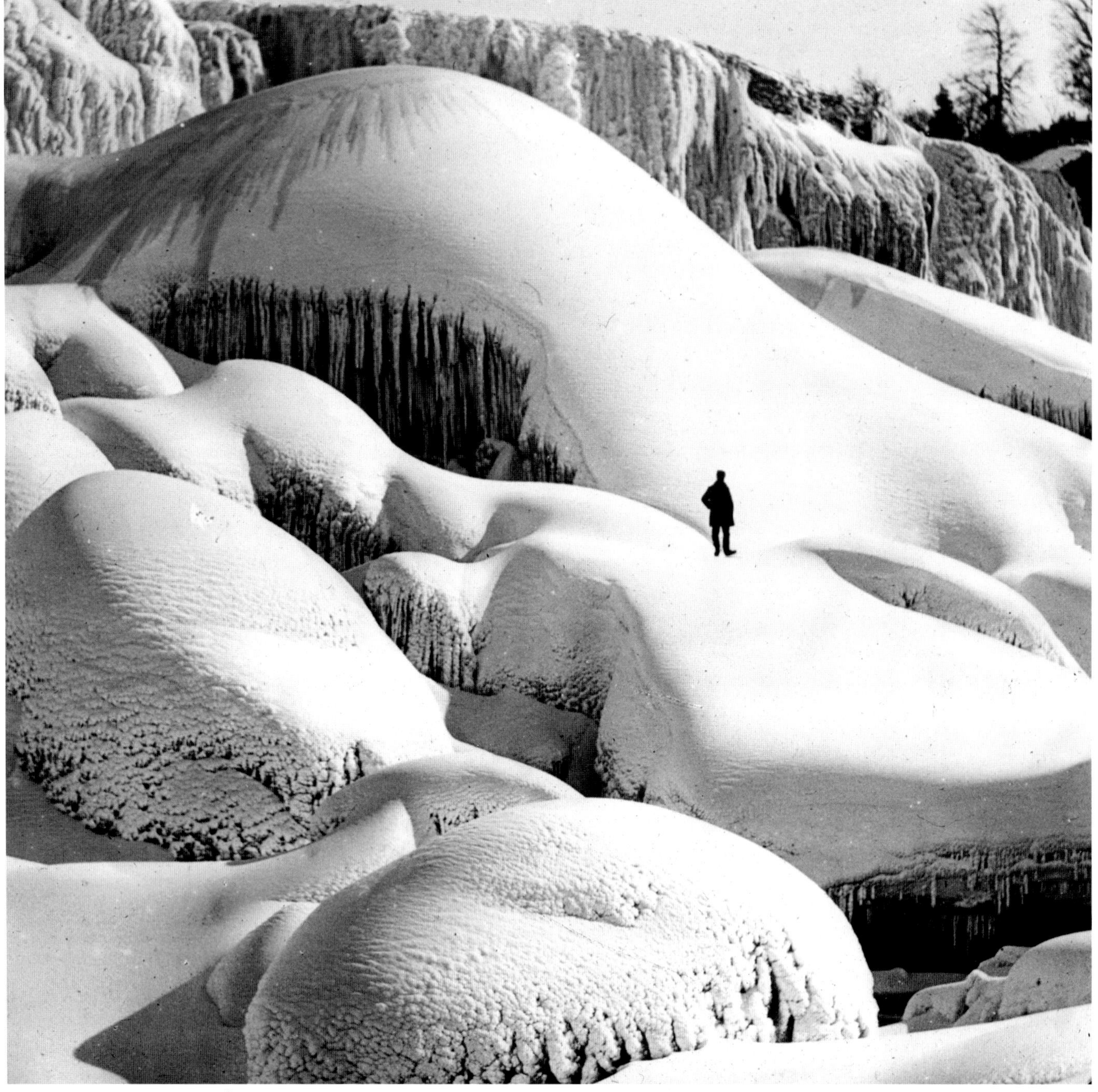

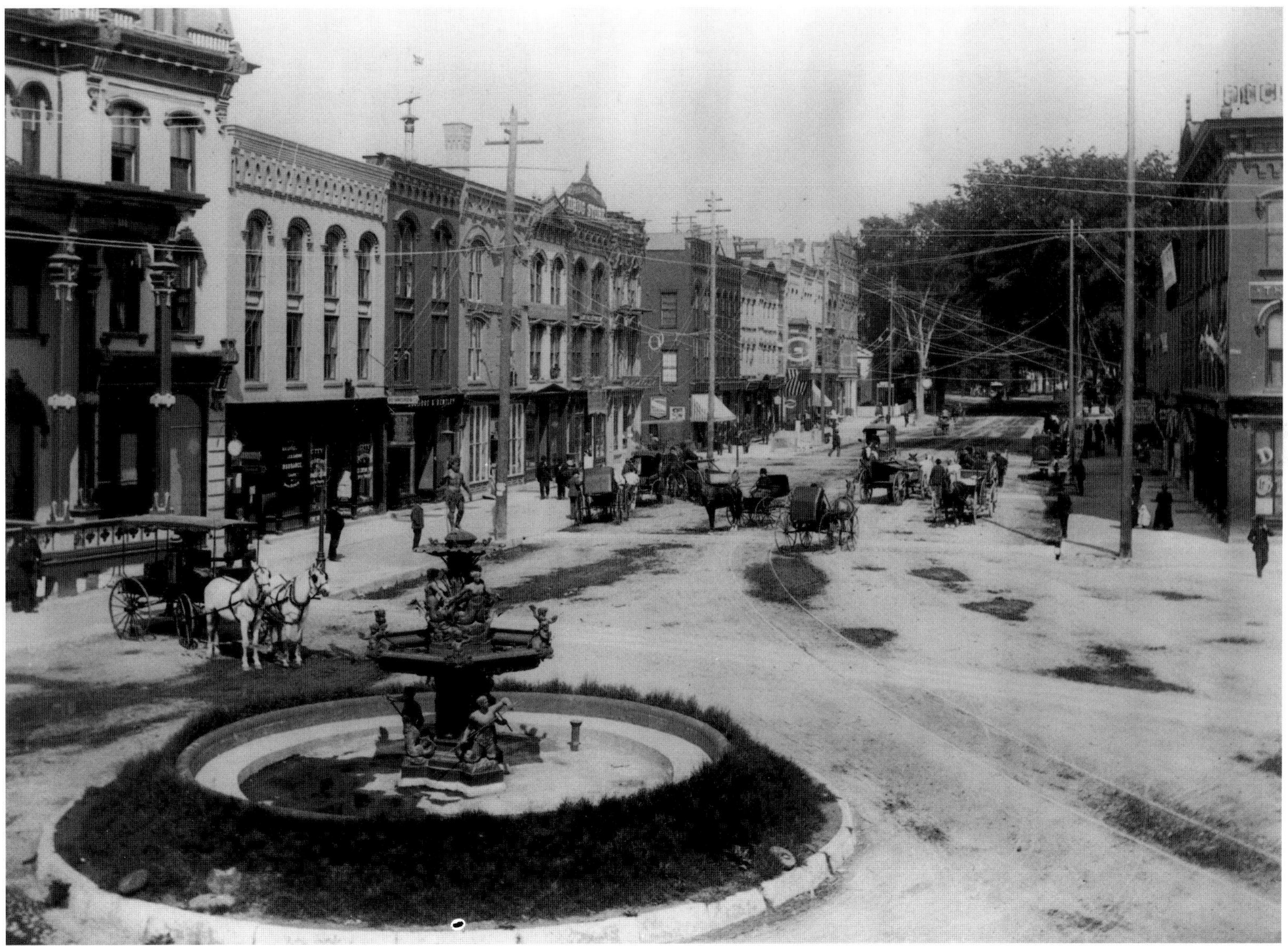

Glens Falls is a city on the Hudson River in the Adirondacks. This 1889 view shows the town square with its cast-iron fountain. The square forms Centennial Circle where five streets intersect. Although settlement here dates to 1766, Glens Falls was incorporated as a village in 1839 and chartered as a city in 1908, celebrating its centennial in 2008. A canal connected Glens Falls to the Champlain Canal and New York State Canal system, through which lumber, marble, lime, and agricultural products were shipped from the area in the nineteenth century.

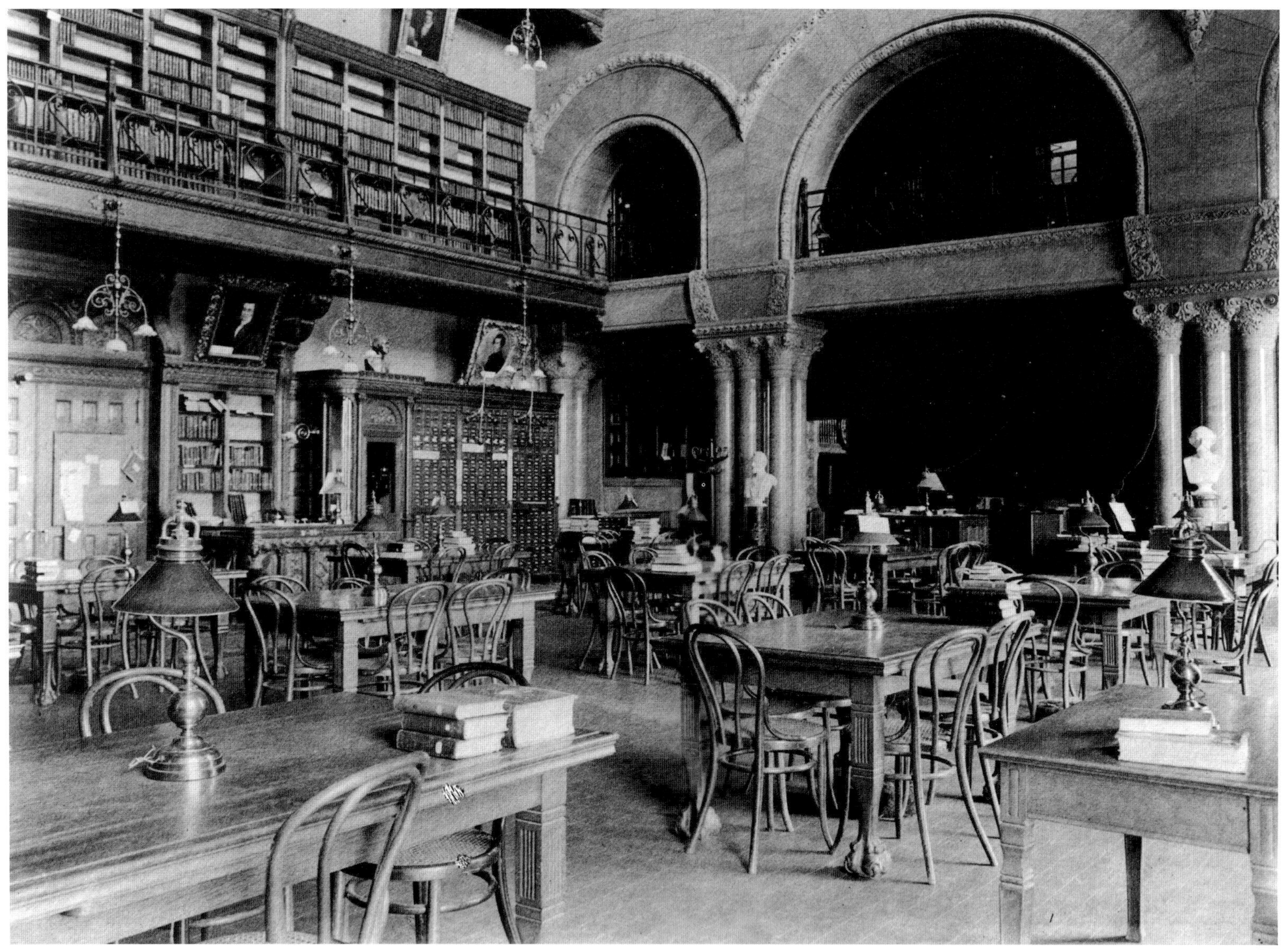

The construction of the New York State Capitol was a model of government inefficiency. It took 32 years to design and build and involved four separate architectural firms. Henry Hobson Richardson finally completed the project in 1899. Richardson's signature architectural style, Romanesque, dominates the building as shown here in the prevalent arches of the New York State Library. The Capitol is one of the last monumental, all-masonry buildings constructed in America, and it cost twice as much as the nation's capitol in Washington, D.C.

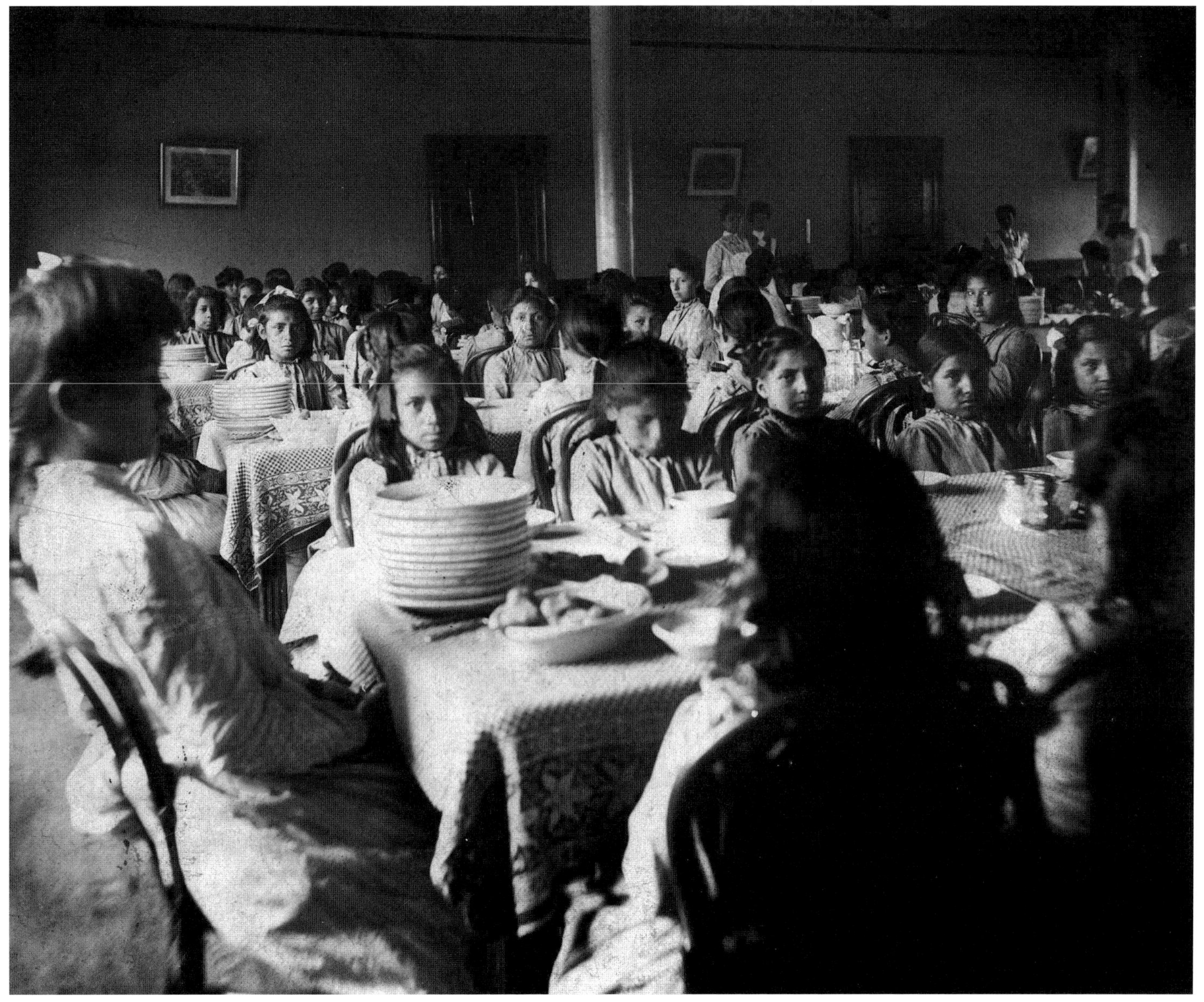

Shown here in the 1890s, young girls at the Thomas Indian School on the Cattaraugus Seneca Indian Reservation in western New York wait for a meal to be served. The plates will be filled at the head of each table and then passed around. Teachers and serving staff also wait at rear. The school was formed in 1855 to educate destitute and orphaned children from Indian reservations across the state.

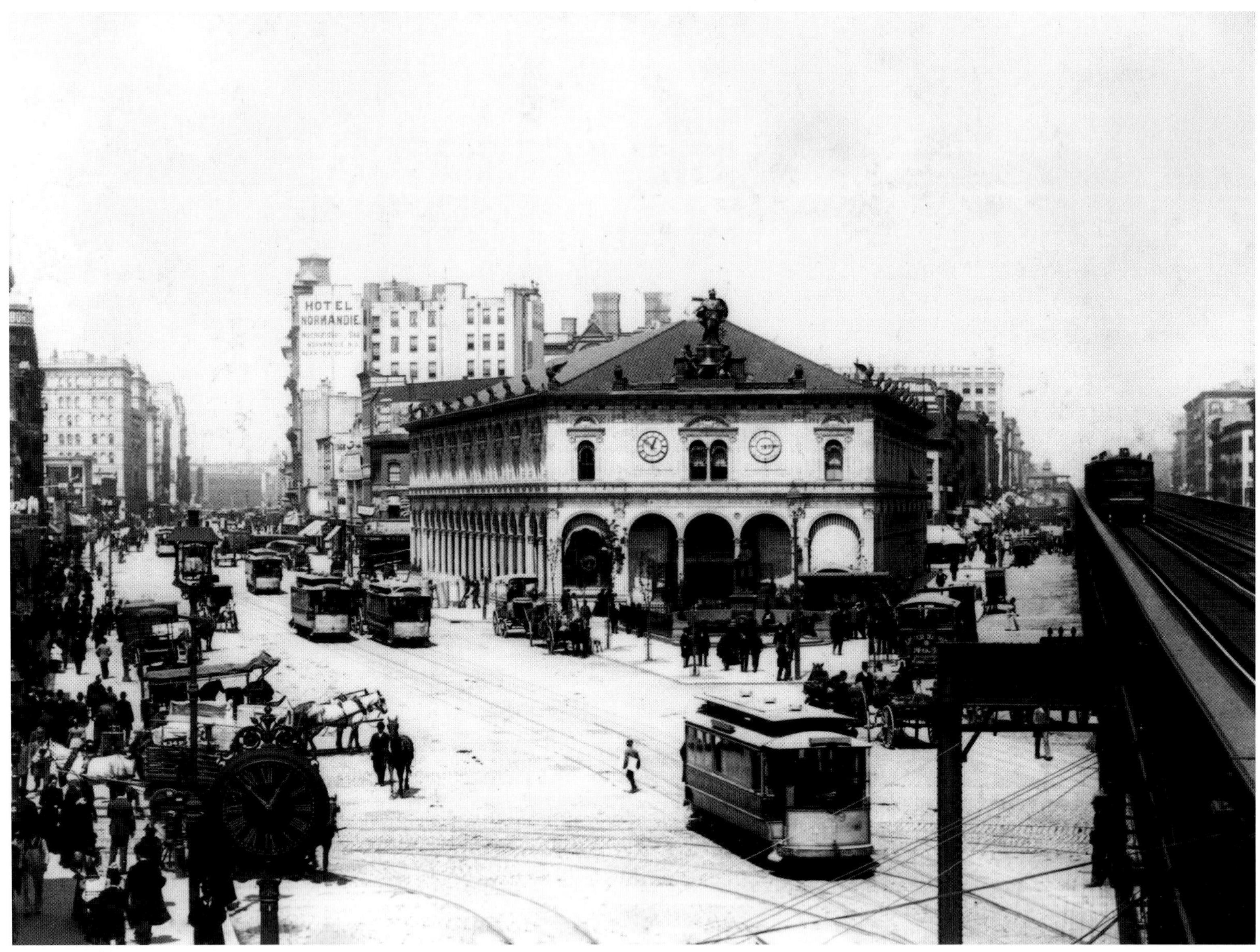

Herald Square is formed by the intersection of Broadway, Sixth Avenue, and 34th Street in Manhattan. The distinctive edifice with a five-arched entrance is the New York Herald newspaper building as it appeared in 1895. The Sixth Avenue elevated railroad runs at right. The most notable business at Herald Square today is Macy's flagship department store. The wooden escalator there still runs, and visitors still stop to shop.

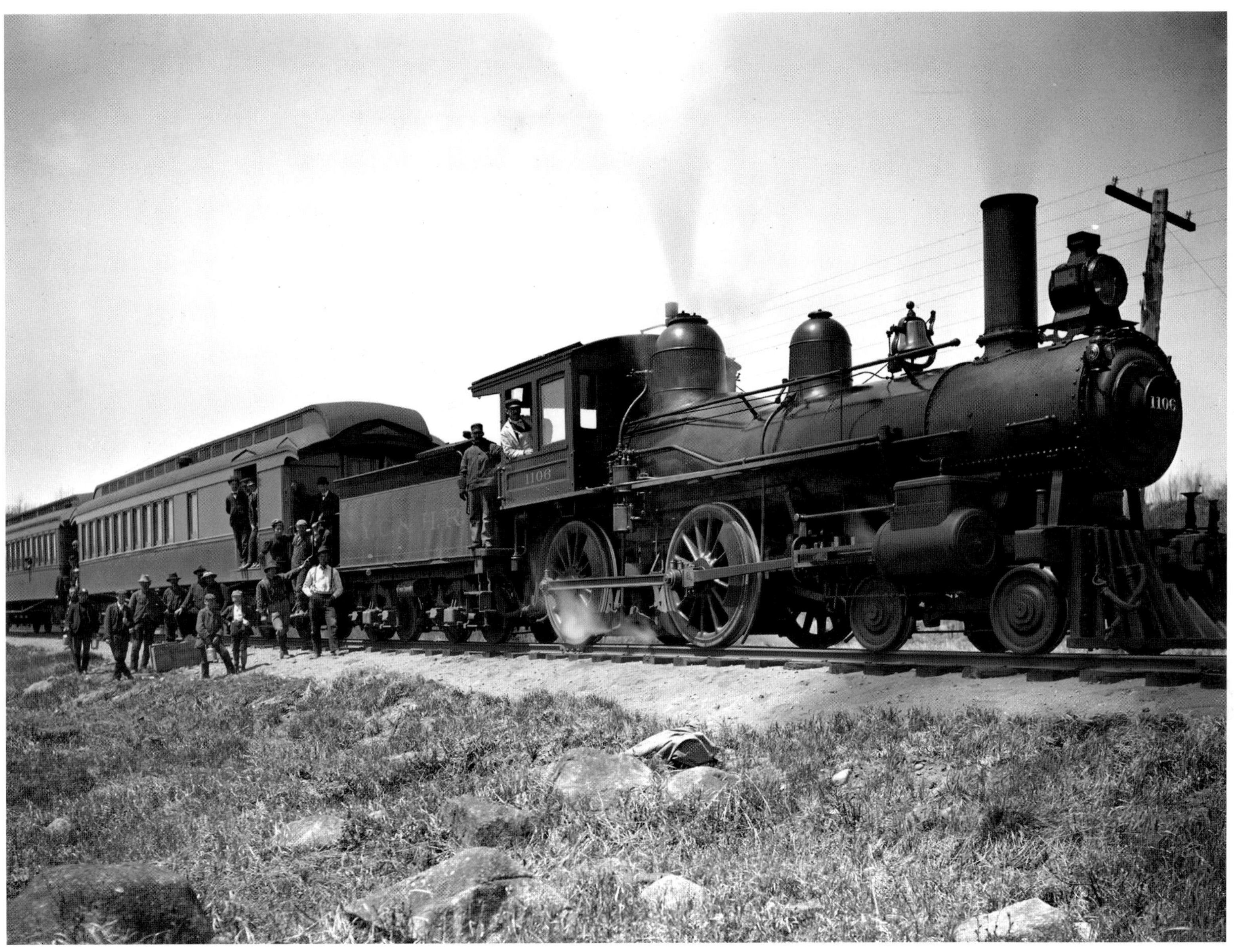

As part of a New York State reforestation project in the late 1890s, a New York Central train transported tree planters from Lake Clear Junction in the Adirondacks to nearby planting grounds each weekday for a period of two weeks. Men and boys are shown here debarking for their day of planting.

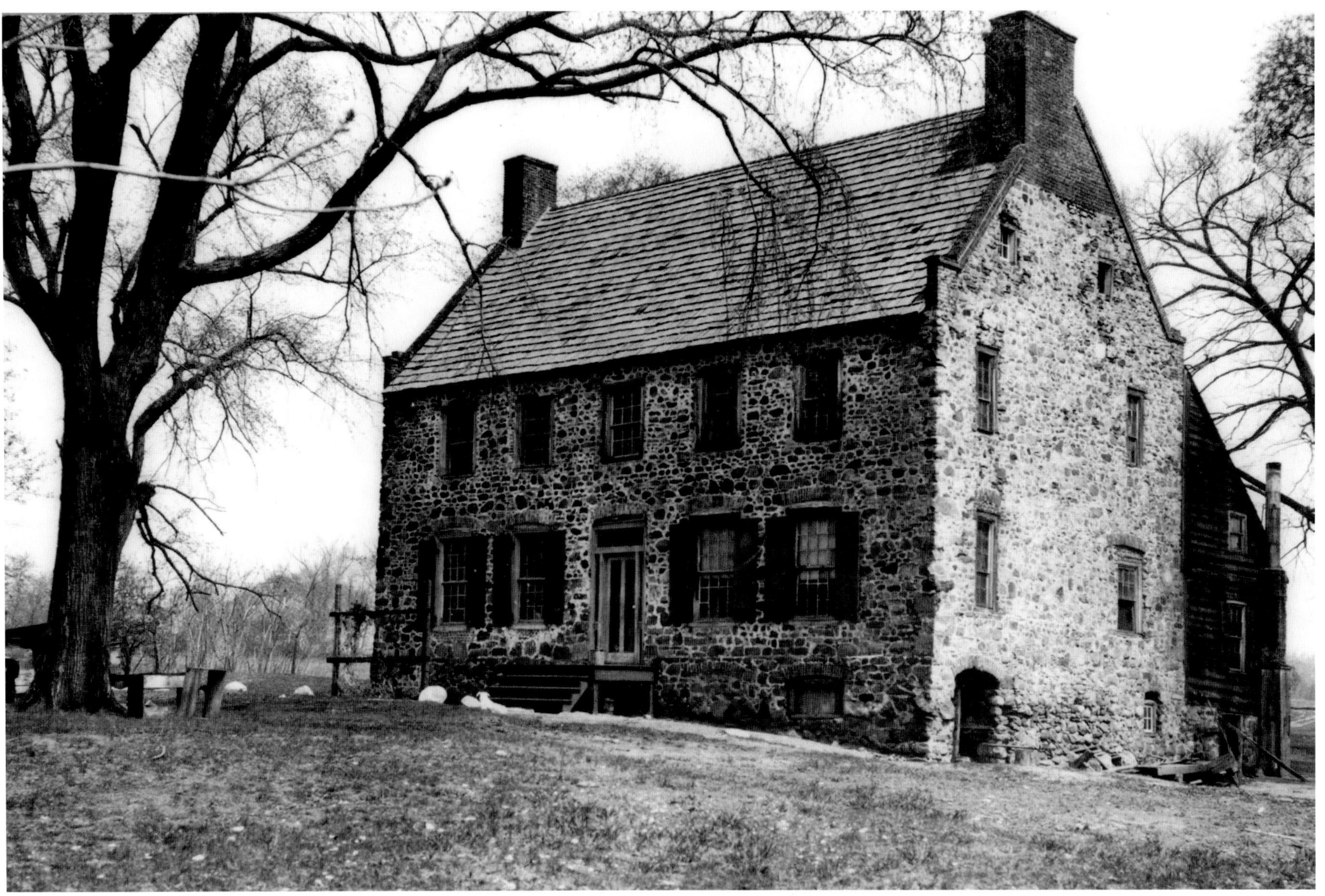

Shown here in the 1890s, the Conference House, as it is known, on Hylan Boulevard in Staten Island is a large Colonial vernacular stone residence built around 1680 by Christopher Billop and enlarged in 1720. It became the site of a conference on September 11, 1776, to achieve a peace agreement between England and the American colonies. The British were represented by Lord Richard Howe and the Americans by John Adams, Benjamin Franklin, and Edward Rutledge. Negotiations failed and the Revolutionary War proceeded.

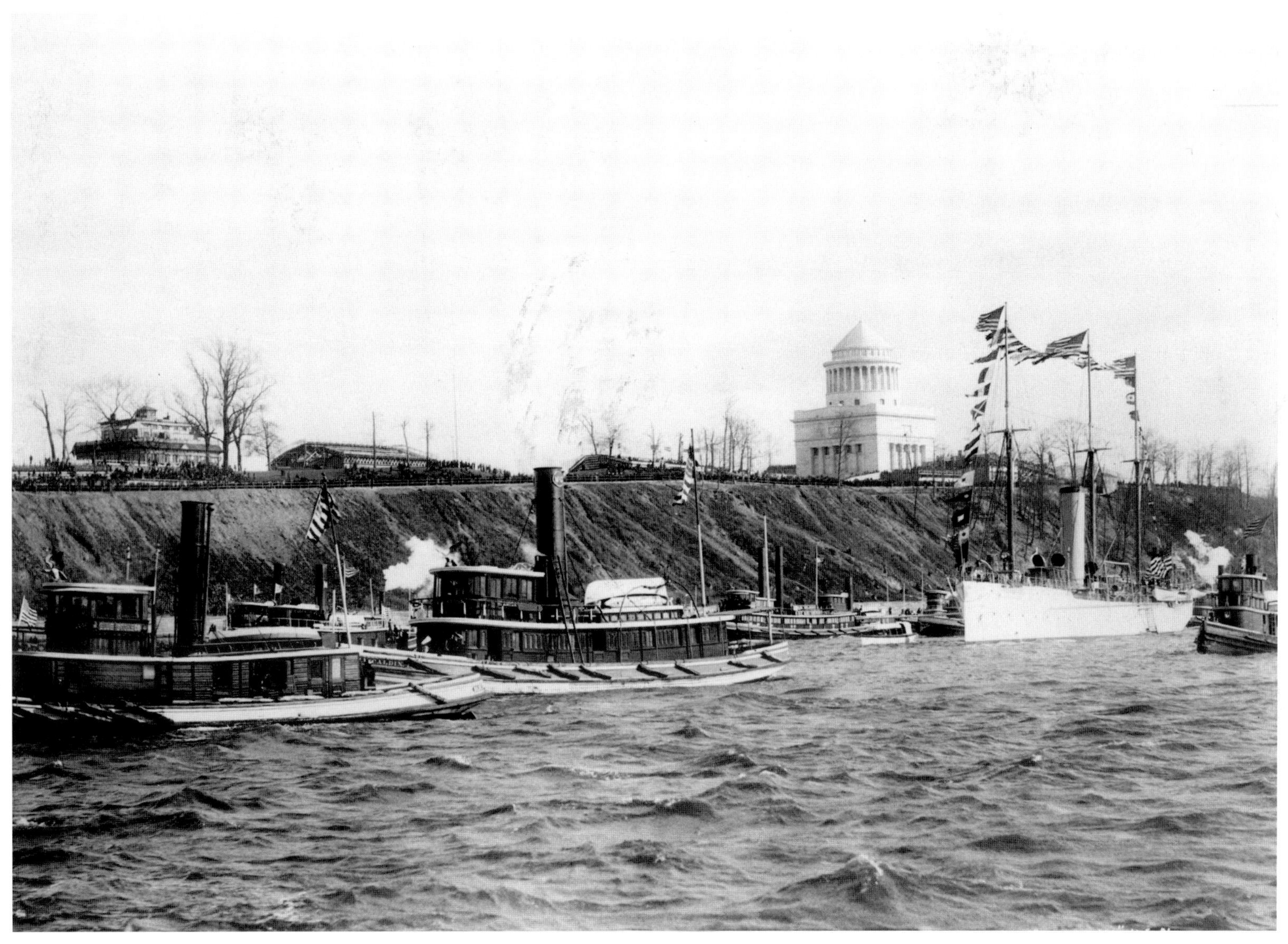

Tugboats and the USS *Dolphny* lie at anchor on the Hudson River in 1897, fronting the newly completed General Ulysses S. Grant National Memorial, on Riverside Drive at West 122nd Street, New York City. Designed by John H. Duncan, the monumental Classical Revival building is constructed of granite with Doric columns and a colonnaded drum. The marble interior holds the tombs of President Grant and his wife.

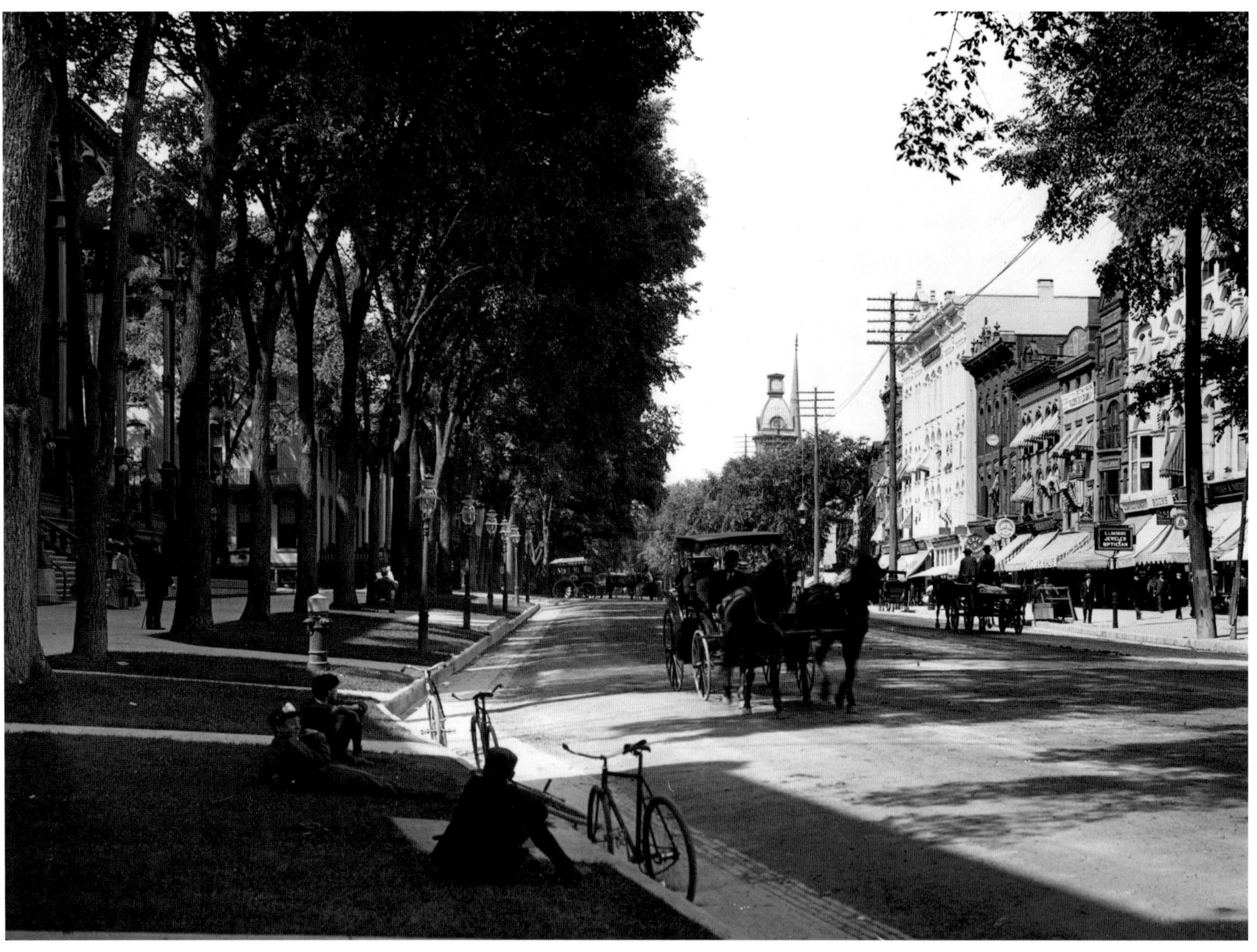

A favorite summer destination for wealthy New Yorkers was Saratoga Springs in the foothills of the Adirondack Mountains. The air was clean and cool, and there was much to occupy one's time in this attractive resort city: mineral baths, horse racing, casino gambling, and lavish parties. Shown here in the late 1890s, tree-lined Broadway featured grand hotels and elegant shops. Even the children enjoyed the ambiance—three boys have curbed their bicycles to take pleasure in the posh avenue.

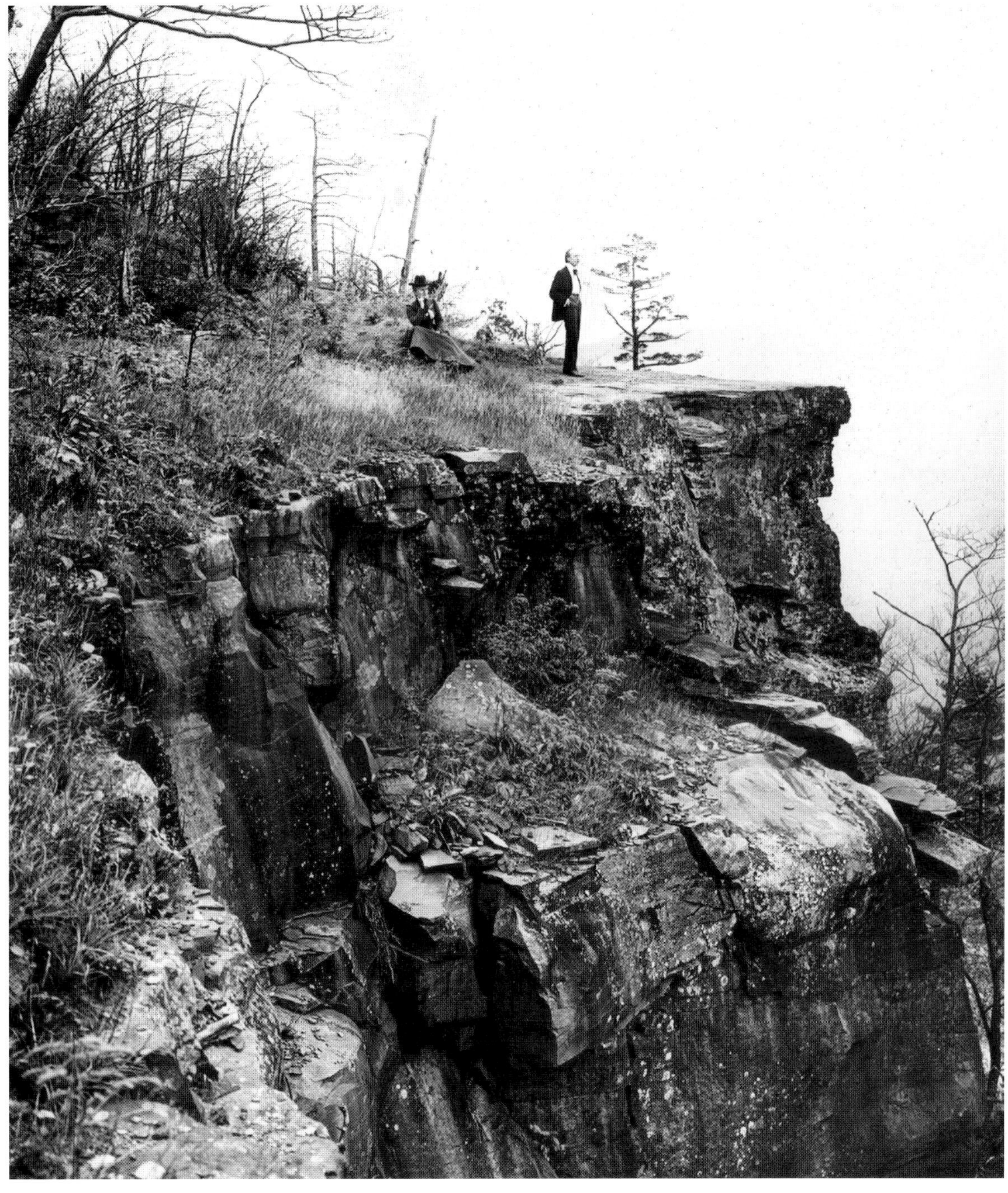

About two miles from Kaaterskill Falls in the Catskill Mountains is Inspiration Point, with panoramic views of the surrounding mountains and the Hudson River. This and other places in the Catskills inspired artists of the Hudson River School, founded by the painter Thomas Cole. The preeminent painter in the group was Frederic Edwin Church, who wrote, "Nature has been very lavish here in the gifts of her beauty." Inspiration Point is a precipitous ledge that this couple respect at a safe distance.

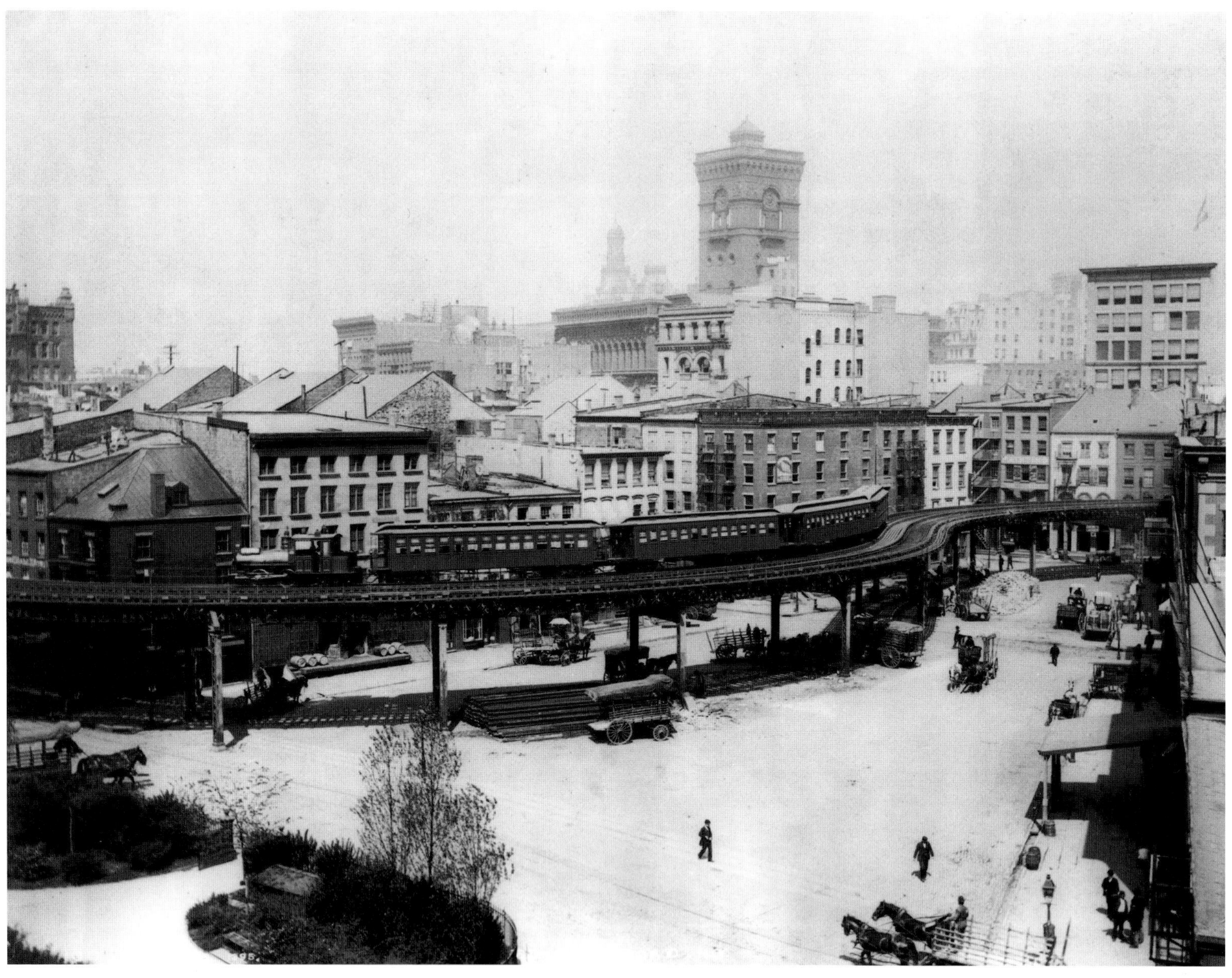

The first elevated railroad in New York City was constructed between 1867 and 1870 along Greenwich Street and Ninth Avenue. Here in 1895, the El winds through the Coentes Slip along the waterfront in lower Manhattan. The slip was a busy produce market area.

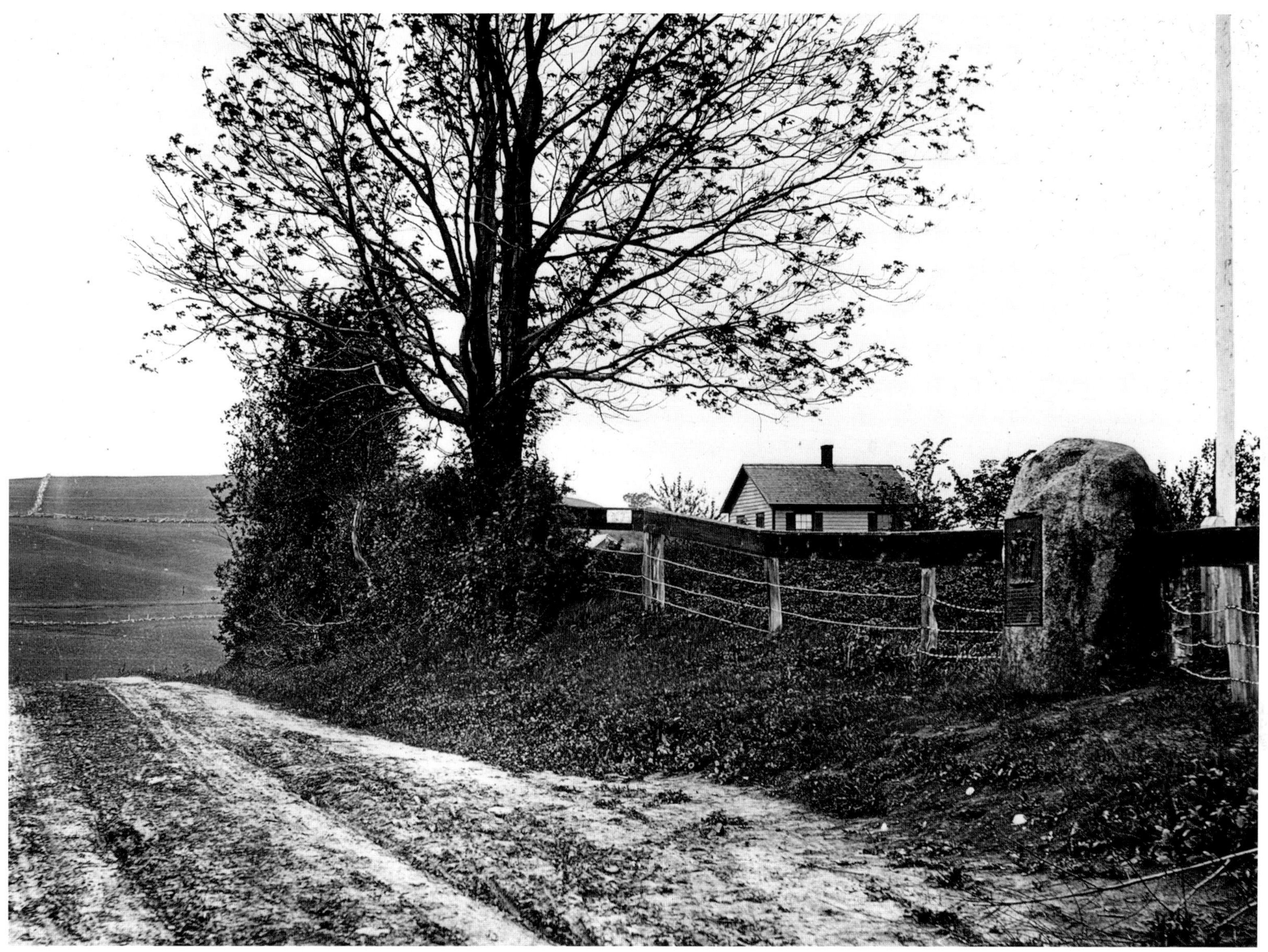

The historic marker (a bronze plaque on a stone boulder) on Johnson Avenue in Johnstown commemorates the Battle of Johnstown, which took place in the fields around Johnson Hall on October 25, 1781. British Loyalist forces were commanded by Major John Ross and Captain Walter Butler, and the Continentals were led by Colonel Marinus Willett. The battle ended with Loyalist forces retreating as night fell. It was one of the last battles of the Revolutionary War, taking place a week after the British surrender at Yorktown, Virginia.

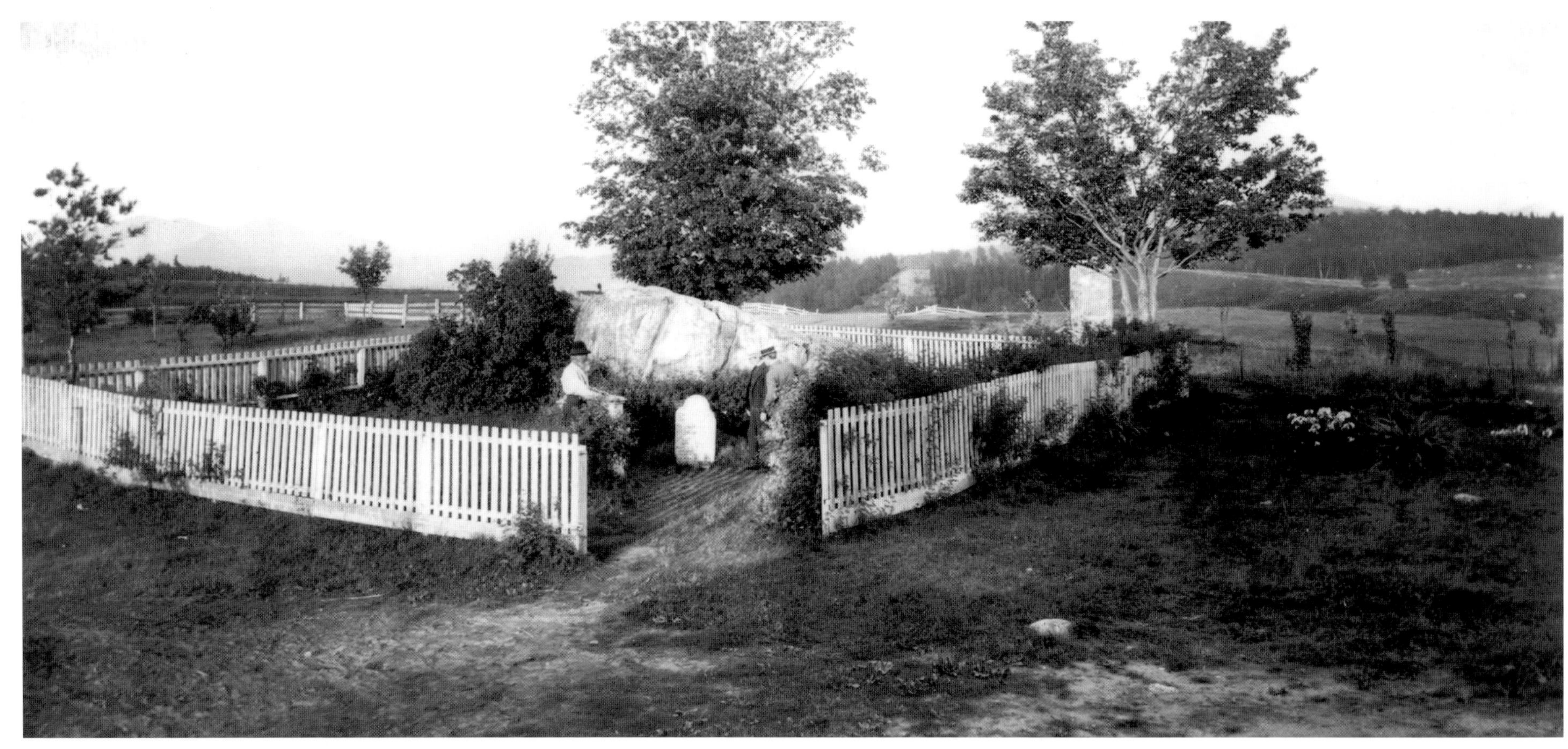

John Brown (1800–1859) was a man with a moral vision and the courage and determination to pursue it. At a time when America was tolerant of slavery, he became one of its principal opponents. He was arrested for his attempt to launch a slave insurrection and was convicted and hanged. His martyrdom was commemorated with the song "John Brown's Body," rewritten by Julia Ward Howe to become "Battle Hymn of the Republic." Brown's body, as well as those of family members, is buried inside this picket fence next to his house at his Adirondack farm in North Elba, near Lake Placid.

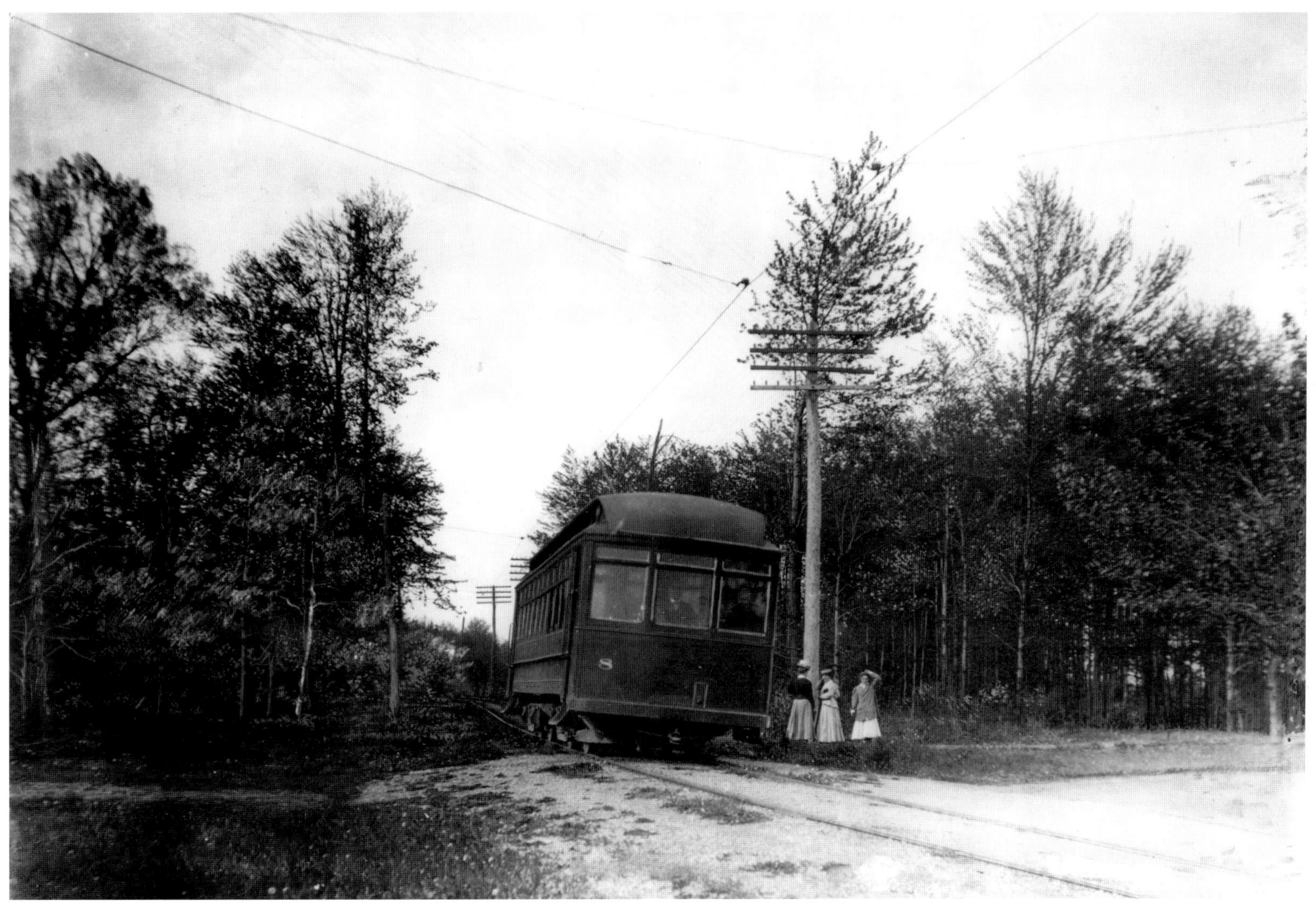

The village of Hamburg is located in western New York just commuting distance south of Buffalo. After the Civil War, Hamburg built a village streetcar system, eventually electrified. One of the electric trolley cars is pictured here in the late 1890s.

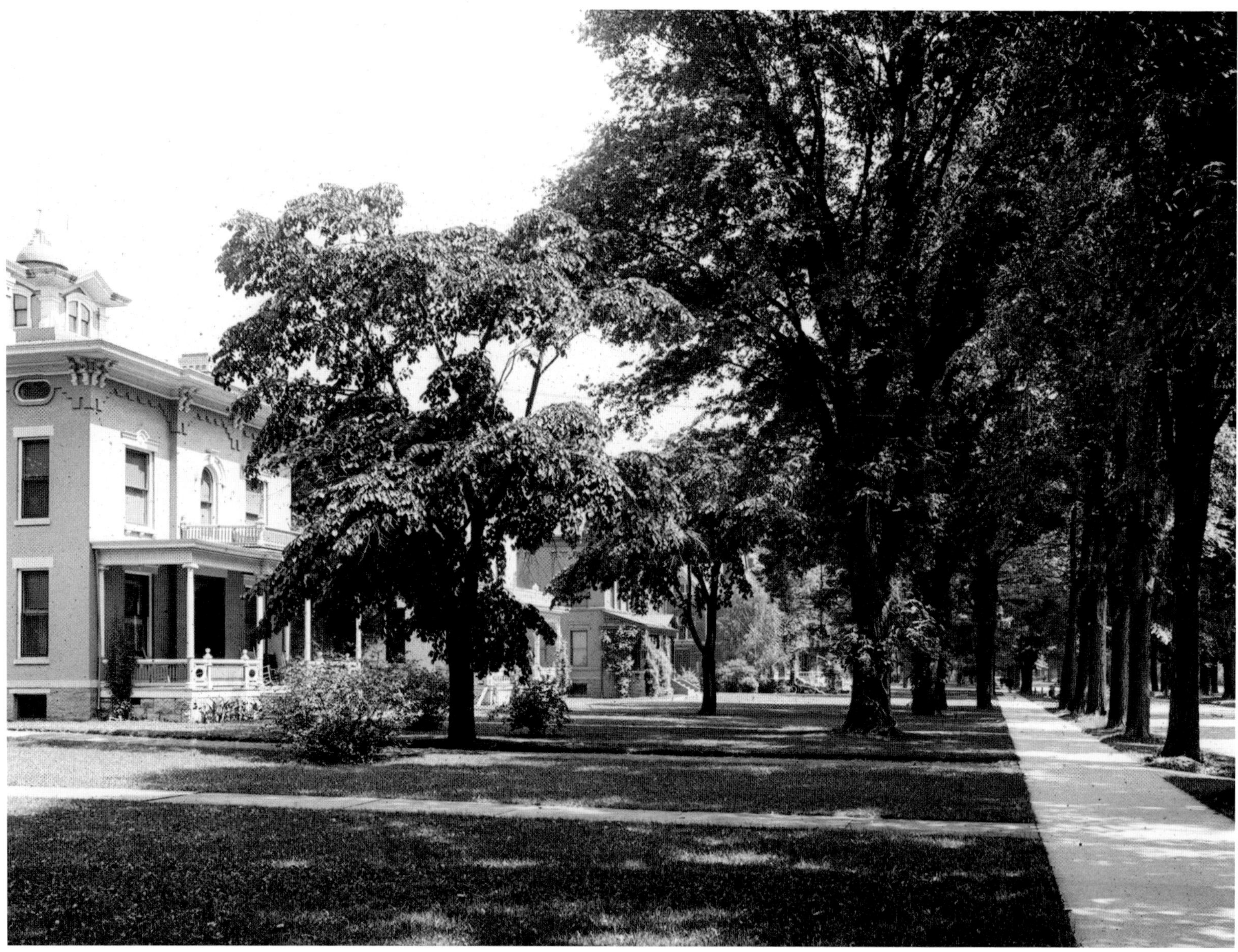

Onondaga Street in Syracuse was lined with stately elms in the late 1890s. Dutch elm disease would later decimate the landscape of many city streets like this one. Fine residential streets like Onondaga have deep front-lawn setbacks, and the houses, like the Italianate-style house in the foreground, often had broad front porches for relaxation and visiting with neighbors on summer evenings.

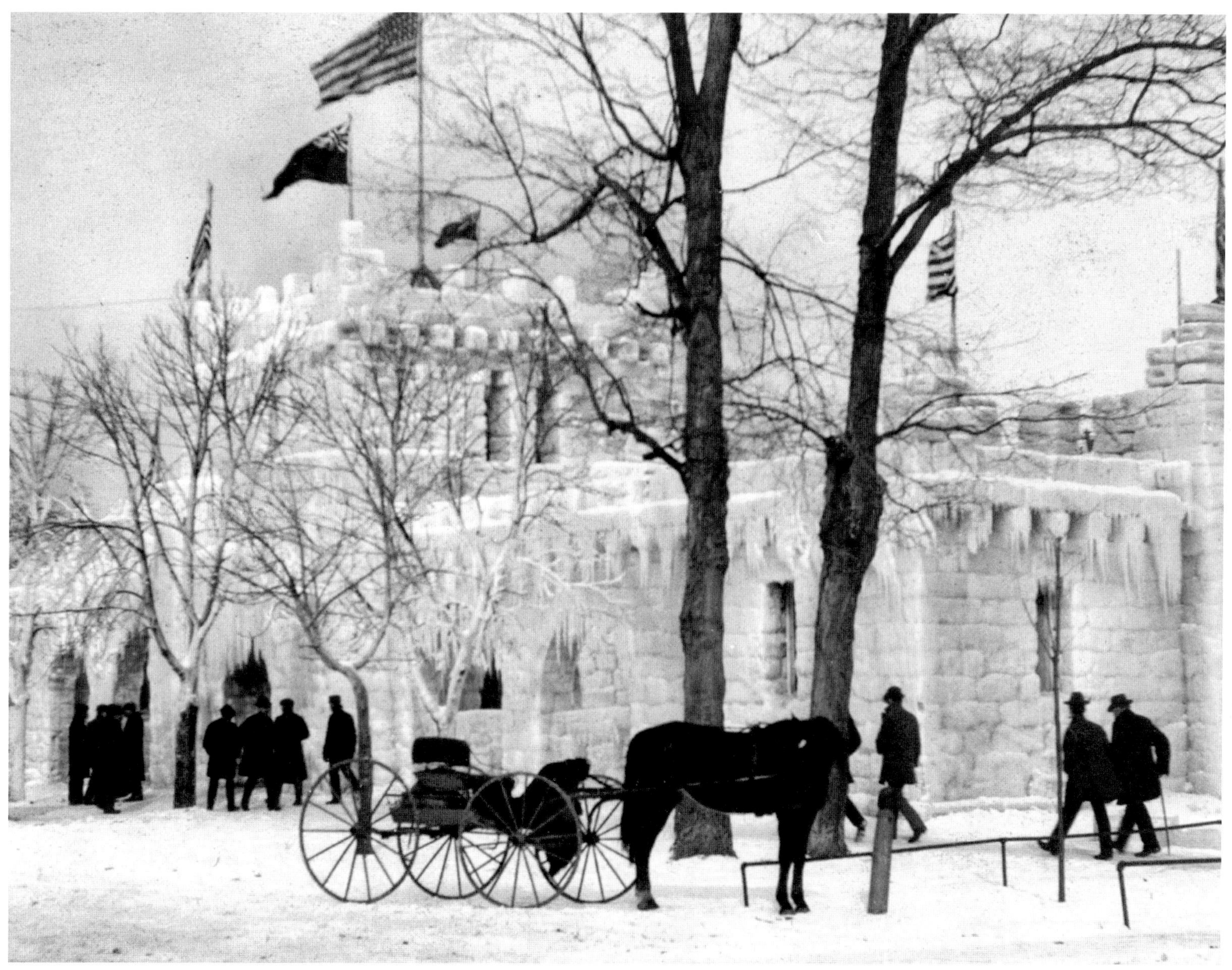

The "Great Ice Palace" was built near the American Falls for a winter festival held at Niagara Falls during 1898–1899. Constructed of large blocks of ice, the palace's walls were seven feet thick, and the structure supported three ice towers. At night, the ice palace was illuminated with colored lights.

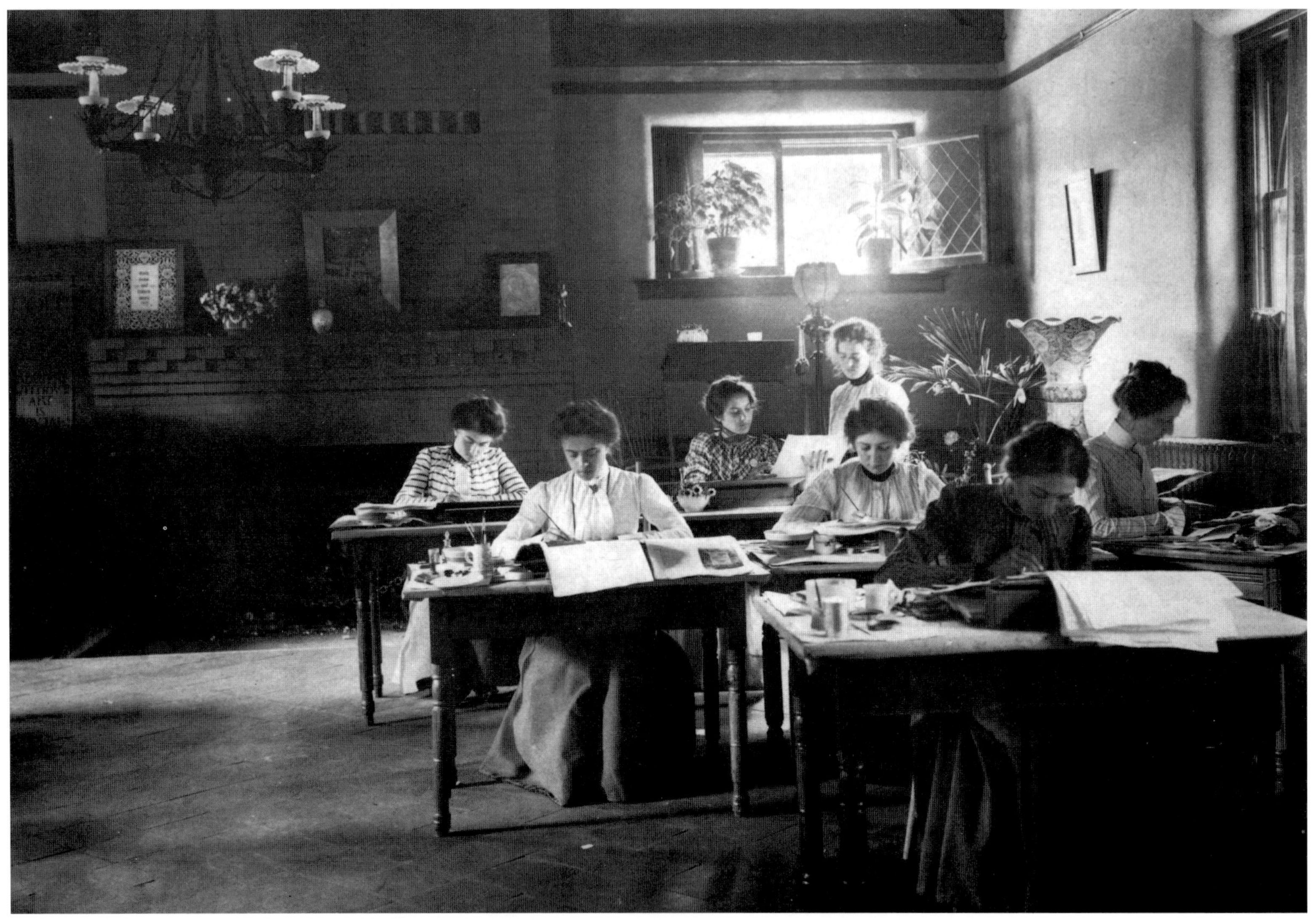

In 1900, seven women at the Roycroft colony in East Aurora, just outside Buffalo, are engaged in the crafts efforts for which Roycroft became internationally famous. On the walls are framed quotations urging industry and creativity.

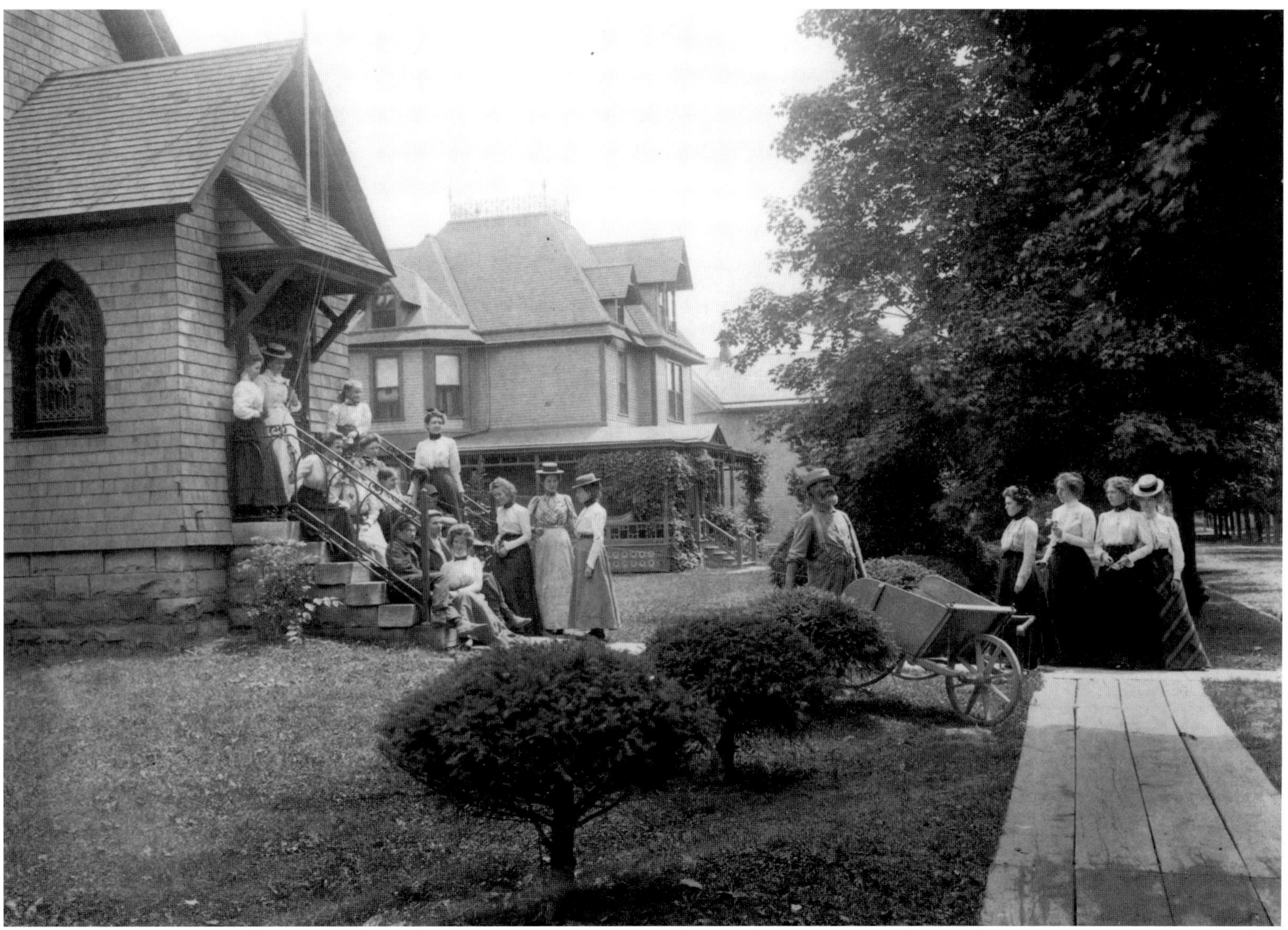

In the foreground is one of several buildings on the Roycroft campus, photographed in 1900. The Roycroft was established in 1895 by Elbert Hubbard, a charismatic business entrepreneur and writer, as part of the Arts and Crafts movement in America. Roycrofters did expert printing, fine bookbinding, hand-fashioned glass and copperware, handsome leather goods, and Mission-style furniture. One of Hubbard's best-known essays, *A Message to Garcia,* on accepting responsibility and getting the job done, has sold more than 80 million copies. The Roycroft community began to decline following the deaths of Hubbard and his wife aboard the *Lusitania,* which was torpedoed by a German U-boat in 1915.

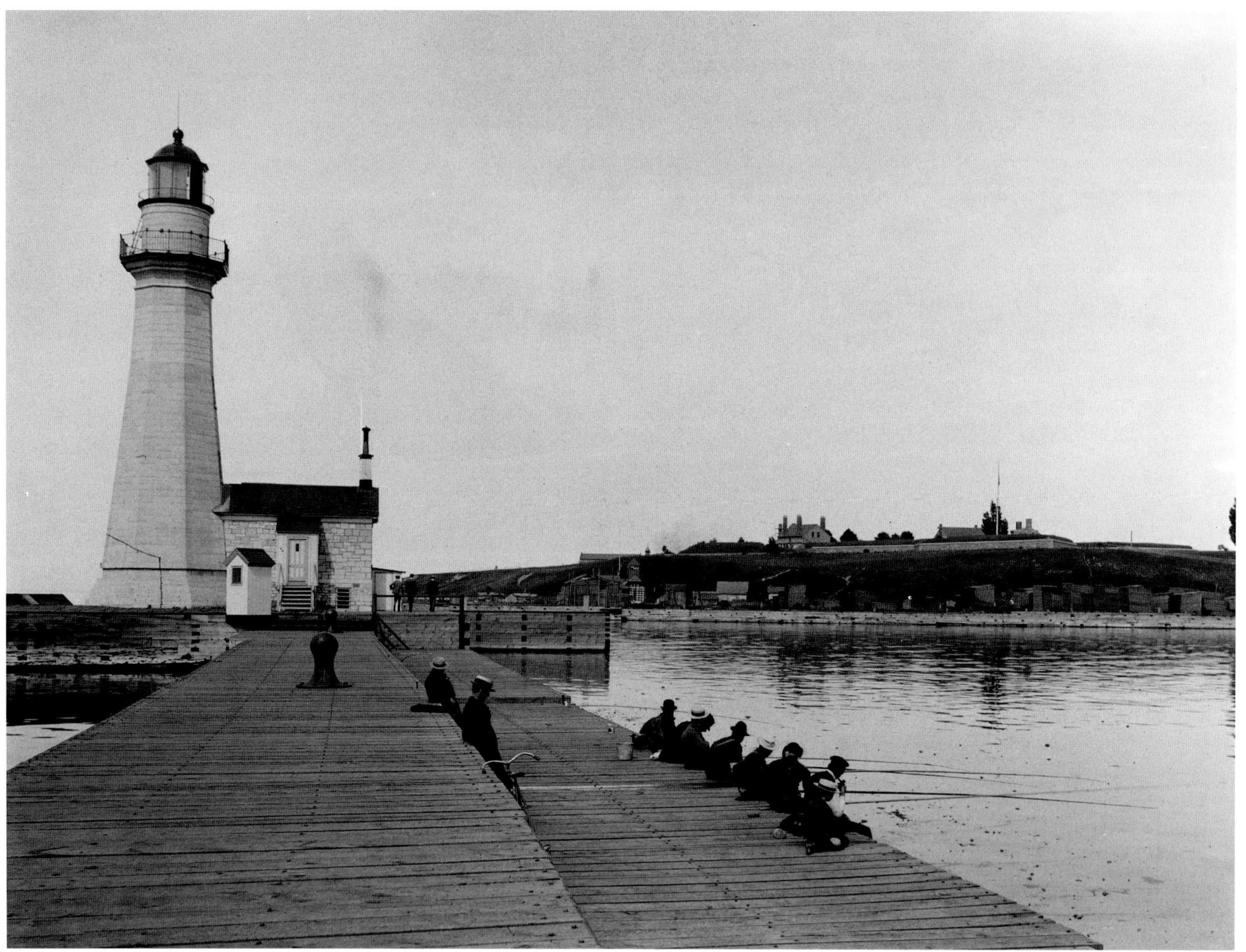

Oswego is a port city on the eastern shore of Lake Ontario. The Oswego Canal, built in 1828, connected Lake Ontario to the Erie Canal, making the city a prominent trading center. The lighthouse alerted ships to the Oswego port. In the distance is Fort Ontario, which dates to 1755. It was destroyed and rebuilt several times. The shape of the fort is pentagonal with five arrowhead-shaped bastions atop an earth embankment, which could repel attacks from any direction, by sea or by land.

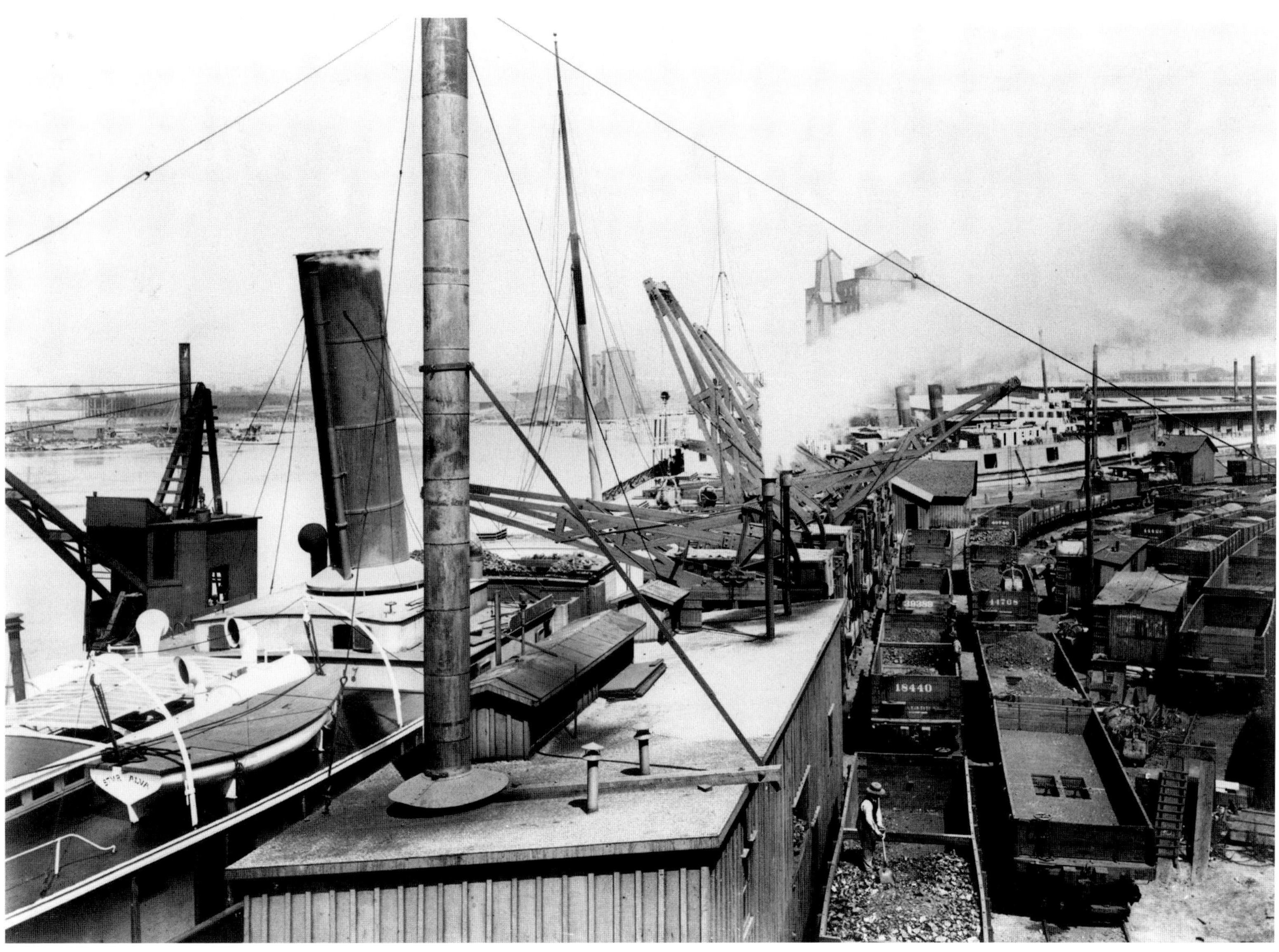

In 1900, Buffalo was a major steel town. Iron ore was shipped on the Great Lakes from the Midwest and unloaded at this Lake Erie dock in Lackawanna. Thornberger hoists were used to unload ore from the lake ships and deposit it in railroad cars that transported it to the steel mills. Coal to fire the blast furnaces came by train from Pennsylvania. Lackawanna Steel would be acquired by Bethlehem Steel, one of America's largest steel producers, in 1922.

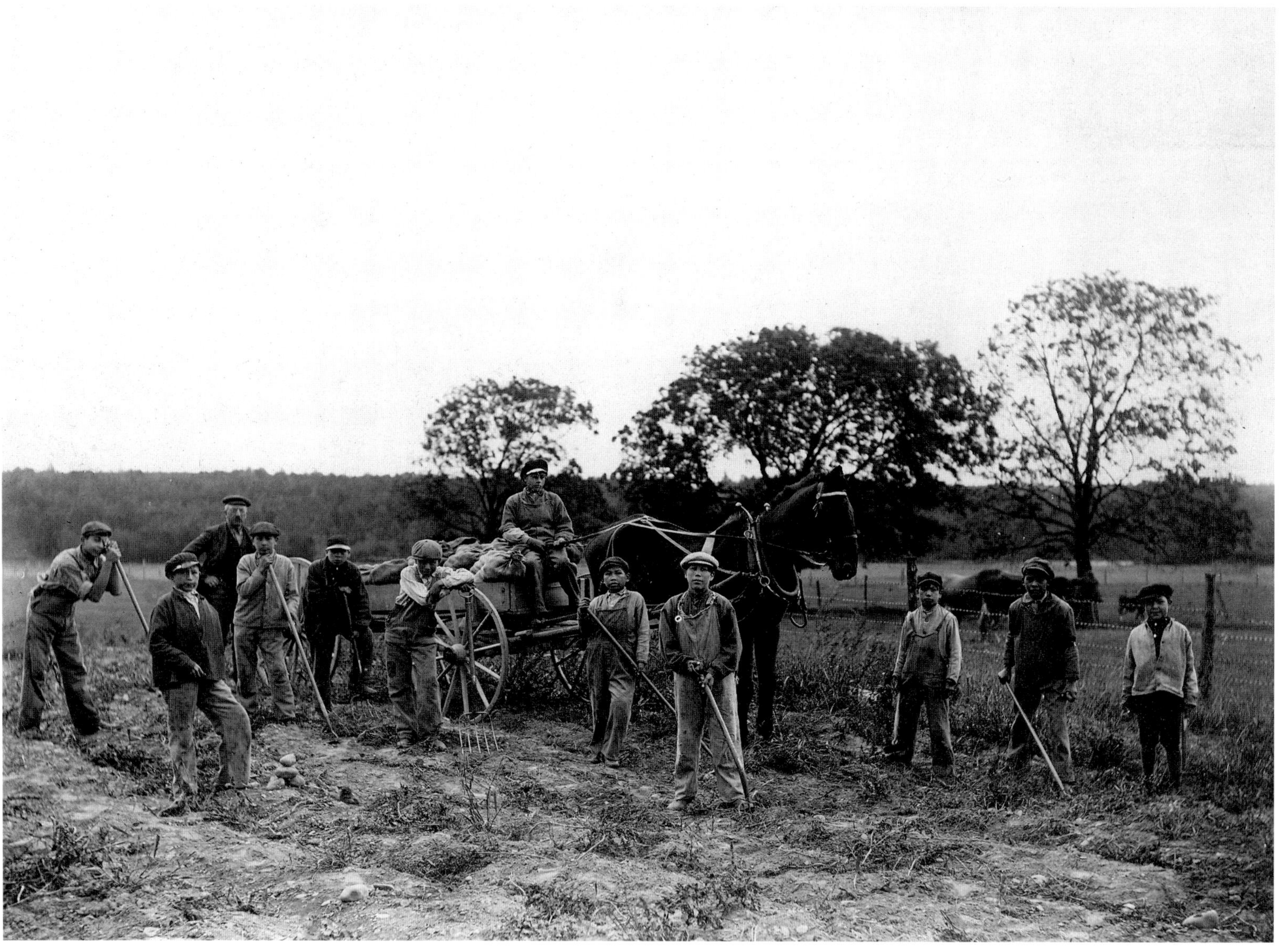

Around 1900, Thomas Indian School boys are shown harvesting potatoes and loading them on a horse-drawn cart.

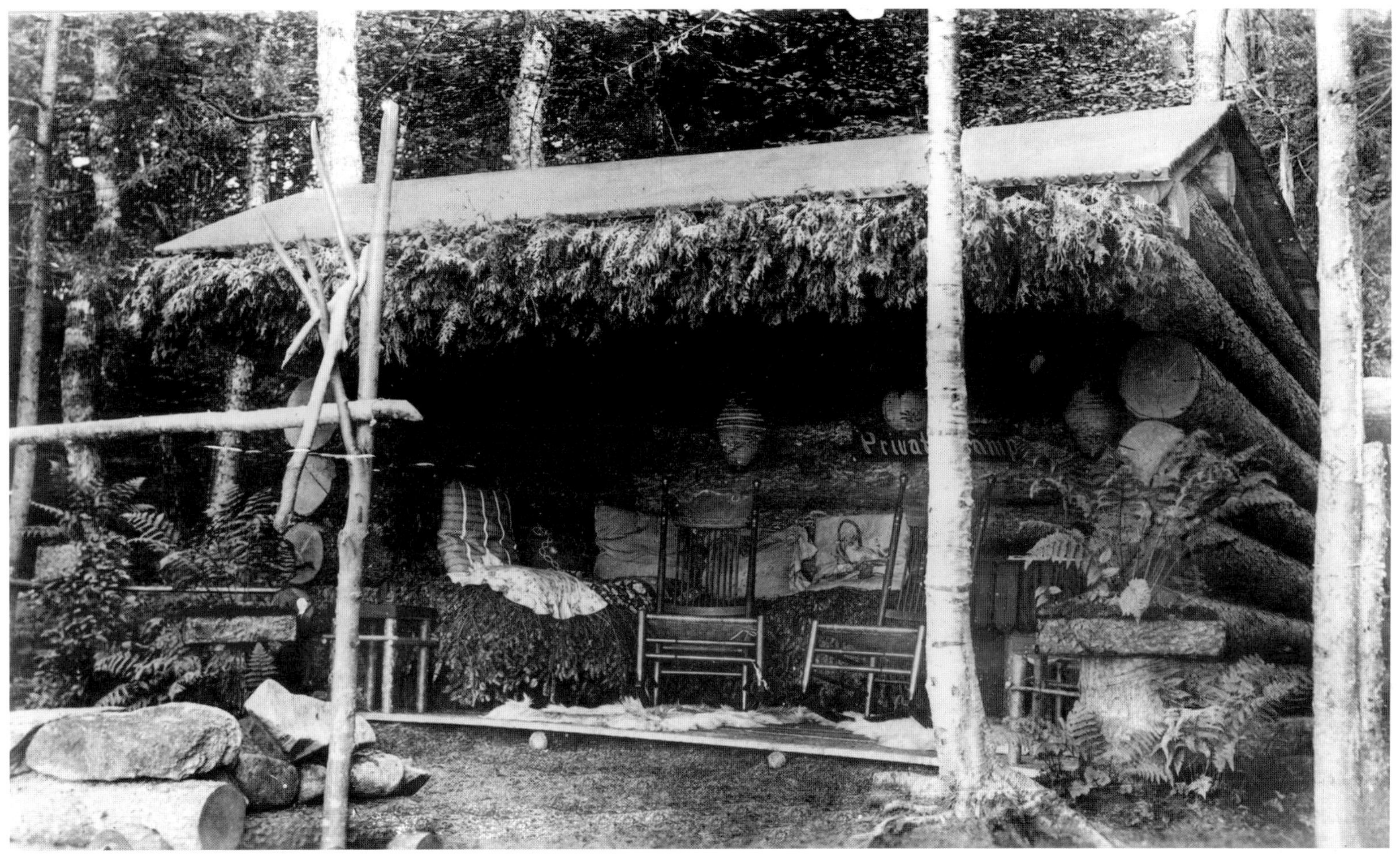

This rustic, open-sided log cabin was situated in the Adirondacks, in a wooded area on the Hotel Glennmore grounds at Big Moose Lake. It was fitted with animal-skin rugs, rocking chairs, cushions, potted ferns, and Japanese paper lanterns. The small sign on the back wall reads, "Private Camp."

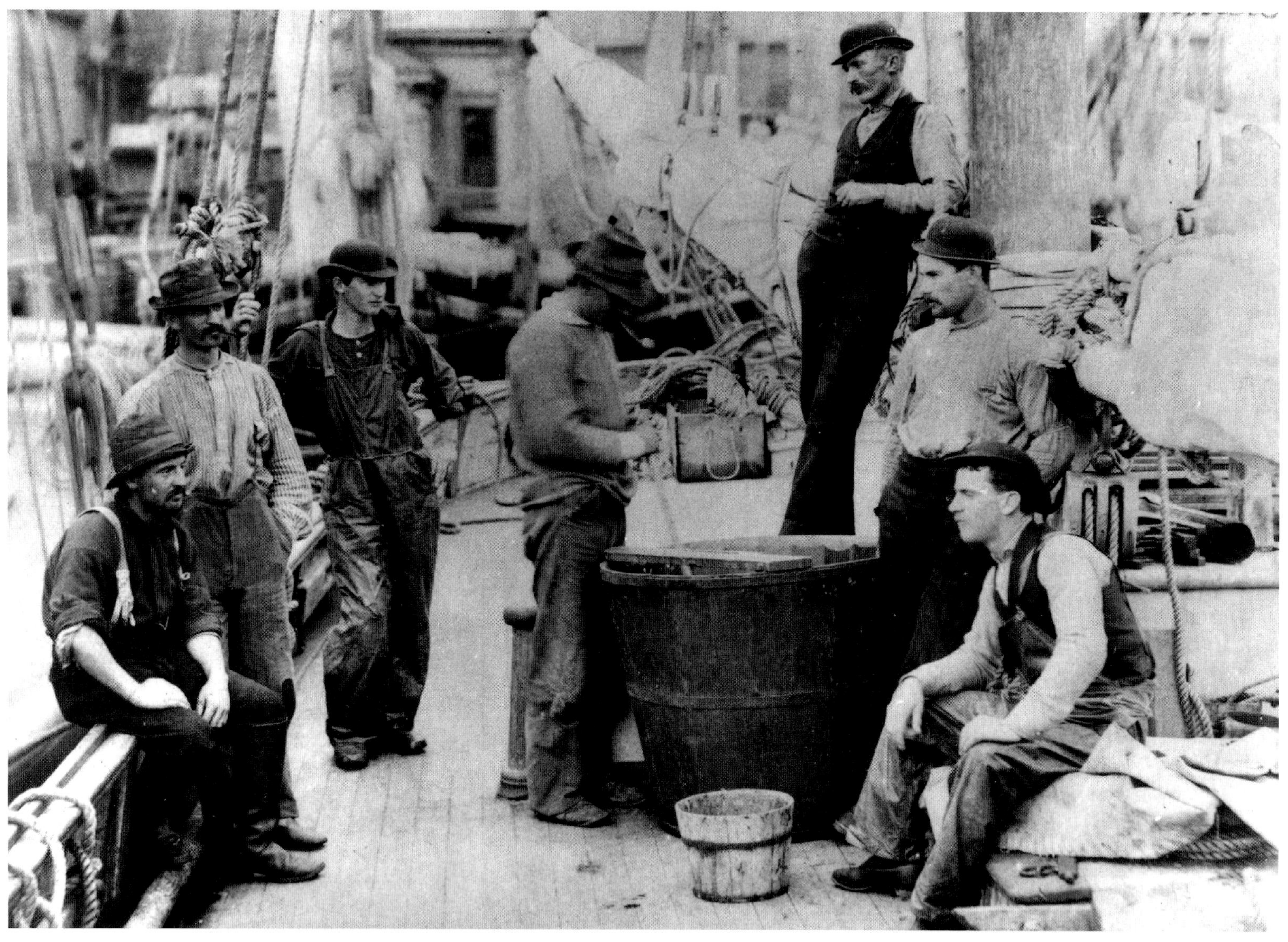

While anchored in the port of New York City, the crew of a fishing sailboat gather on the deck for a photograph around 1900. Ropes and rigging to manage sails and fishing nets, as well as wooden barrels and boxes, are visible on the deck.

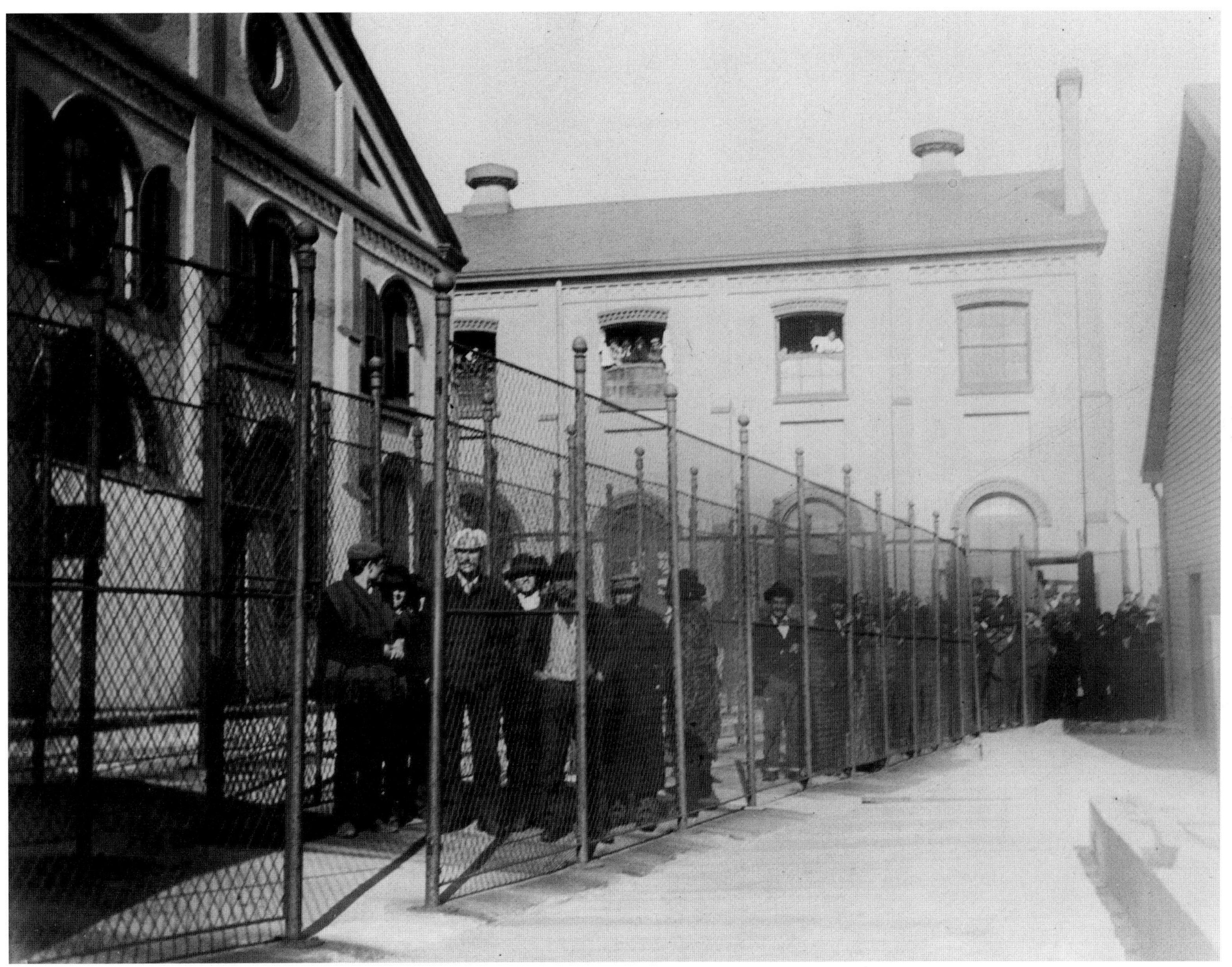

Hoffman Island is a small, 11-acre artificial island off Staten Island. When this photograph was made in 1901, Hoffman Island was used as a quarantine station to house immigrants believed to be carrying contagious diseases, principally smallpox. The picture shows immigrants from a smallpox ship being registered for their stay at housing facilities on the island.

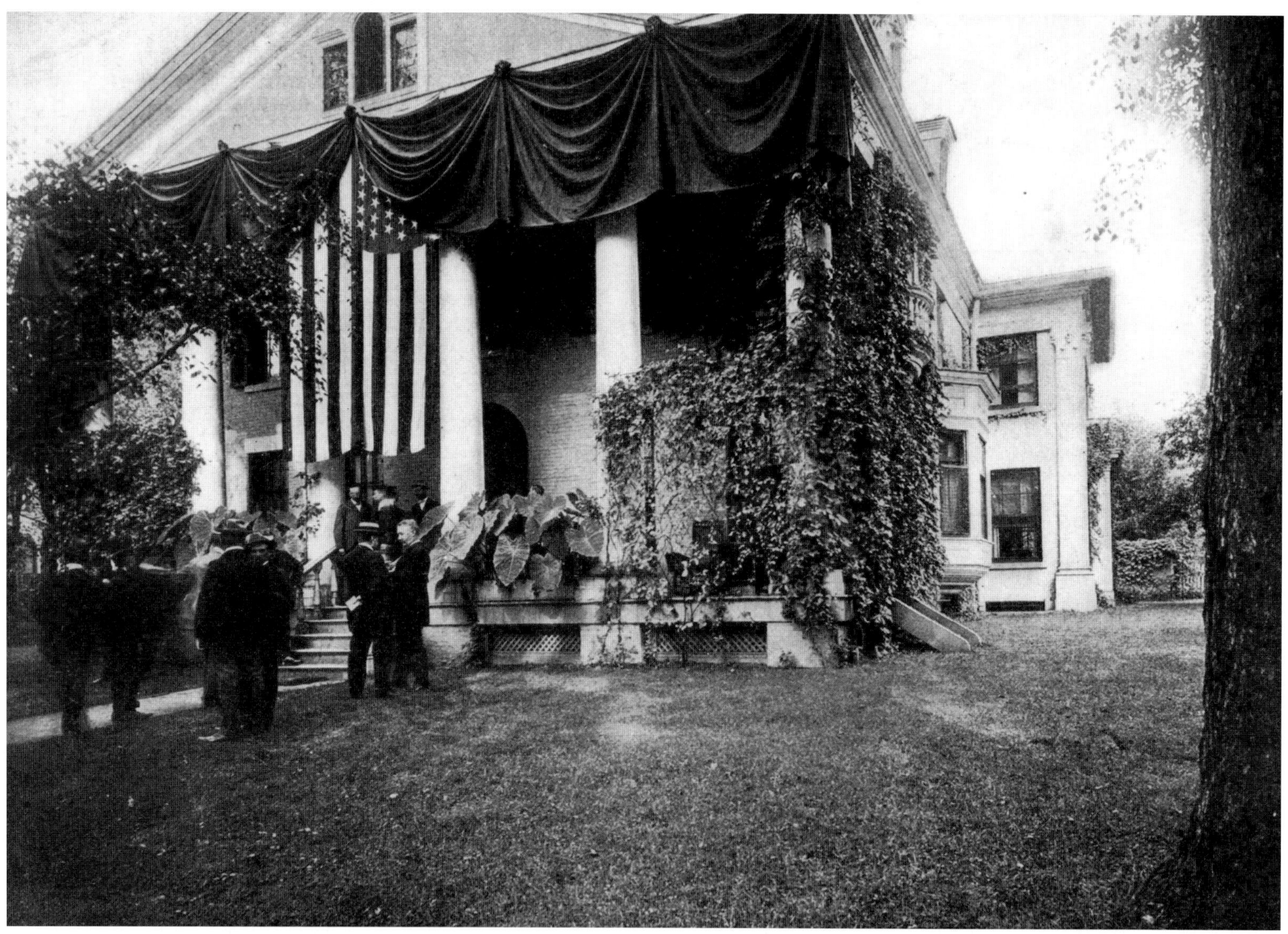

Featuring an imposing Greek Revival façade, the Ansley Wilcox House, at 641 Delaware Avenue, was built in 1838 in Buffalo. Vice-president Theodore Roosevelt was inaugurated as the 26th president of the United States here after President William McKinley was assassinated while attending the 1901 Pan-American Exposition in Buffalo. On vacation in the Adirondacks at the time, Roosevelt rushed to Buffalo and, with the Wilcox family and dignitaries in attendance, took the oath of office in the living room.

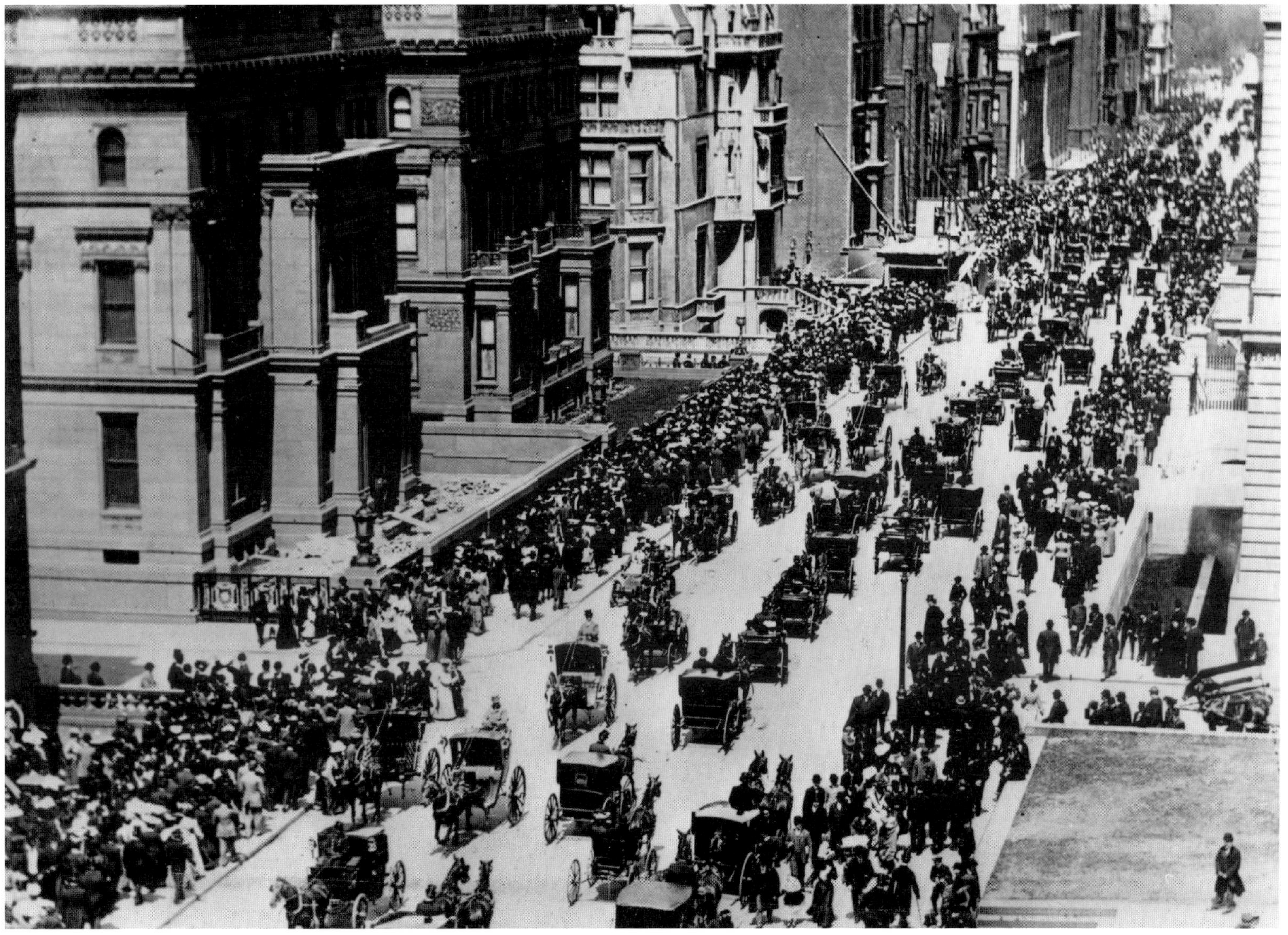

This is Easter Sunday morning in 1900 on Fifth Avenue in New York City. The sidewalks are jammed with churchgoers and other celebrants, and the street itself is bustling with two-way traffic. Most of the vehicles are horse-drawn carriages, but there are at least two motorcars, one driving uptown in the center of the photograph. The elegant mansions of the wealthy line the avenue at left.

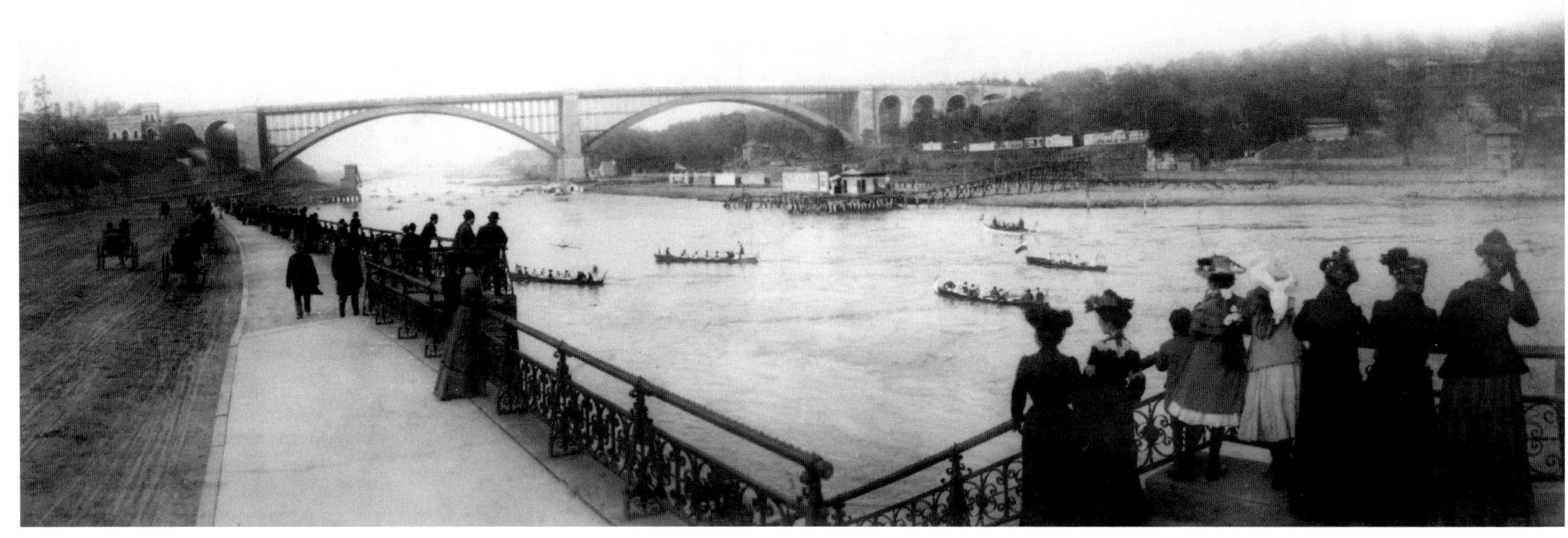

This is the Harlem River, which separates Manhattan Island from the Bronx, around 1902. Spectators are watching a regatta staged by a New York boat club. In this era, rowing was highly popular as a sport in the New York City area, which was home to dozens of rowing clubs. The Harlem River Regatta, attended by thousands, was an annual event in the spring of the year.

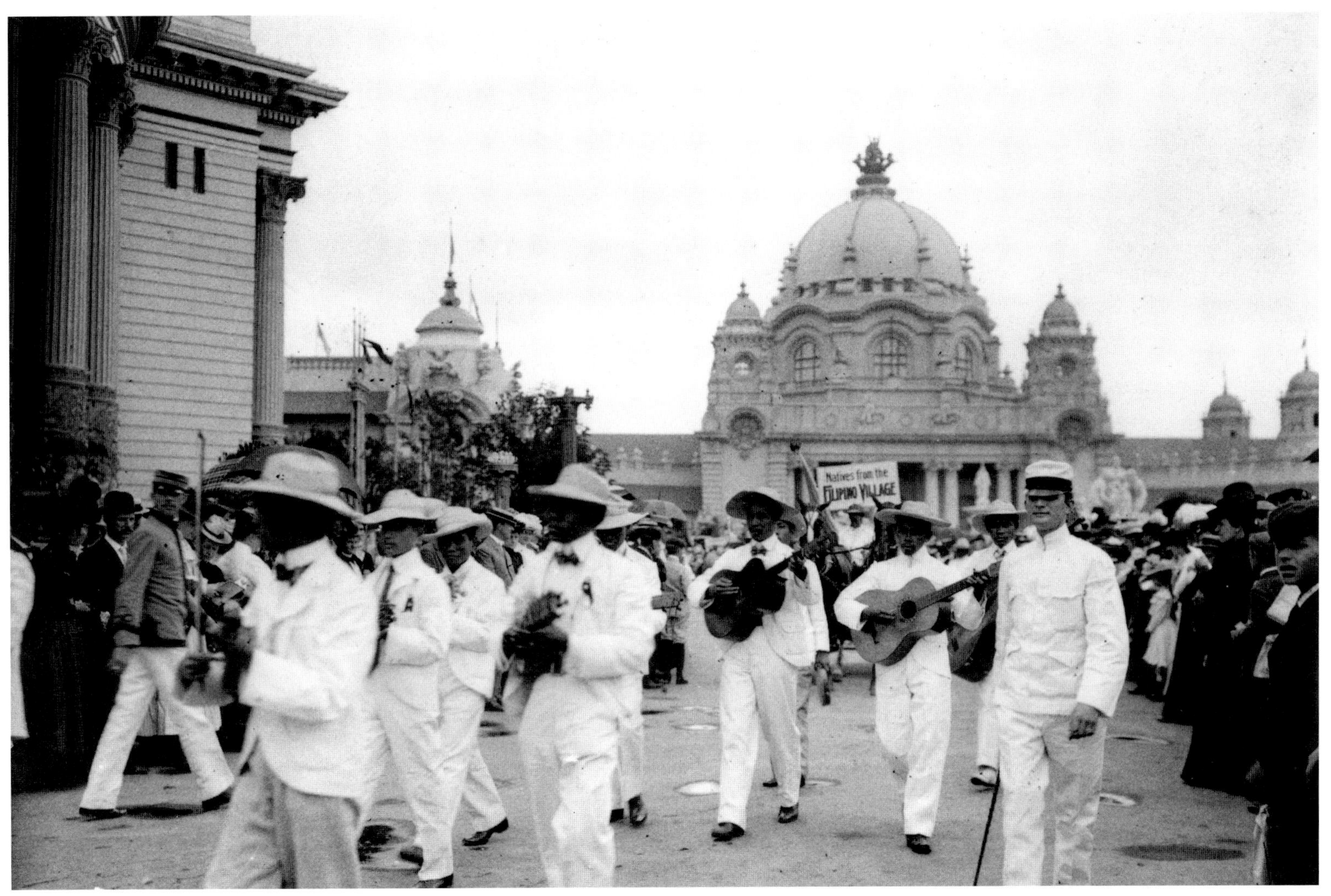

The World's Fair of 1901 was held in Buffalo. It was called the Pan-American Exposition and occupied 350 acres on the north side. As the name of the exposition implies, this fair celebrated progress among western-hemisphere countries and featured electric lighting and the newly invented X-ray machine. On Midway Day, a parade on the fairgrounds included representatives of many nations, among them these men dressed in white, some of them playing guitars. The domed building in the background is the U.S. Government Building.

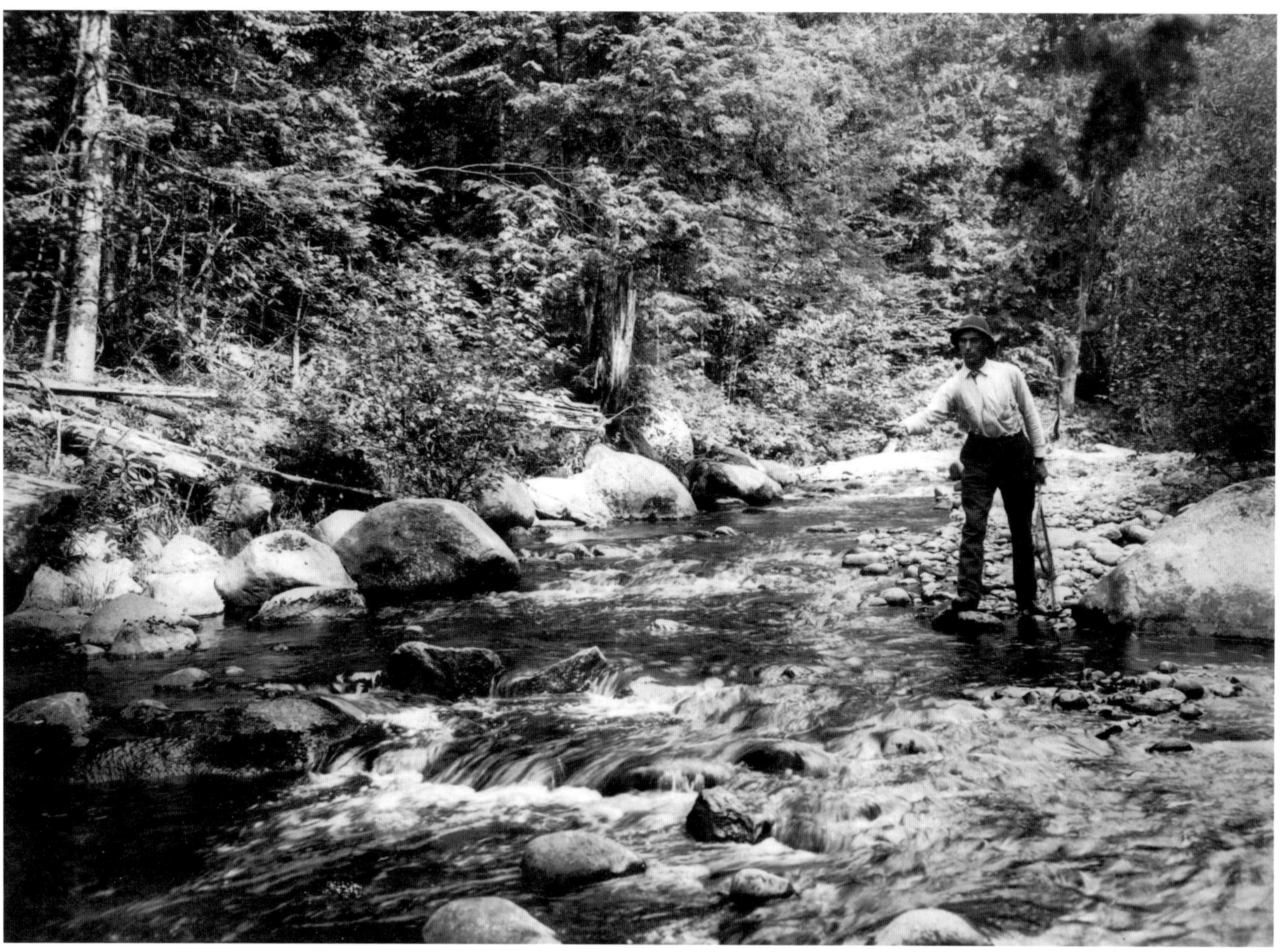

The lakes, creeks, and rivers of the Adirondacks were an angler's paradise in 1902 and remain so today. The waters are home to brook trout, lake trout, landlocked salmon, muskellunge, great northern pike, pickerel, walleye, small-mouth and large-mouth bass, bullhead, whitefish, as well as exotics like brown trout, rainbow trout, splake, and tiger muskie.

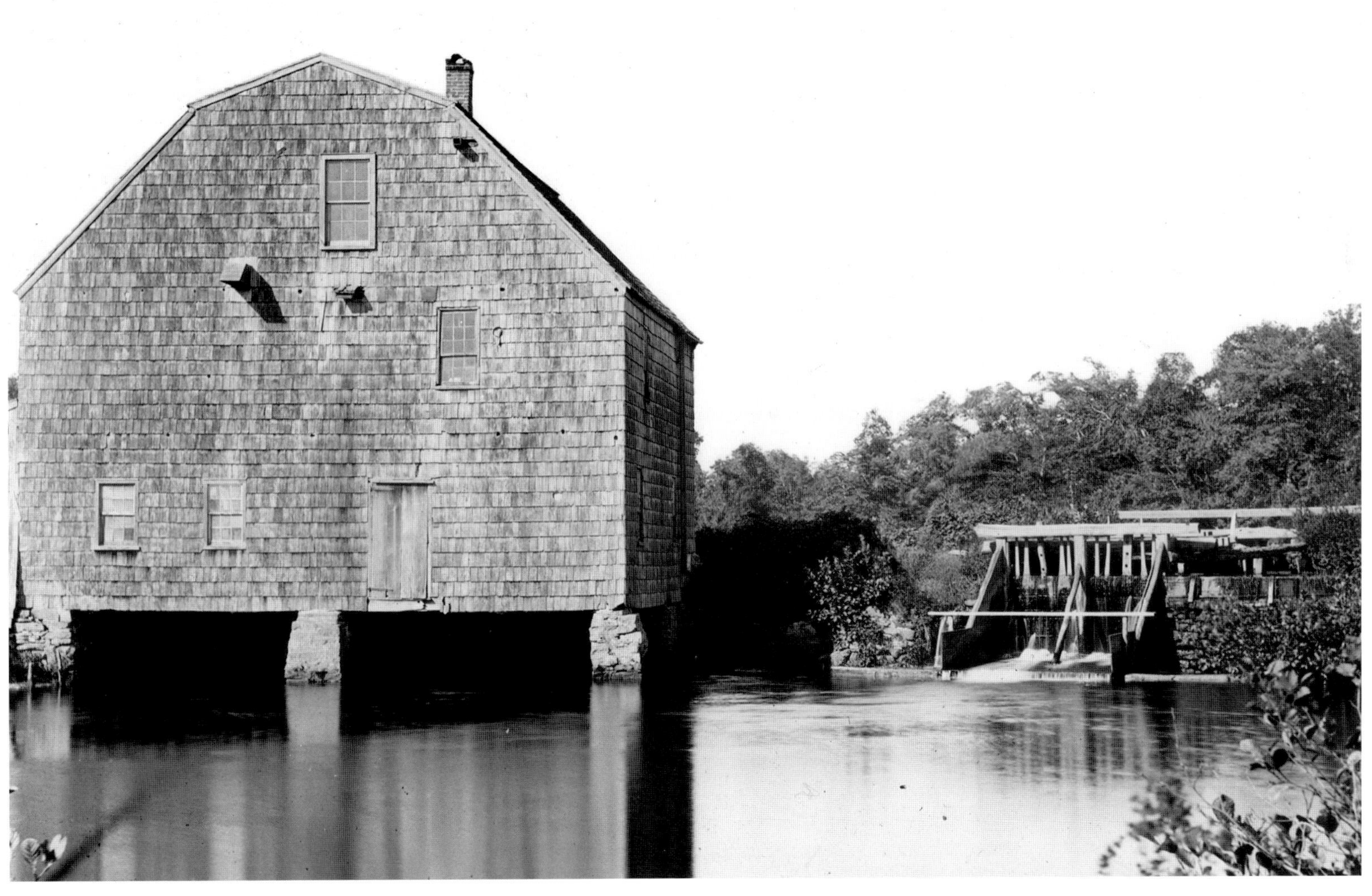

Shown here in 1900 is the watermill at Smithtown, Long Island, on the Nissequogue River. Mills like this one, which employed a waterwheel powered by falling water, were once relied on to grind wheat into flour and saw trees into lumber.

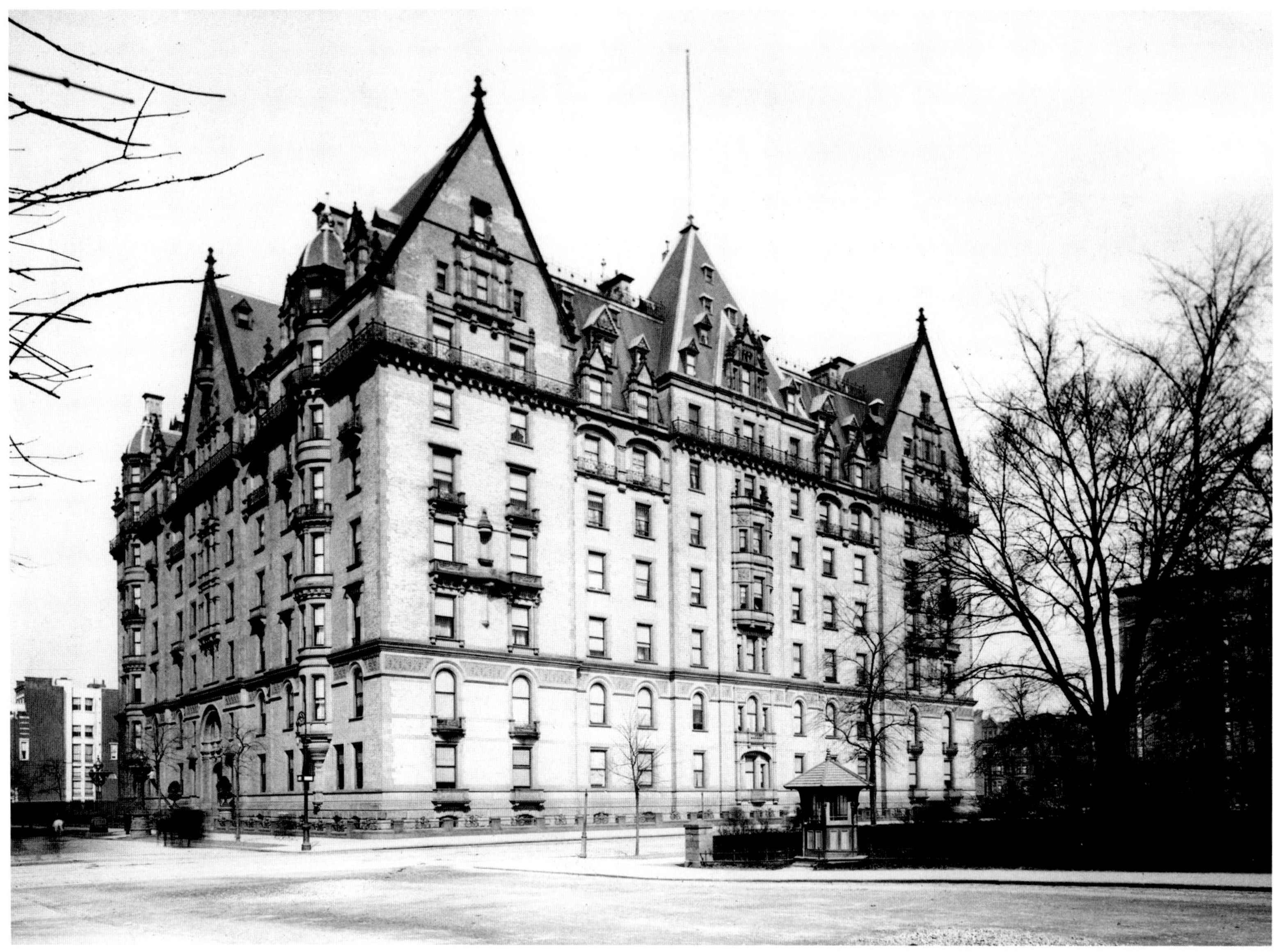

The Dakota is arguably the most famous apartment building in New York City. The architectural style is German Renaissance. It was built in the years 1880 to 1884 on Central Park West at 72nd Street, which was a remote address at that time, giving rise by some accounts to the name. The apartments were designed for wealthy New Yorkers who maintained a staff of servants. The Dakota's many famous residents have included Judy Garland, Carson McCullers, Leonard Bernstein, and singer-songwriter John Lennon of the Beatles. Lennon was shot and killed on the sidewalk outside the Dakota in December 1980.

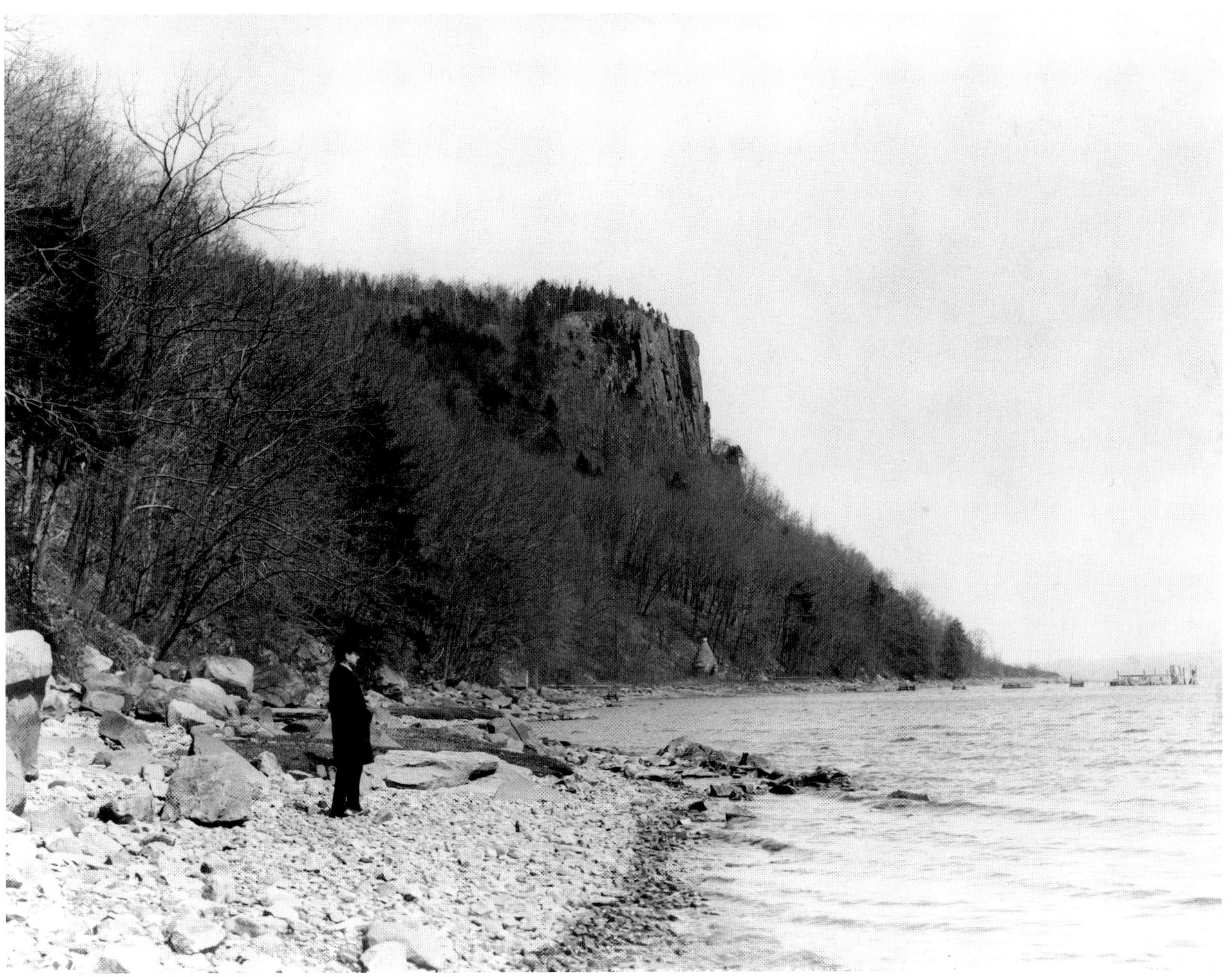

The Palisades is a line of lofty, steep cliffs on the west side of the Hudson River in Rockland County. The town of Palisades is a residential hamlet in the vicinity, and Columbia University operates an observatory in the area. In this 1903 image, a visitor looks east across the Hudson from a point below the cliffs.

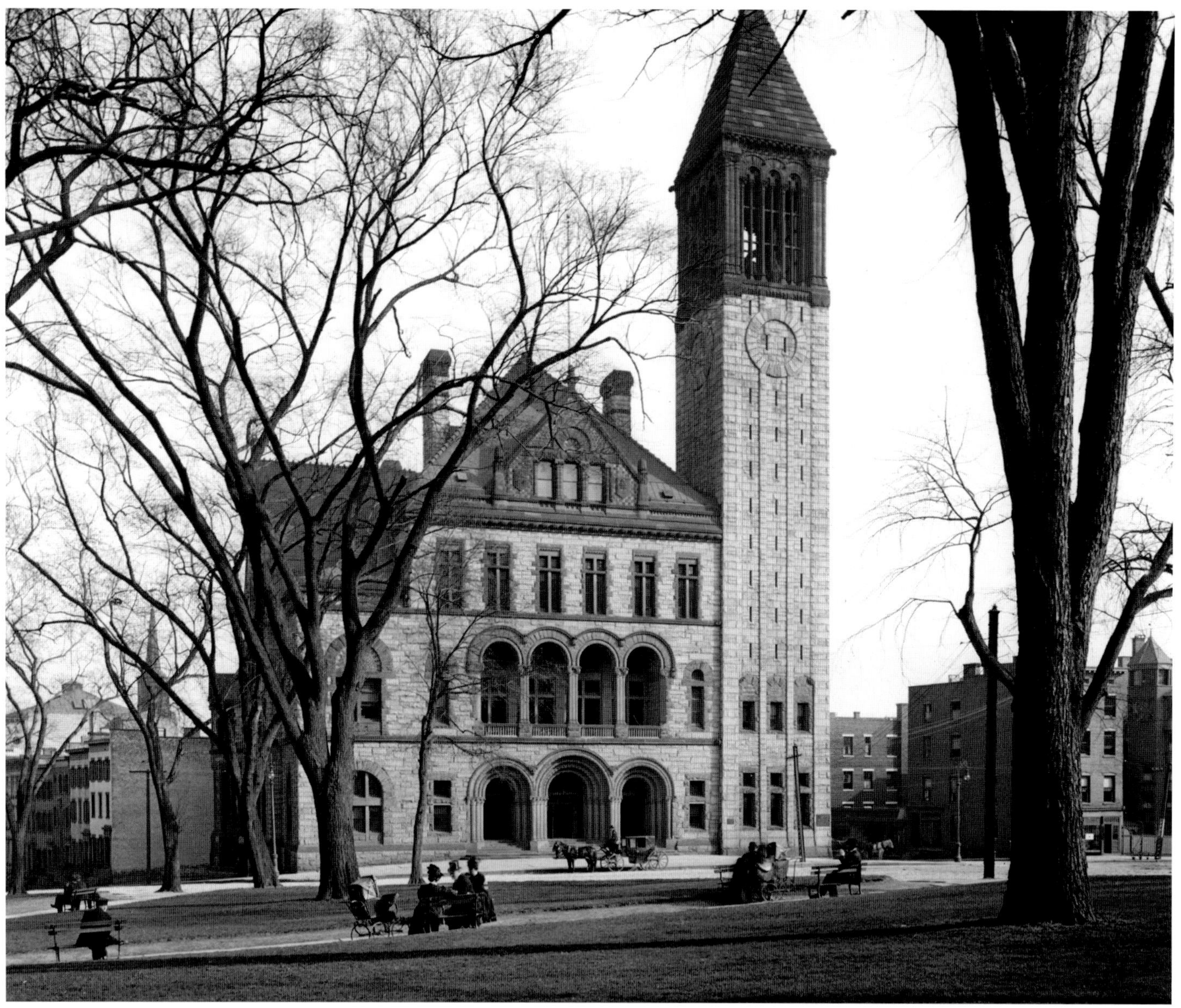

Albany City Hall, completed in 1883 at Eagle Street and Corning Place, is a magnificent Romanesque structure designed by Henry Hobson Richardson, America's preeminent architect of the period. The arch was Richardson's signature design motif, which is amply demonstrated in this building. City Hall features rusticated granite and brownstone trim to separate the stories and highlight fenestrations. There are 60 bells in the tower, which play music and ring the hours daily.

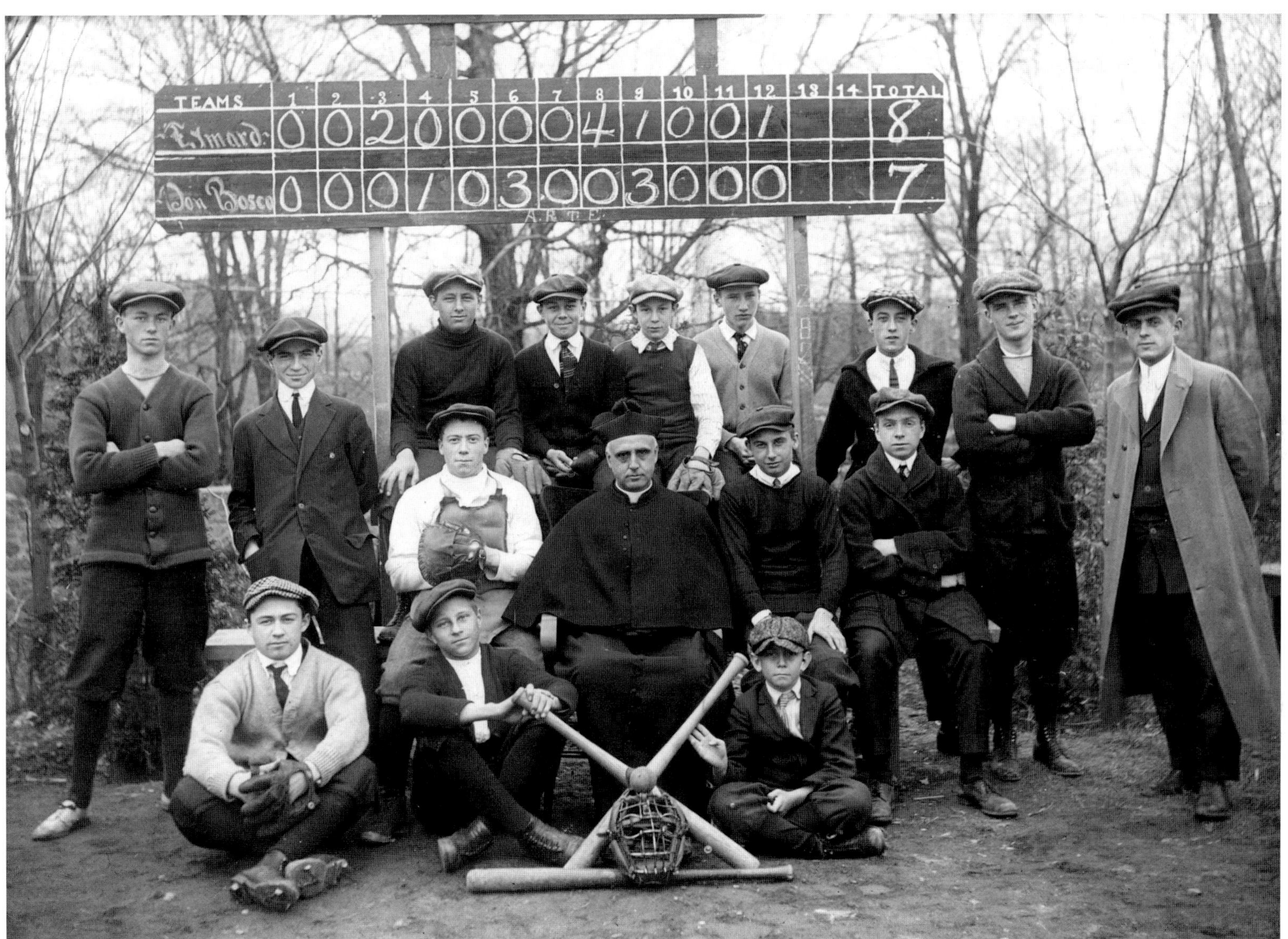

Posing for a group shot around 1890 is the baseball team of Eymard Seminary, a Catholic school in Suffern, located in southern New York near the New Jersey border. A Roman Catholic monsignor, wearing a cape and biretta, is seated at center. Team members are gathered around, with an adult in a long overcoat, perhaps the coach, standing at right. The scoreboard indicates that the Eymard team scored a run in the 12th inning to beat the Don Bosco team by a score of 8 to 7.

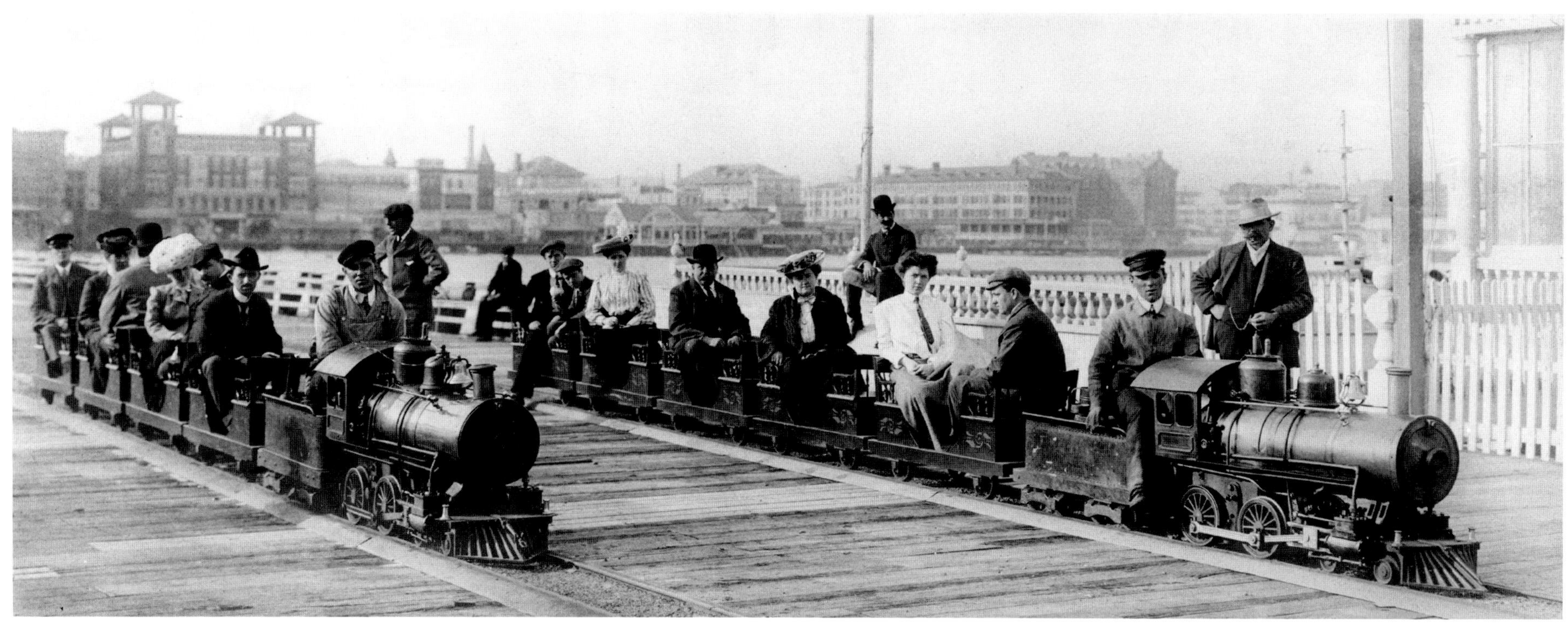

A miniature railway system transports visitors around Dreamland, an amusement park on Coney Island in south Brooklyn that operated for seven years beginning in 1904. It would appear that the rail cars were made for children, but in this image only adults are aboard. Reportedly, the trains could haul ten tons of weight, pulled by genuine 4-4-0 steam engines. Dreamland caught fire in 1911 and burned to the ground, leaving only fond memories of its spectacular rides and attractions.

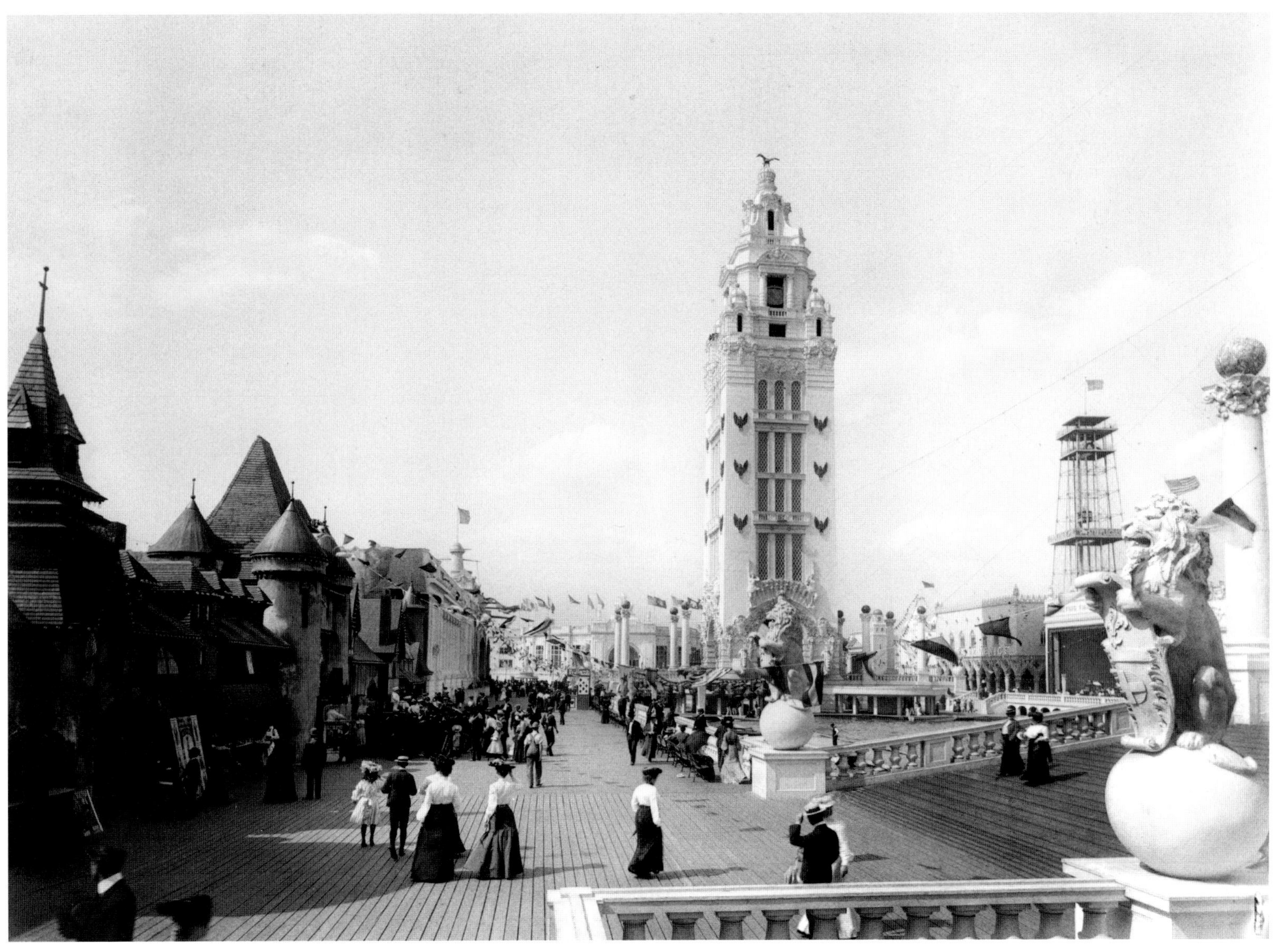

The Dreamland Tower dominated the park at 375 feet in height and fitted with 100,000 lights, including two powerful spotlights, which apparently disoriented ship captains who thought it was a lighthouse. The tower's architecture was based on the Giralda in Seville, Spain, and included a large metal falcon at its summit. Americans smartly attired, which was the norm in 1904 regardless of one's destination, wander the boardwalk taking it all in.

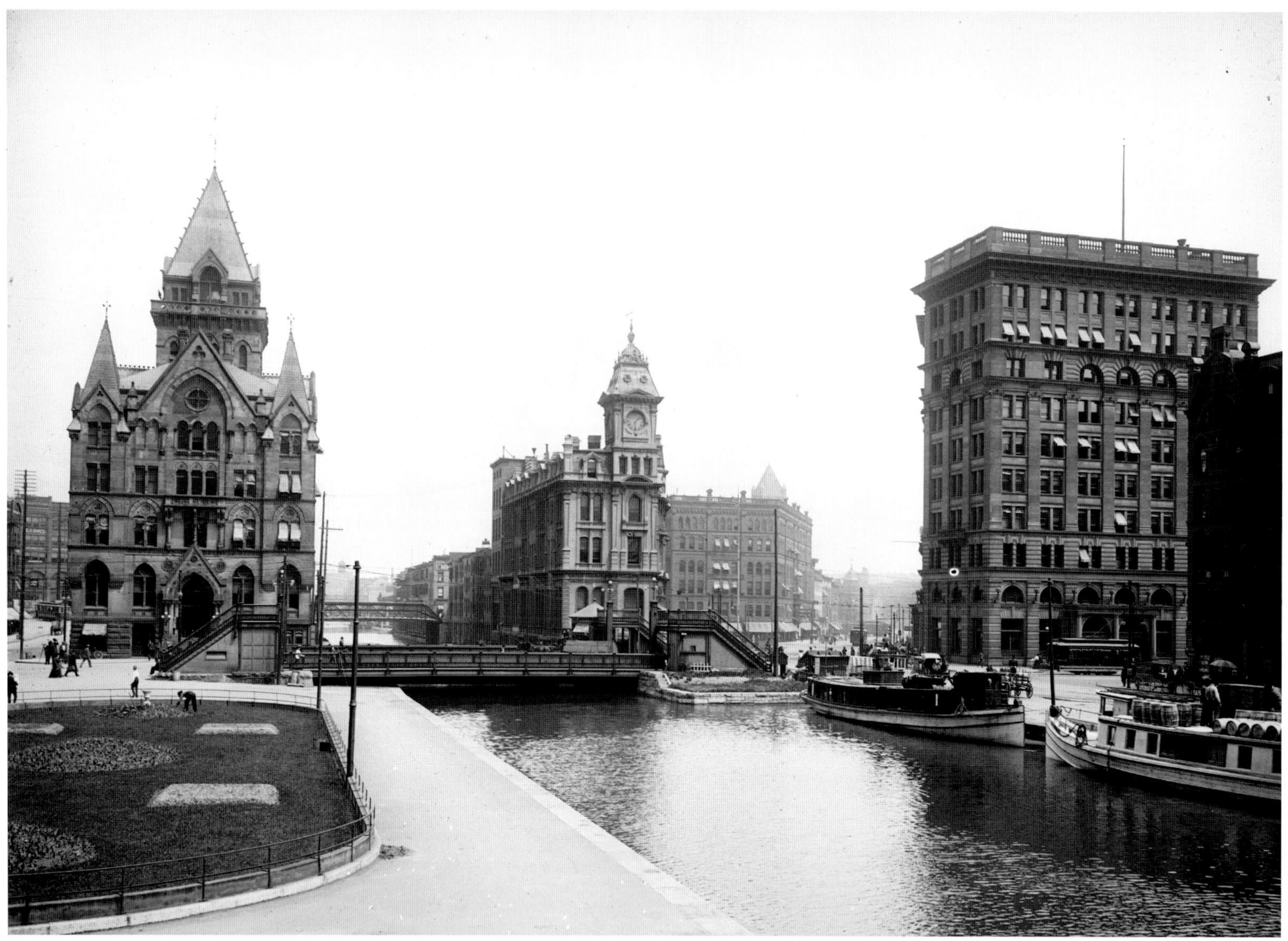

The original Erie Canal ran right through downtown Syracuse. The low bridge, seen here in 1904, could be raised to allow canal boat traffic to pass underneath. At left is the Syracuse Savings Bank, a monumental High Victorian Gothic sandstone building completed in 1876, and an impressive architectural statement to the success that the Erie Canal brought to the city. At center is the Gridley Building, a Second Empire–style edifice designed by the famous Syracuse architect Horatio Nelson White.

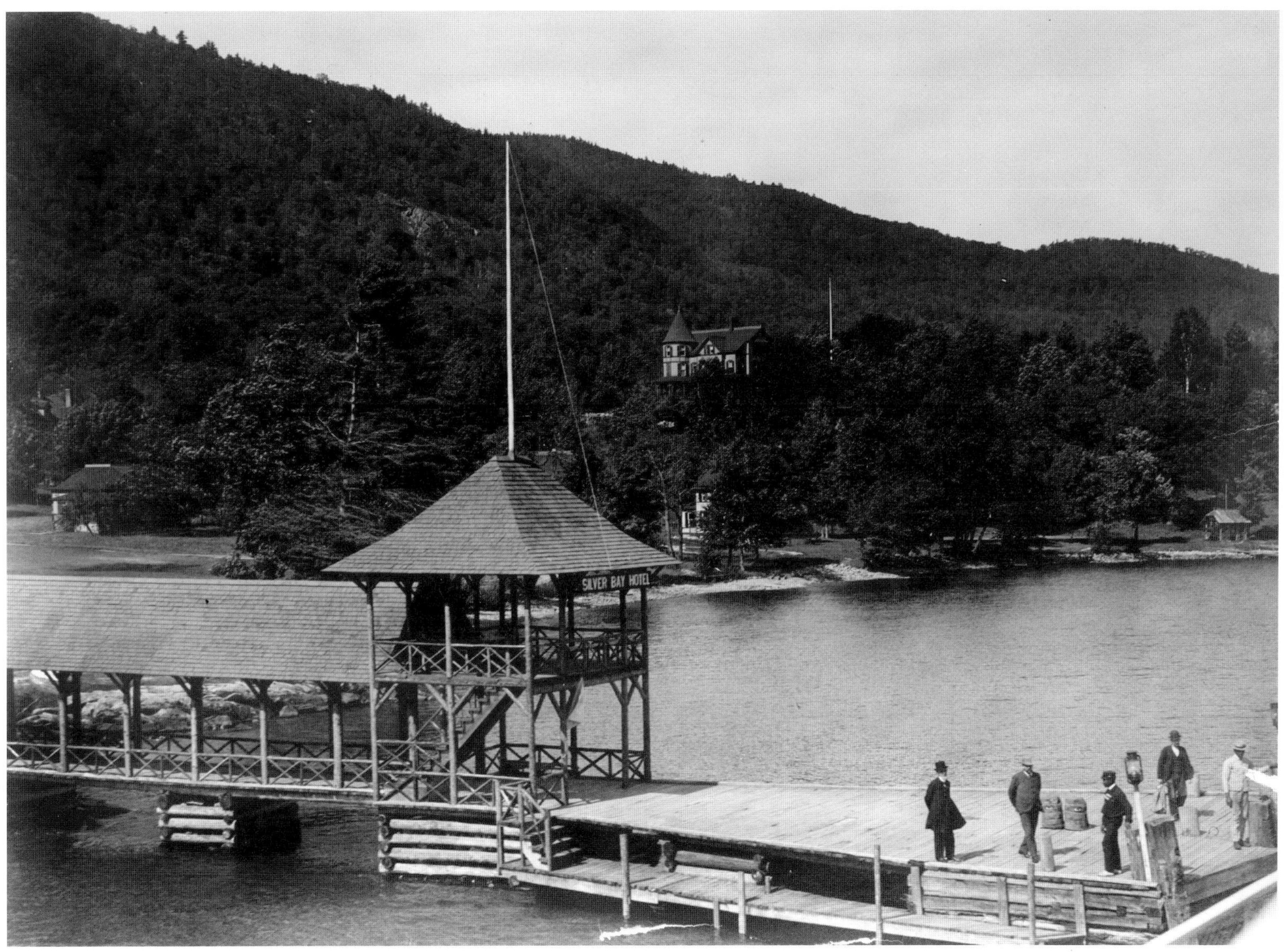

Silver Bay began as a YMCA in 1900 on the west shore of Lake George in the Adirondack Mountains, about 20 miles north of the village of Lake George at the south end of the long lake. Across the lake is Spruce Mountain, and Sugar Loaf and Black Mountain are a little farther to the south. The spectacular scenery at Silver Bay is suggested in this 1904 photograph of the boat dock. Lake George figured importantly in the Revolutionary War and much later as a destination for the nation's rich and famous. James Fenimore Cooper alludes to the lake in his classic Leatherstocking tale *Last of the Mohicans.*

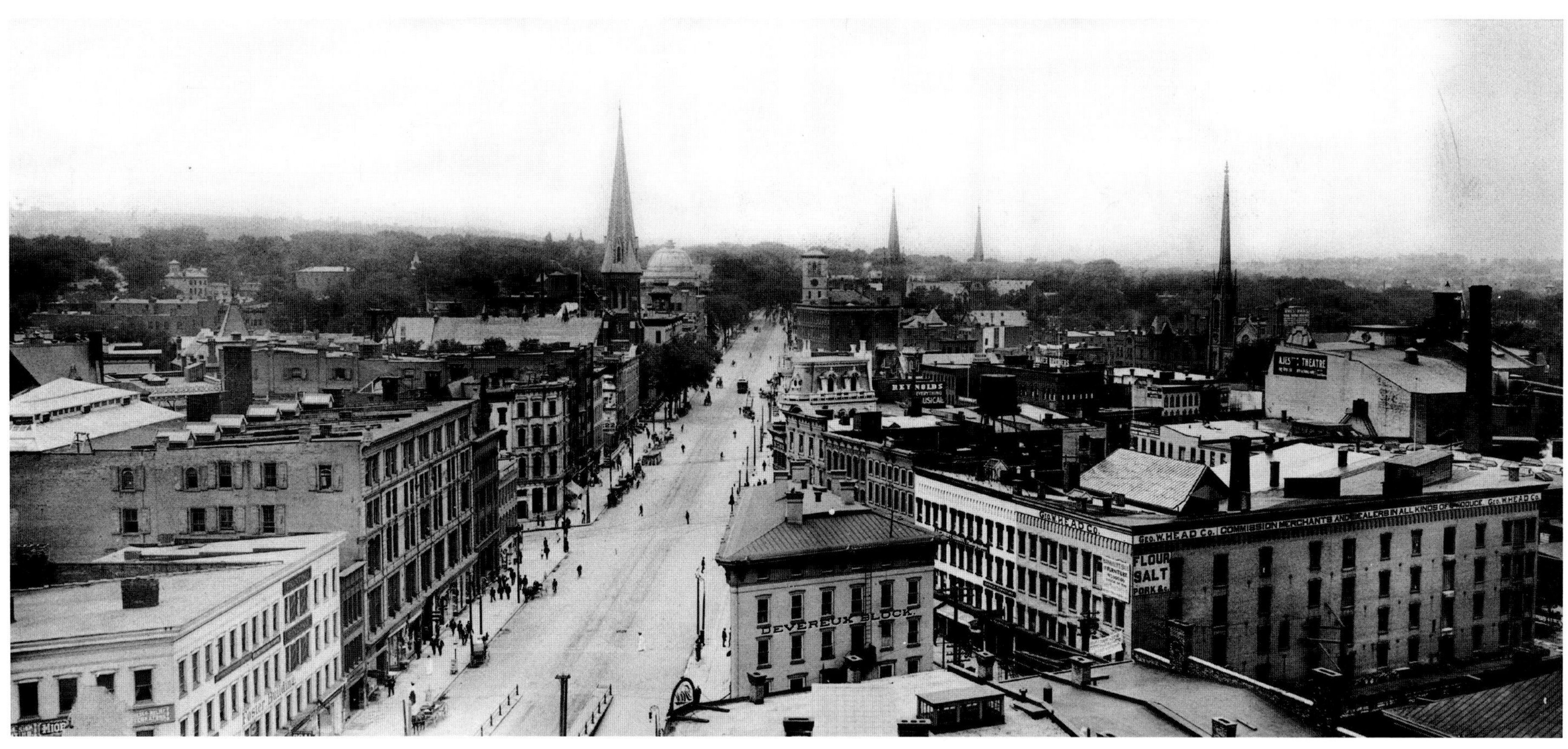

The spires of four churches pierce the sky in this 1905 bird's-eye view of Utica, located on the Mohawk River. The wide avenue is Genesee Street, and on the left beyond the first church steeple is the gold dome of the Savings Bank of Utica, built in 1898 in the Beaux-Arts style. On Saturday, October 23, 1819, the very first trip on the first-completed section of the new Erie Canal between Utica and Rome took place after the canal bed was flooded, a sight that awed many.

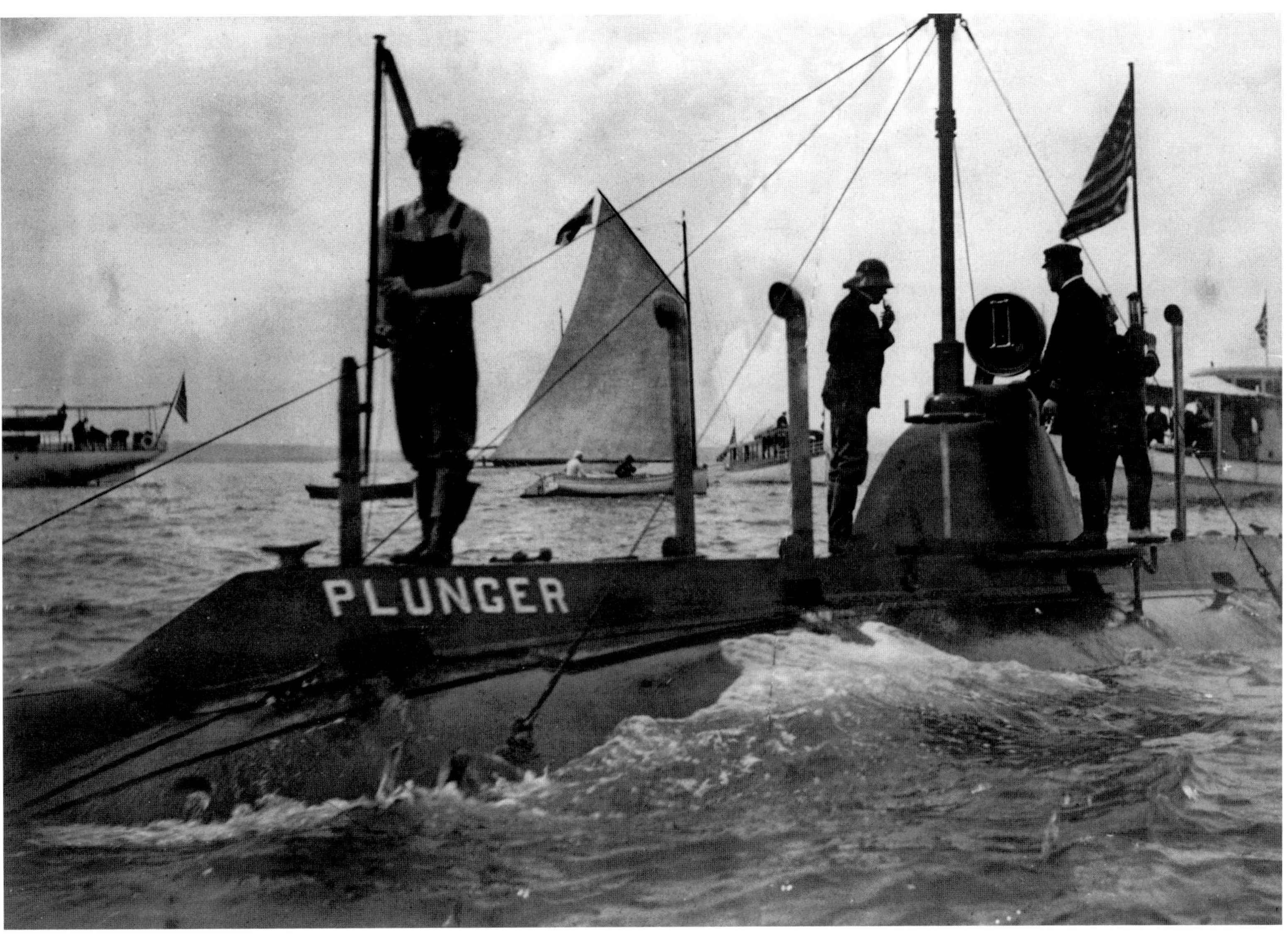

Built in 1902, the USS *Plunger* was one of the earliest submarines of the U.S. Navy. In 1905, when this photograph was taken, it was towed to Oyster Bay on Long Island to conduct trials. Four members of the crew stand on deck while sailboats and yachts move by in the distance. On the afternoon of August 22, 1905, President Theodore Roosevelt, who lived nearby, paid a visit to *Plunger* and boarded the submarine for a series of dives spanning three hours.

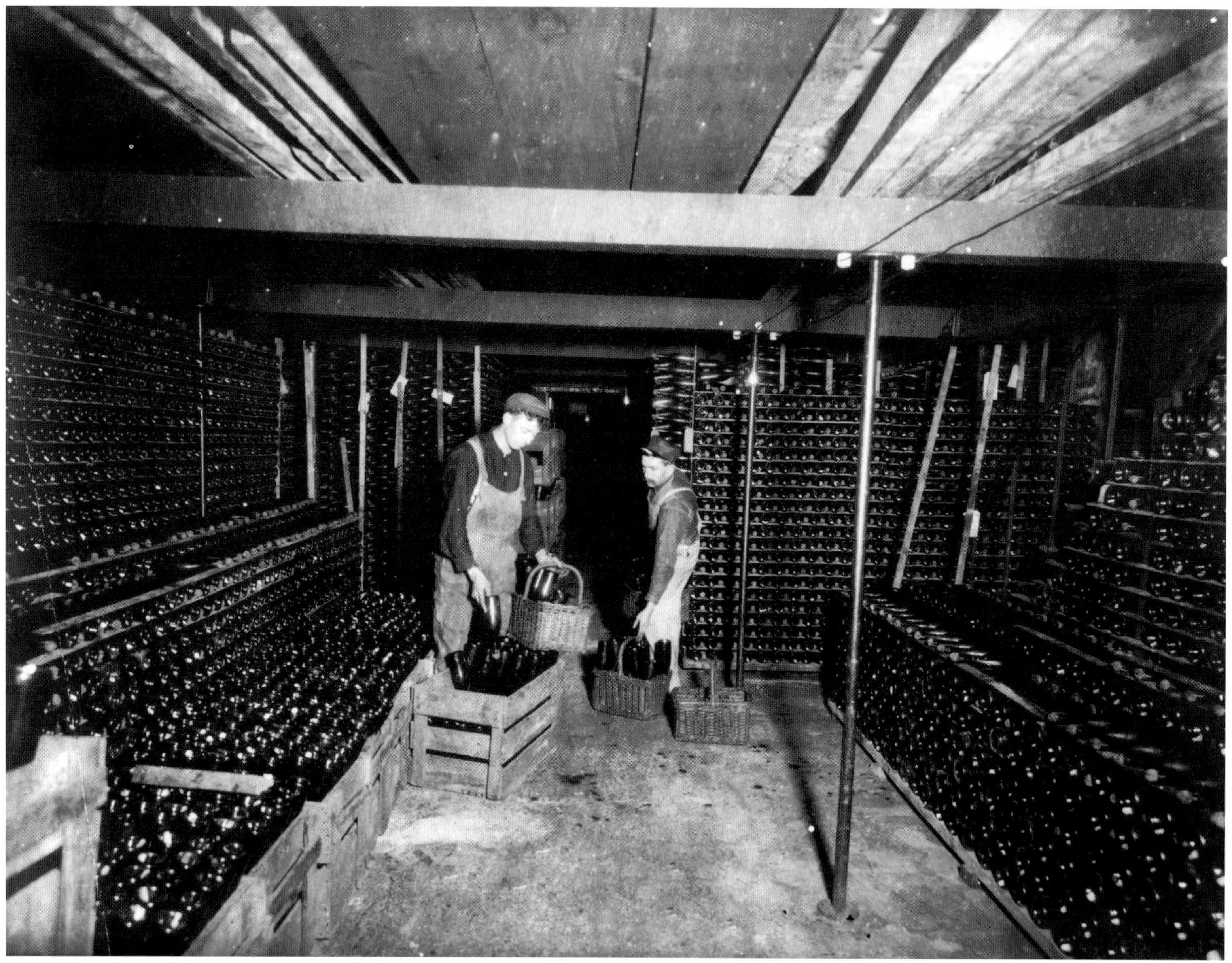

These are the champagne vaults of the Empire State Wine Company in New York City in 1905. Two workers in aprons fill baskets with bottles of champagne to make a delivery.

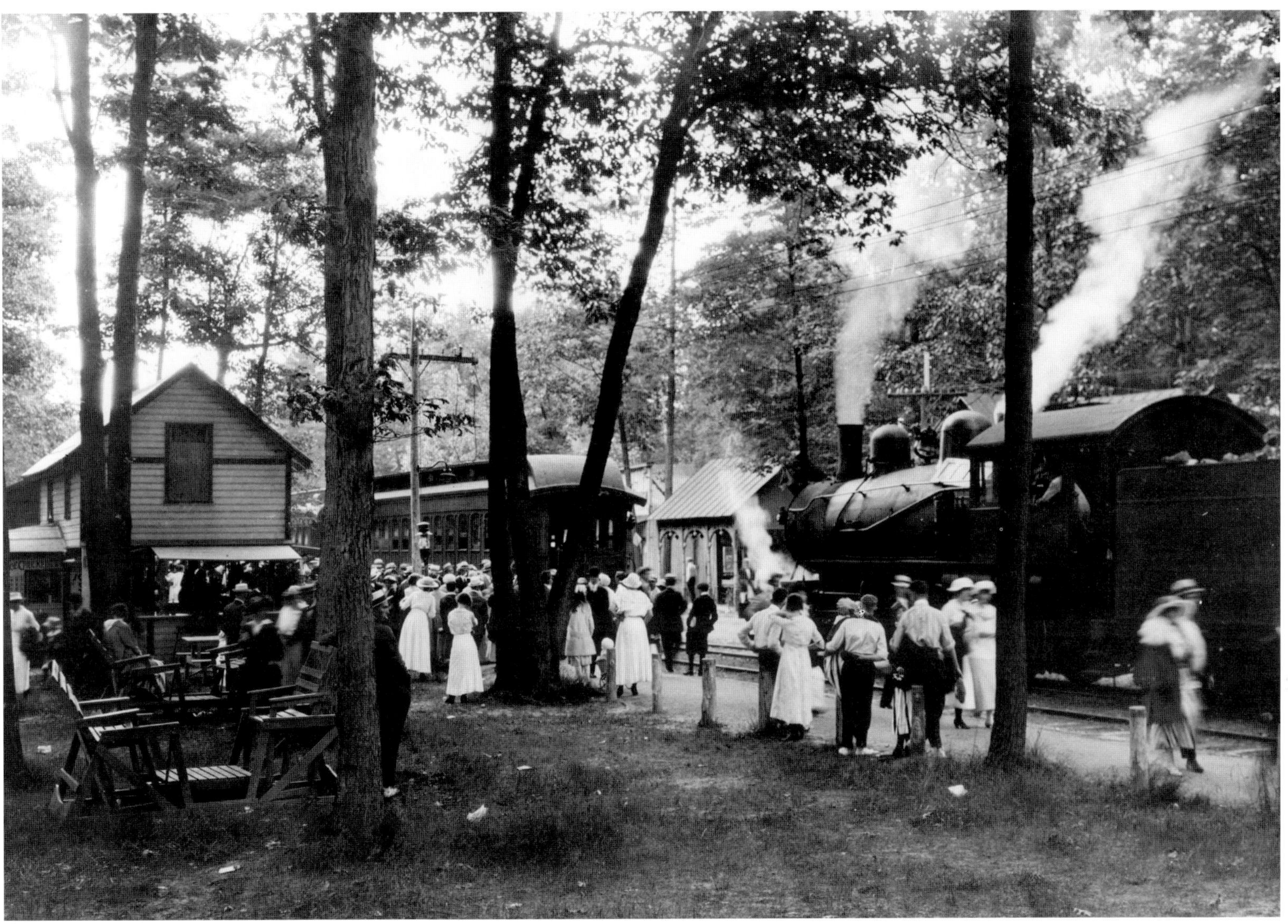

The village of Sylvan Beach on the eastern shore of Oneida Lake in the Finger Lakes region of upstate New York is a resort community offering fishing, swimming, boating, and the Sylvan Beach Amusement Park. In the late nineteenth century, before the advent of the automobile, such resorts succeeded only if they could be reached by train.

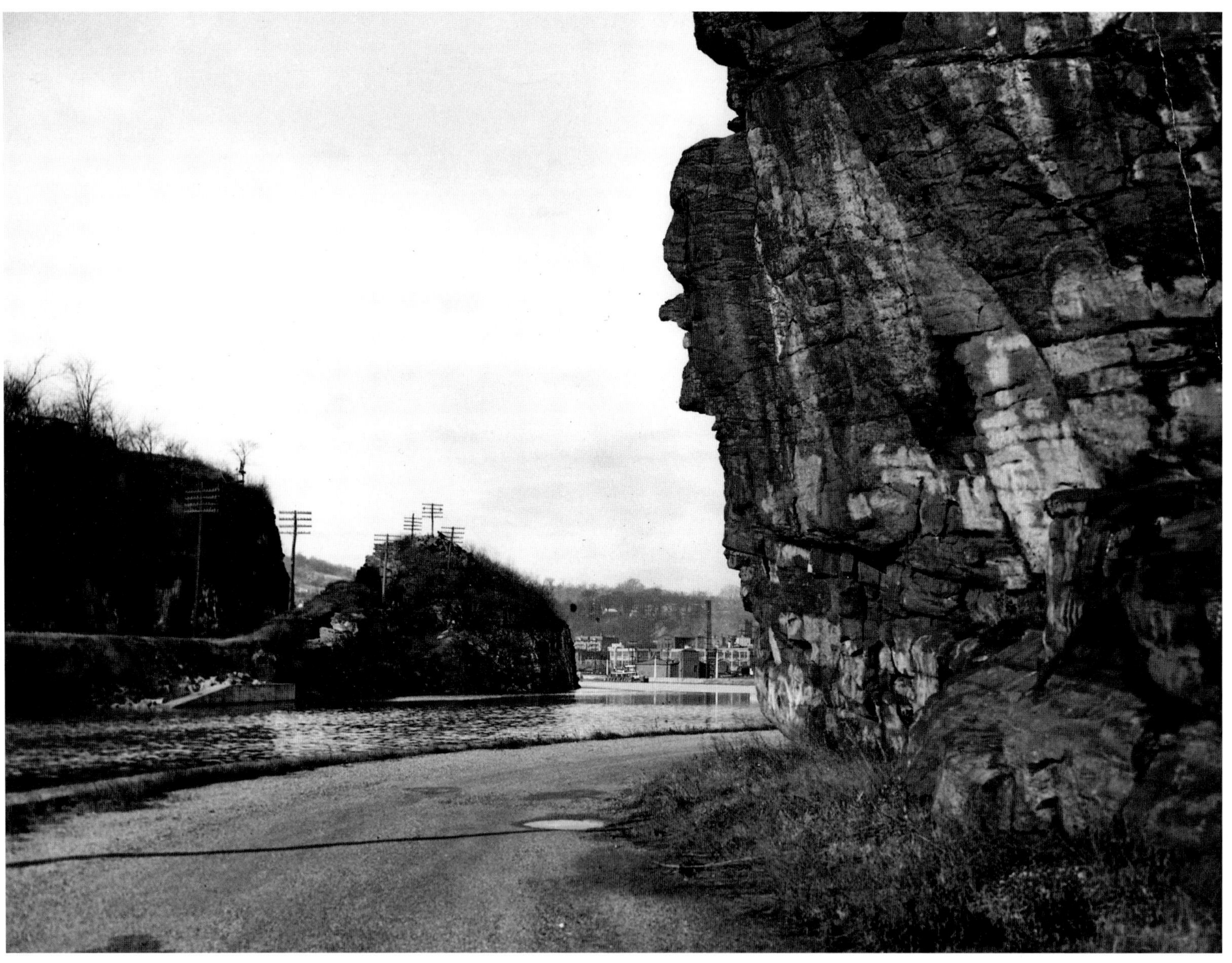

Shown here alongside the Erie Canal in Little Falls is the curious and massive Profile Rock, aptly named for its natural anthropomorphic attributes. Little Falls is also home to the world's highest canal lift lock. In seven minutes, the lock can raise or lower boats 40.5 feet.

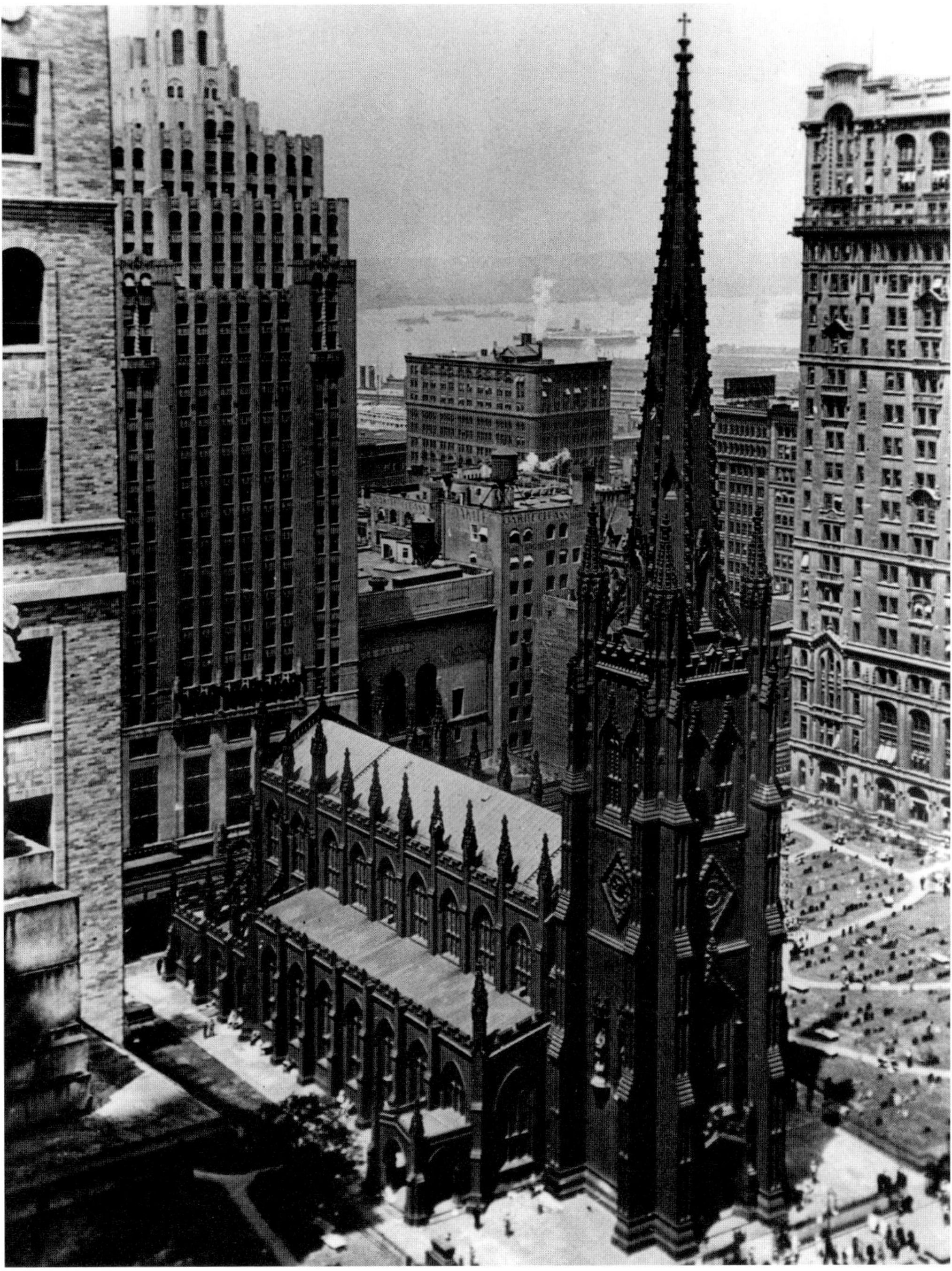

Trinity Church, which faces Wall Street from Broadway in lower Manhattan, was designed by the famous architect Richard Upjohn, whose specialty was Gothic Revival architecture. This church, the second on the site (the first one was built in 1698), was consecrated in 1846. At that time, the soaring neo-Gothic spire was the tallest structure in Manhattan. Trinity Church was designated a National Historic Landmark in 1976.

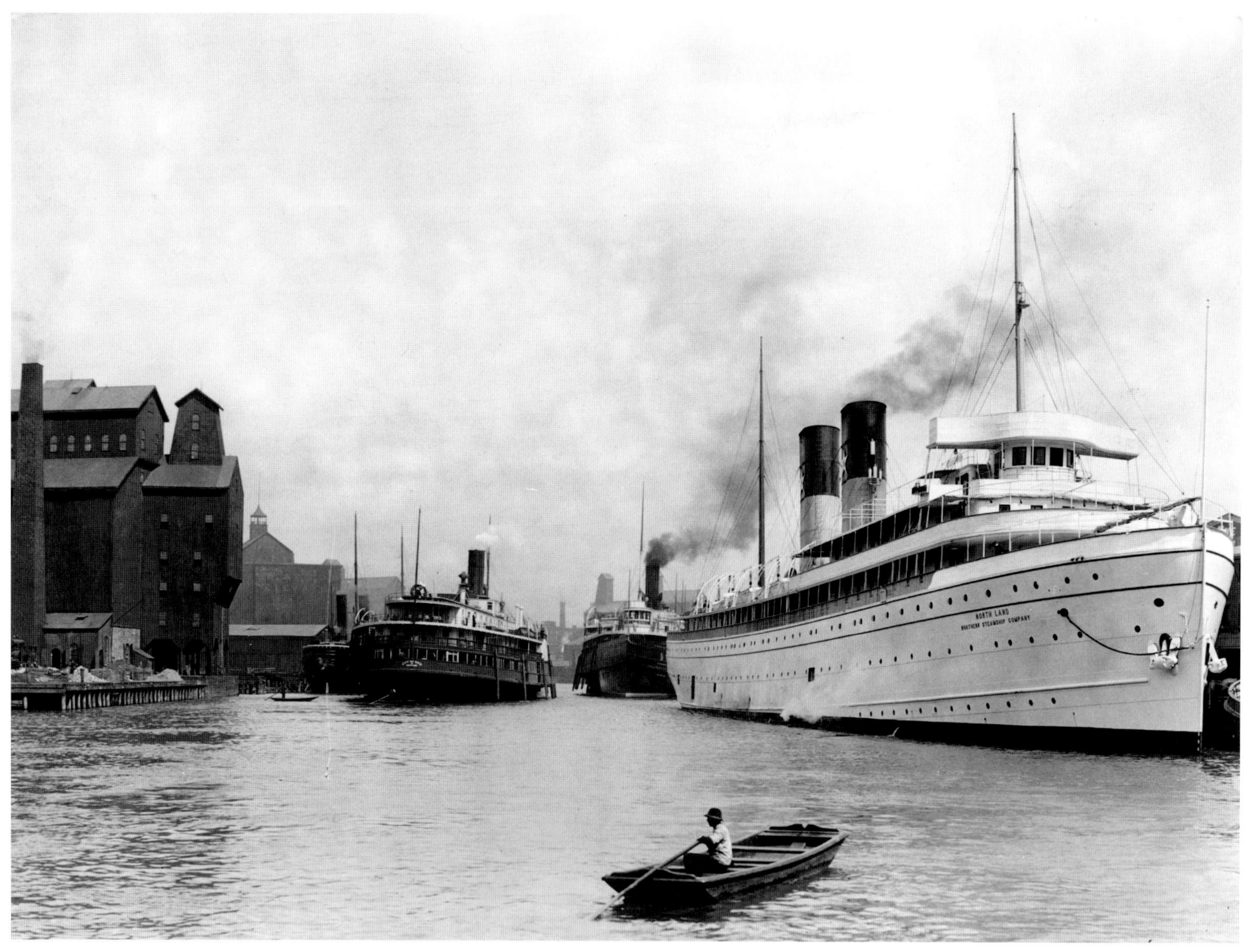

When Buffalo became the western terminus of the Erie Canal, the city grew to be the busiest grain-transfer port in the world. Erie Canal boats had no sails or keels to navigate the Great Lakes, and lake ships were too large for the canal. As a result, cargo had to be unloaded and reloaded at Buffalo. Grain elevators, like those at left, were invented in Buffalo to store grain during the transfer, and steamships like the *North Land* at right, shown here in port, navigated the Great Lakes.

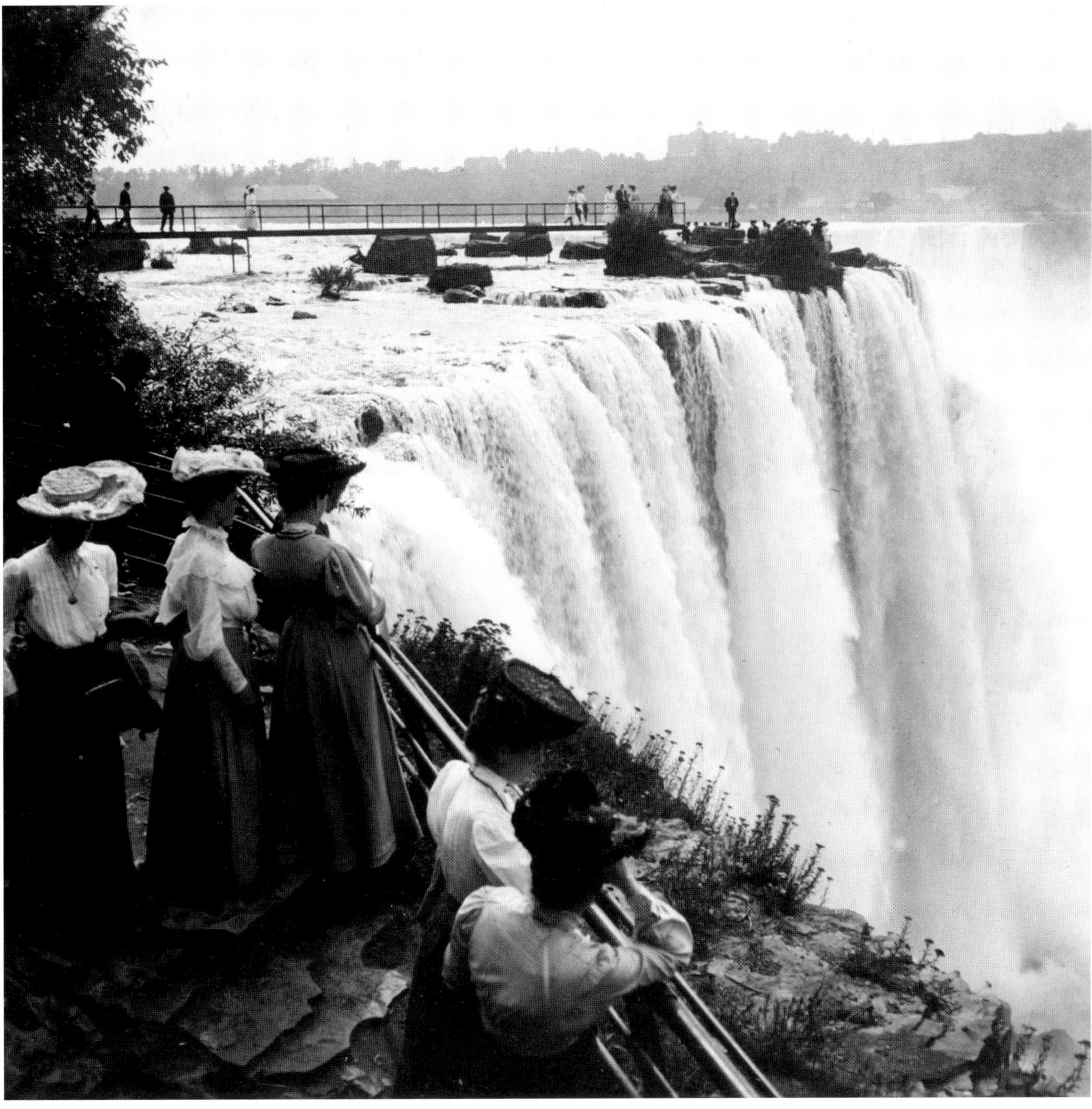

A group of spectators view Niagara Falls from Goat Island, which separates the American from the Canadian Horseshoe Falls. In the distance, a pedestrian bridge leads to rock outcroppings in the rapids. Goat Island gets its name from an early settler, John Stedman, who kept his goats on the island to protect them from wolves. The flank-to-flank width of Niagara Falls is 1,000 feet, and the height varies from 120 to 170 feet.

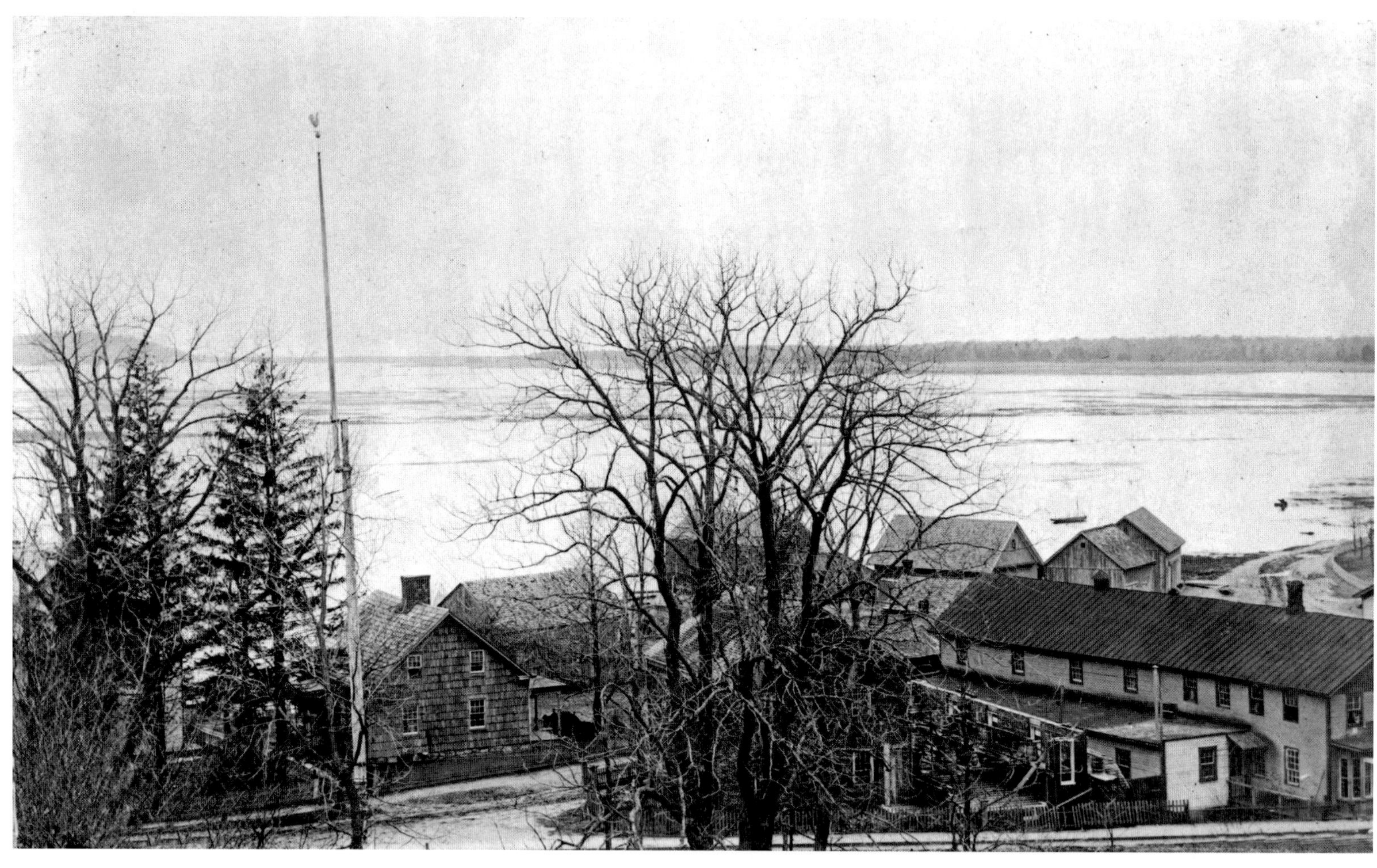

Stony Brook is a village on the North Shore of Long Island. The buildings in this 1906 photograph face Stony Brook Harbor, and the low-lying landmass in the distance is Long Beach. Today the village is primarily a residential community and home to the State University of New York at Stony Brook.

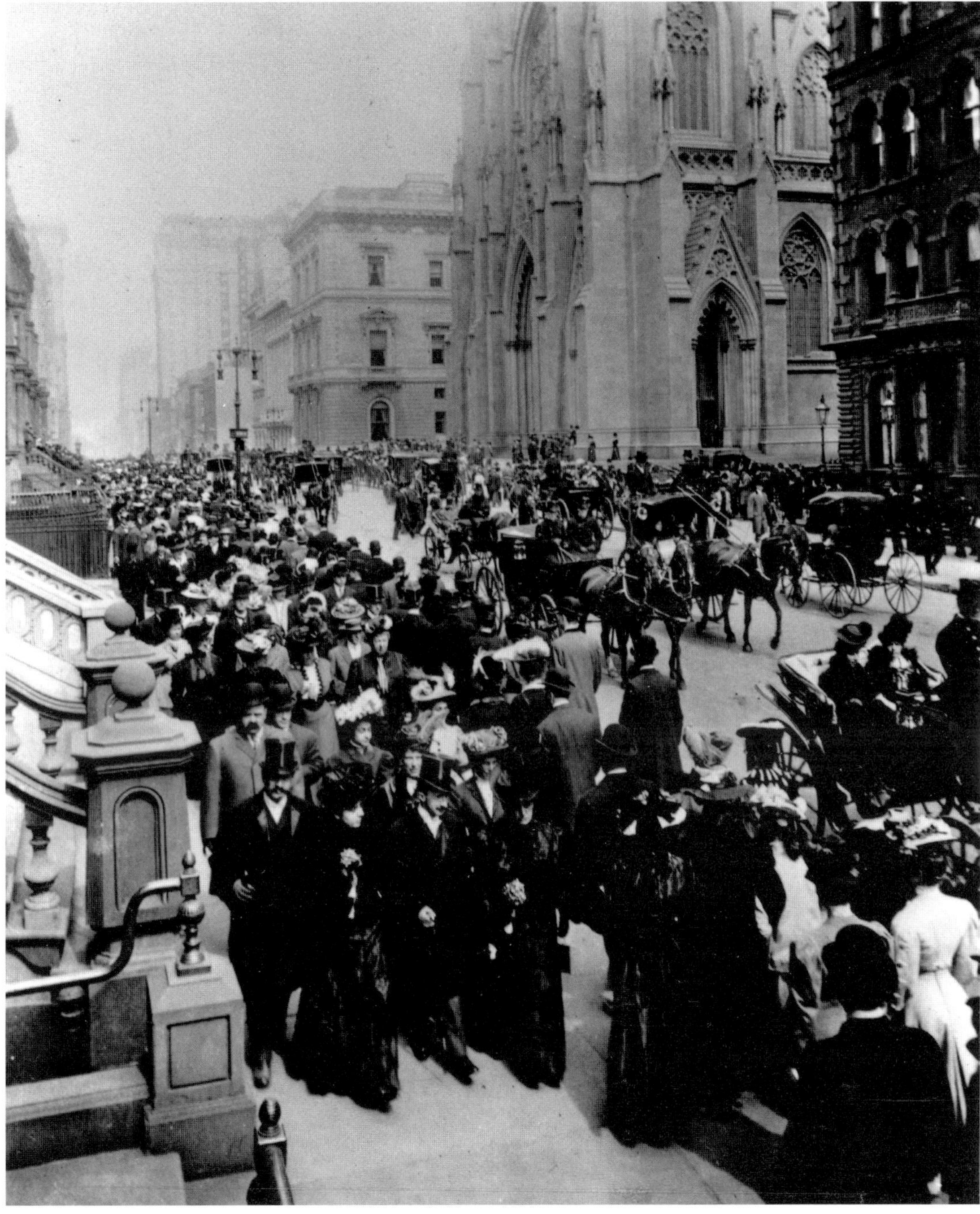

Easter Sunday 1906 finds New Yorkers thronging Fifth Avenue in their finest apparel—men with their top hats and women in long gowns and elaborate bonnets. In the background, between 50th and 51st streets, rises the magnificent neo-Gothic St. Patrick's Cathedral, where as many as 2,400 New Yorkers could have worshiped this morning. St. Patrick's was completed in 1878 on the designs of architect James Renwick, Jr.

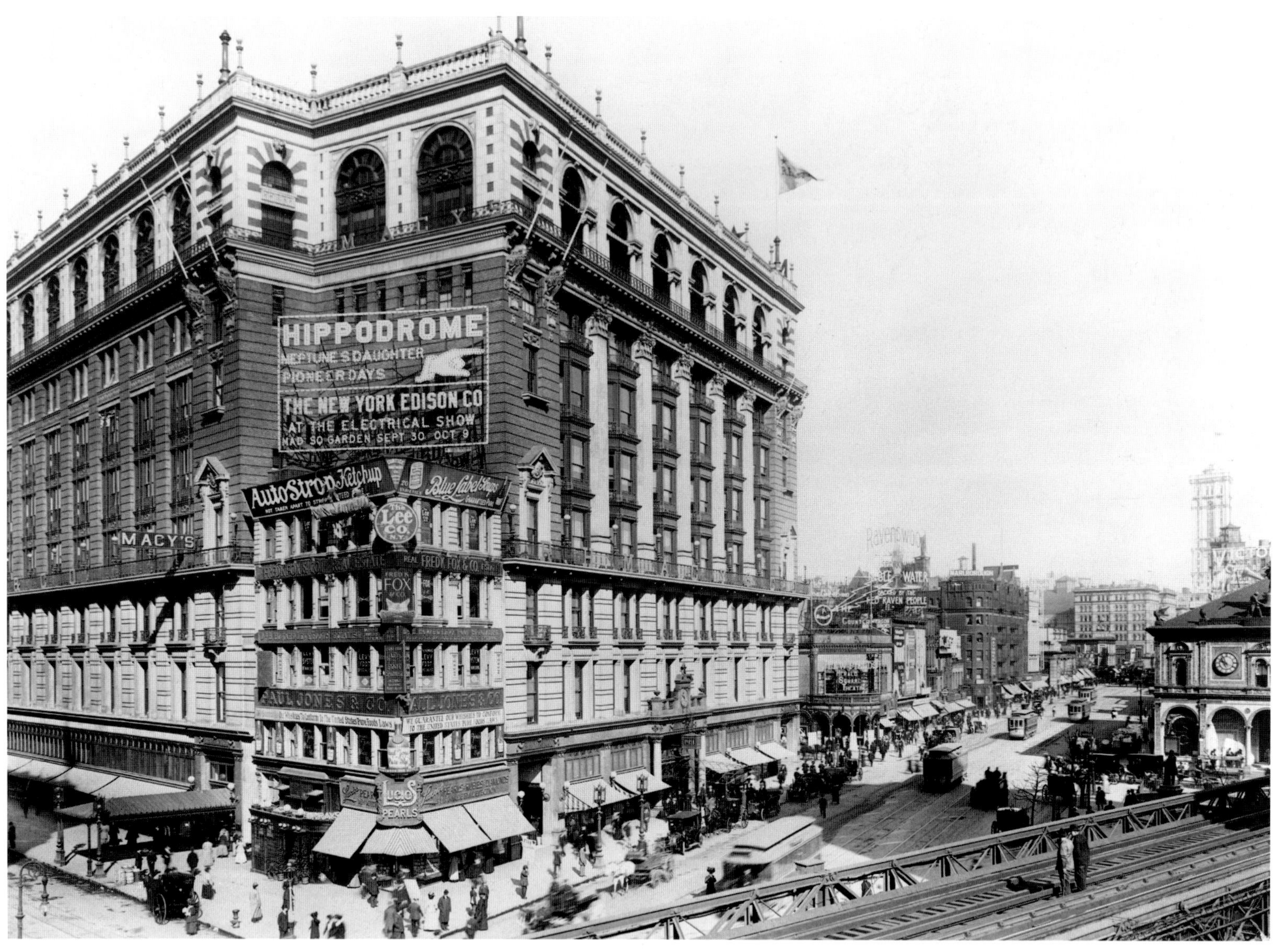

Founded in 1858 by Rowland Macy and touted as the world's largest department store, Macy's at Broadway and 34th Street in Manhattan covers an entire city block. Built in 1902, the stone building in two contrasting colors is nine stories tall, but there are ten shopping floors, including the basement. On the Beaux-Arts exterior, two early-twentieth-century white marble caryatids carved by J. Massey Rhind support an entablature. Huge arched windows adorn the top floor, and four-story-tall columns separate bays on the Broadway façade.

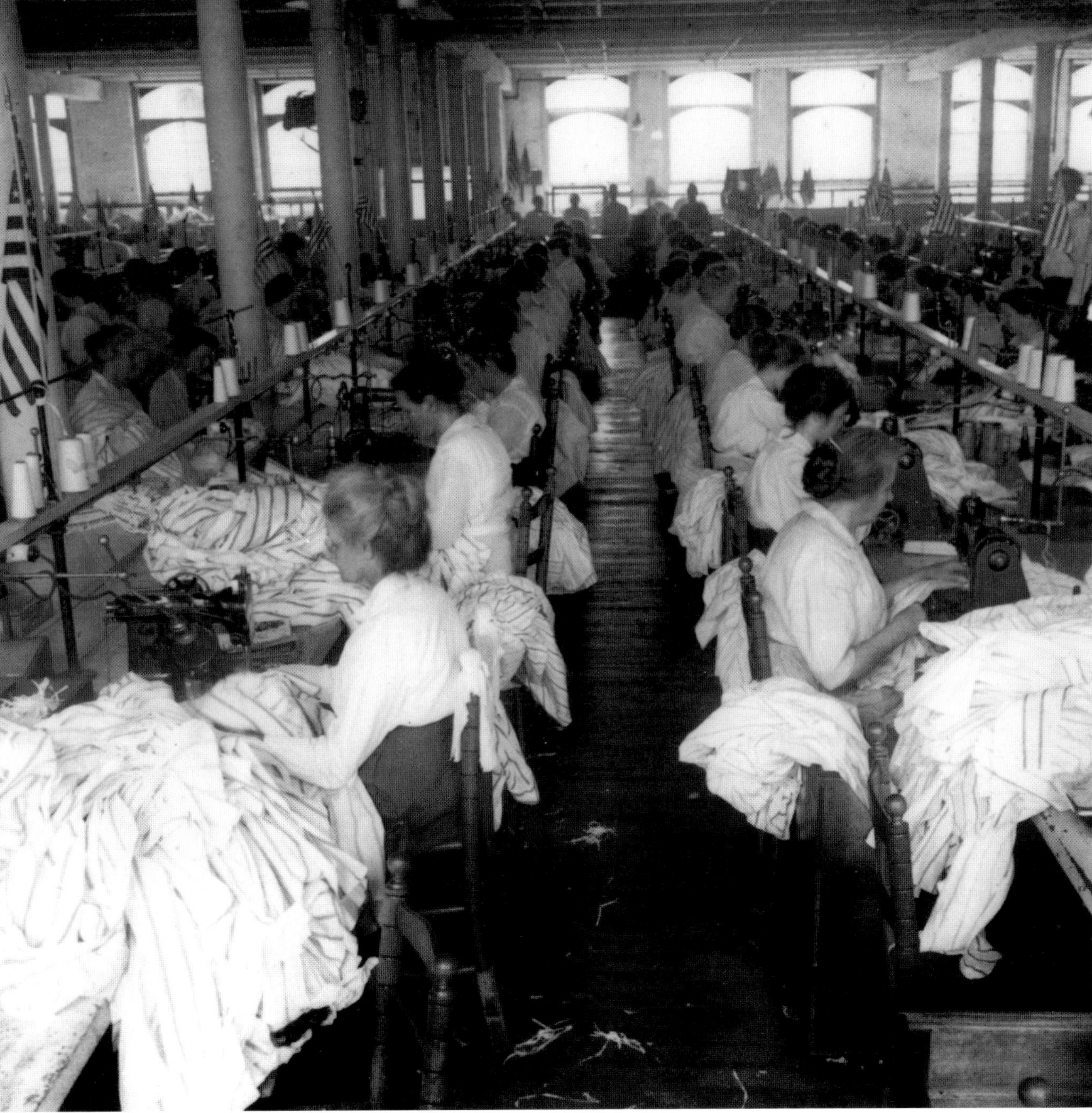

Troy, opposite Albany on the Hudson River, became well known for manufacturing collars, cuffs, and shirts. Cluett, Peabody and Company, the makers of Arrow shirts and collars, became the premier and longest-lasting operation of the kind in the world, manufacturing products into the 1980s. Employees shown here sit at long tables sewing Arrow shirts early in the twentieth century.

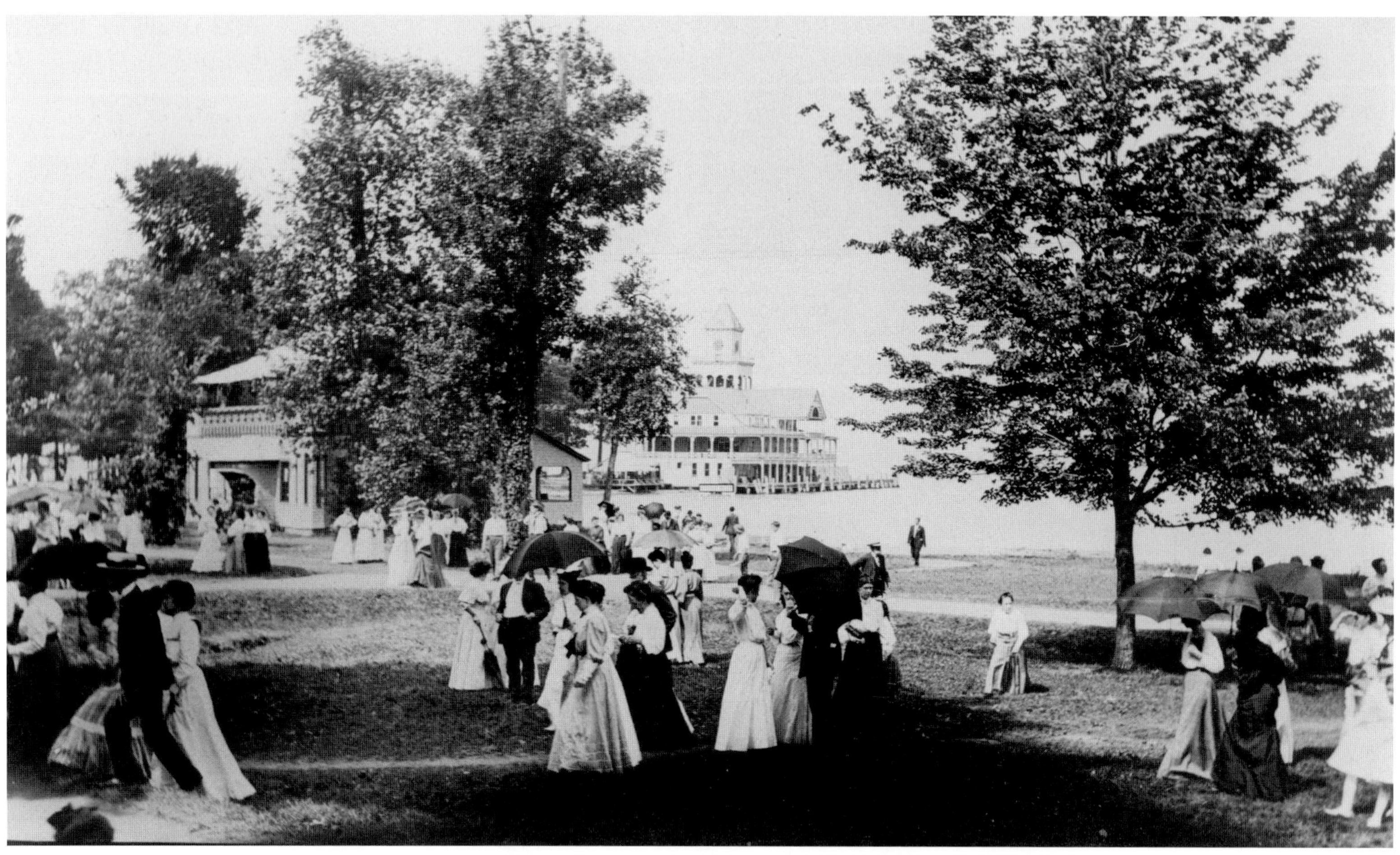

The Chautauqua Assembly in southwestern New York State was founded in 1874 to provide religious meetings for Methodists for two weeks in the summer. It soon expanded to include secular subjects and became nondenominational. Today, Chautauqua Institution offers programs in music, art, politics, religion, education, and science through the entire summer and fall. The 750-acre Victorian village is a designated National Historic Landmark and a remarkable architectural phenomenon. Here in 1908, institution guests socialize on the Promenade next to Chautauqua Lake.

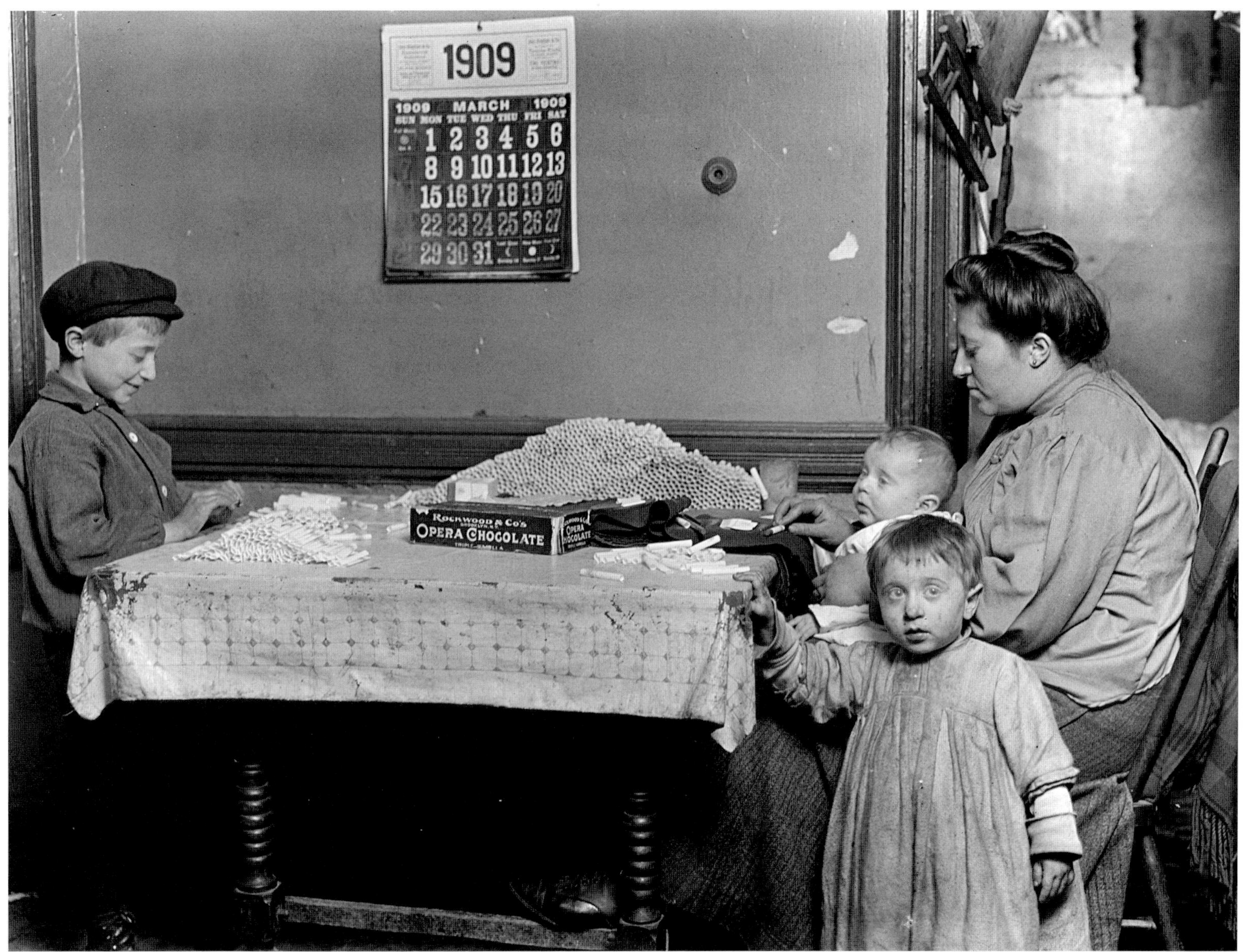

An immigrant widow and her son roll papers for cigarettes on a kitchen table in a dilapidated New York City tenement apartment in March 1909. A pile of completed rolls sits on the table. Well-known photographer Lewis Wickes Hine traveled the nation for ten years beginning in 1907 documenting child labor. His work for the National Child Labor Committee contributed to the effort to end the practice.

On a wintry day in the 1910s, schoolchildren ride sleds down a chute constructed of wood in the playground of a Rochester elementary school. The incline was kept slippery with repeated applications of snow. The children all wear identical hooded winter coats, suggesting that they were enrolled in a private school.

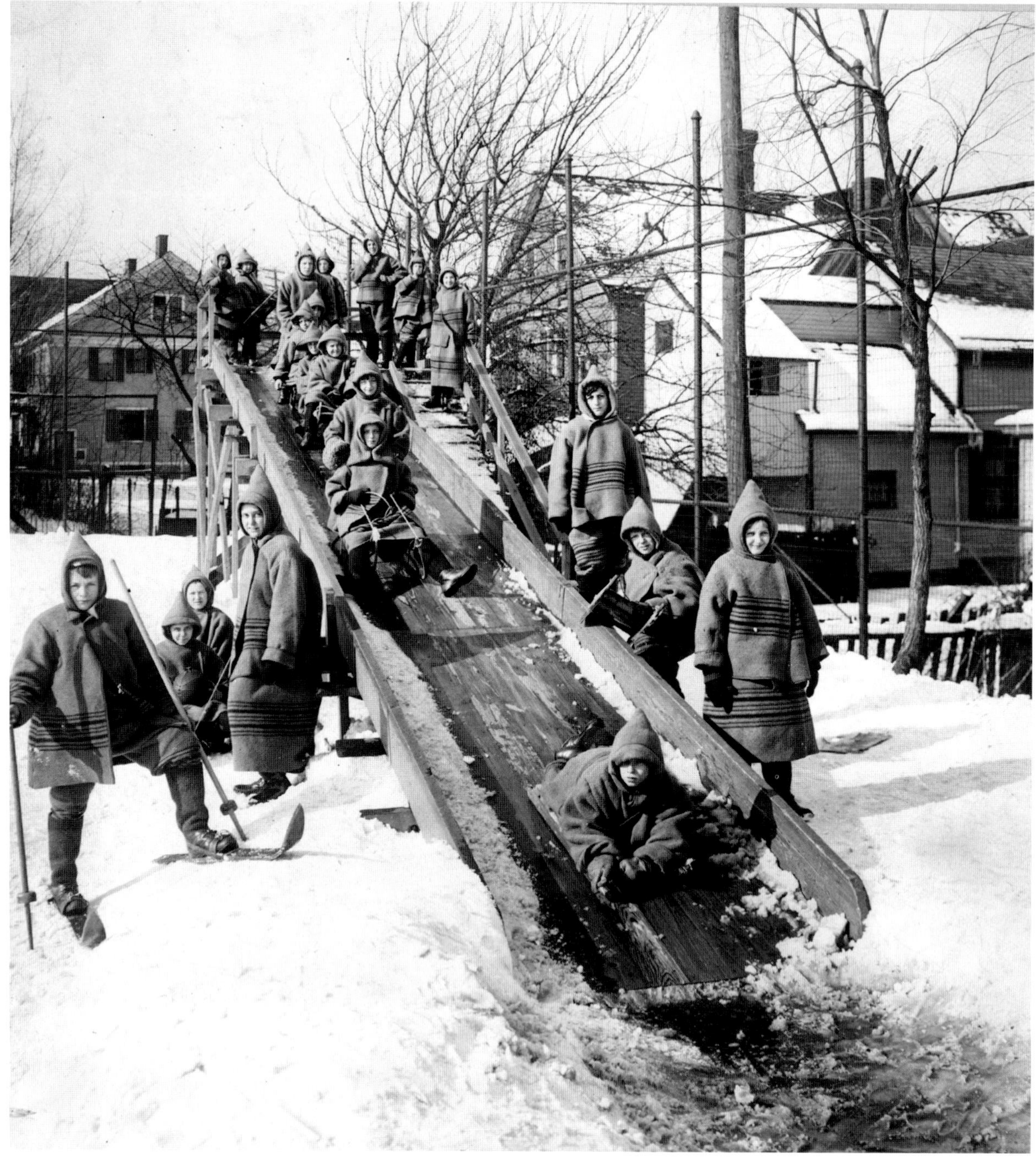

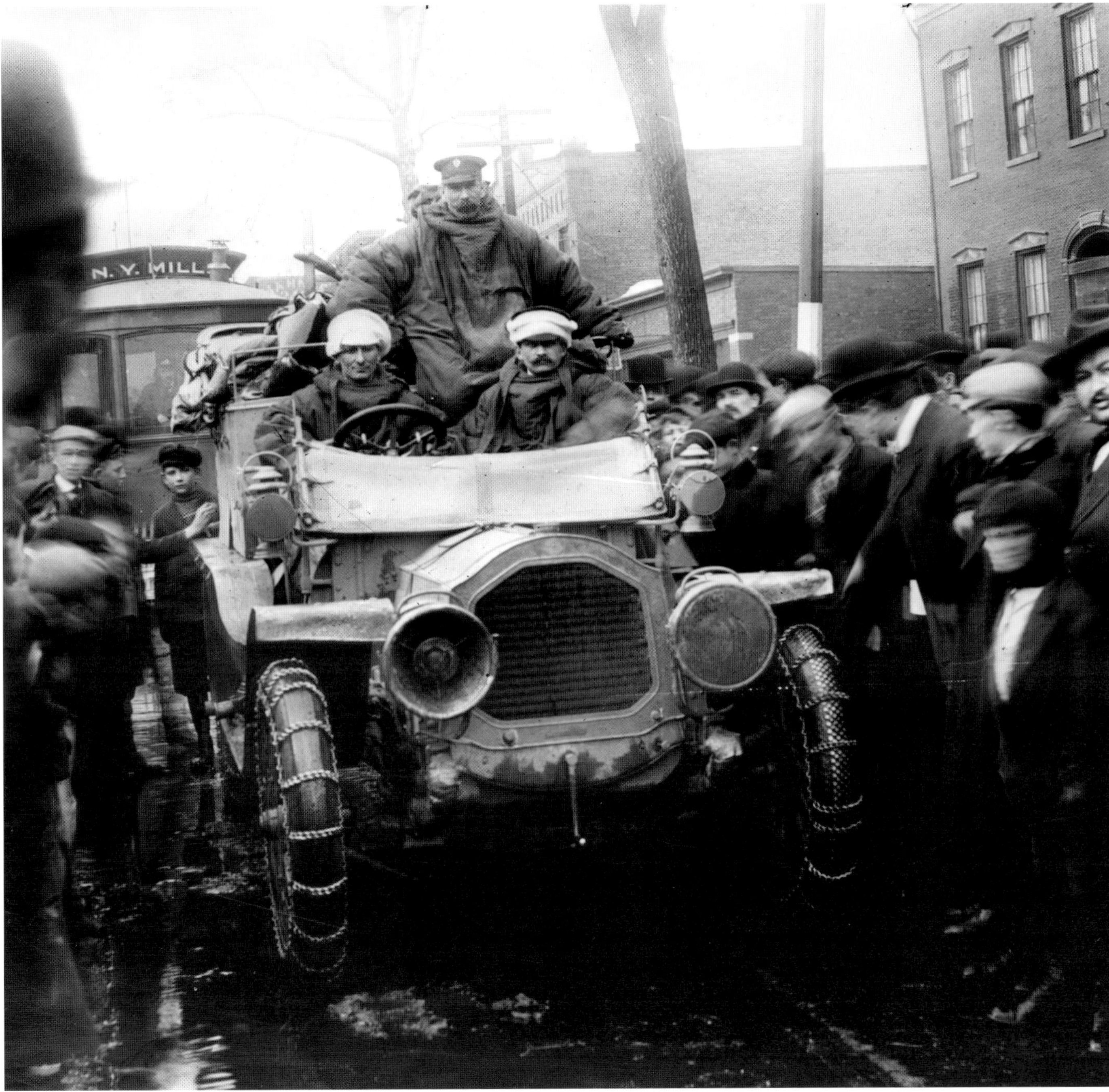

The New York to Paris Auto Race of 1908 is legendary, with teams from France, Germany, Italy, and the United States competing. The race was a grueling around-the-world contest, beginning in Manhattan's Times Square on February 12, then to Chicago, San Francisco, Seattle, north to Alaska, thence by ship to Japan, and on to Asia and Europe through Vladivostok, Berlin, and ending at the Eiffel Tower in Paris. Americans won the event in the Thomas Flyer, built in Buffalo and driven by George Schuster of Buffalo. Here is the De Dion car, competing for France, making its way through Utica near the beginning of the race. The De Dion would fall out of the race in Siberia, where the drivers' nerve was overcome by frigid temperatures and fear of banditry.

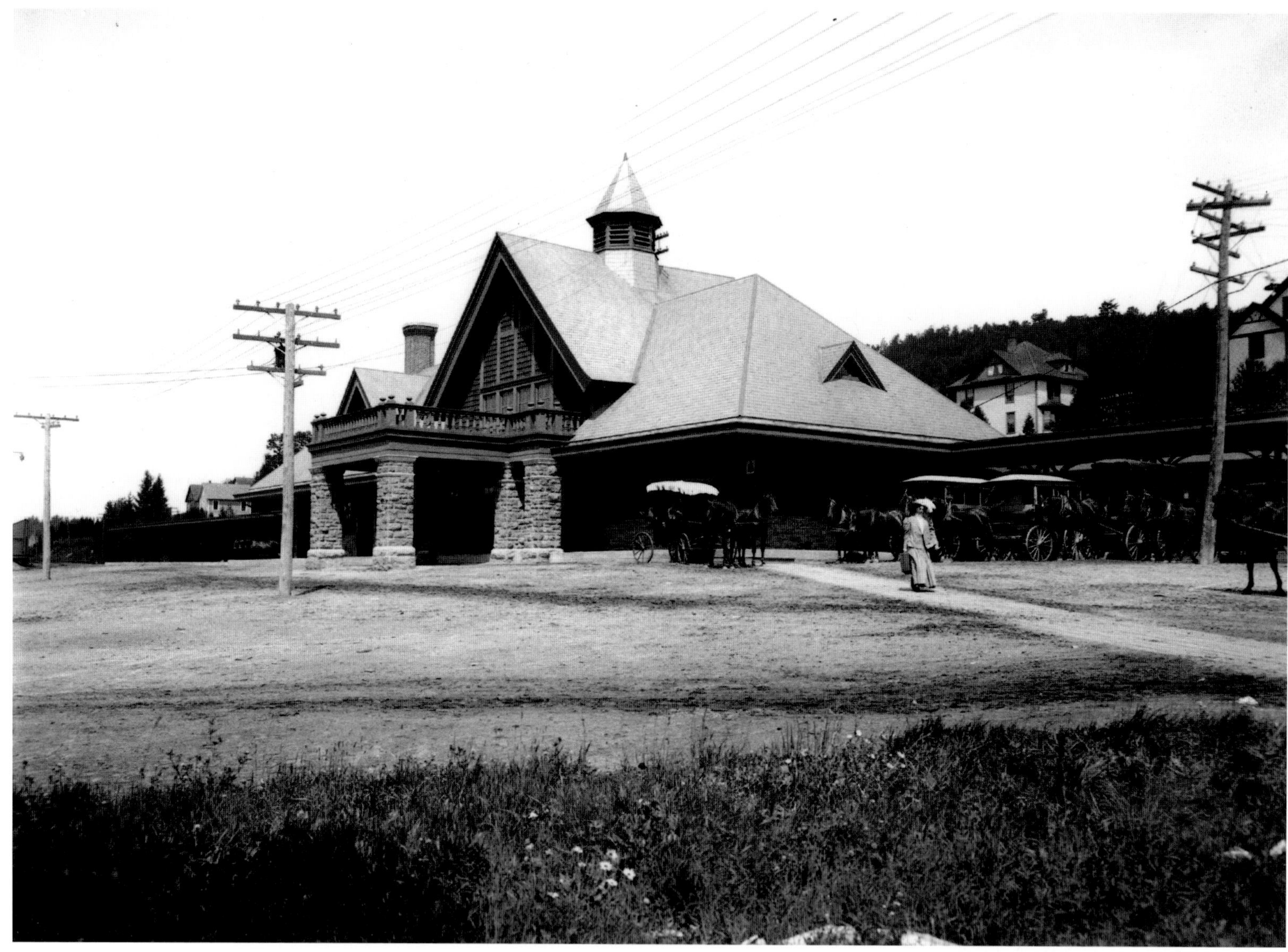

Union Depot in Saranac Lake, in the Adirondack Mountains, was built in 1904 by the Delaware and Hudson Railroad, which consolidated New York Central service from the west and the Chateaugay Railroad from the east. Between 1904 and 1940, railroads were the principal means for visits to the Adirondacks, and the D&H ran 18 to 20 scheduled passenger trains to and from Saranac every day in summer months. The picturesque station now houses historic exhibits, and the ticket office also serves the Adirondack Scenic Railroad, which offers scenic excursions between Saranac Lake and Lake Placid.

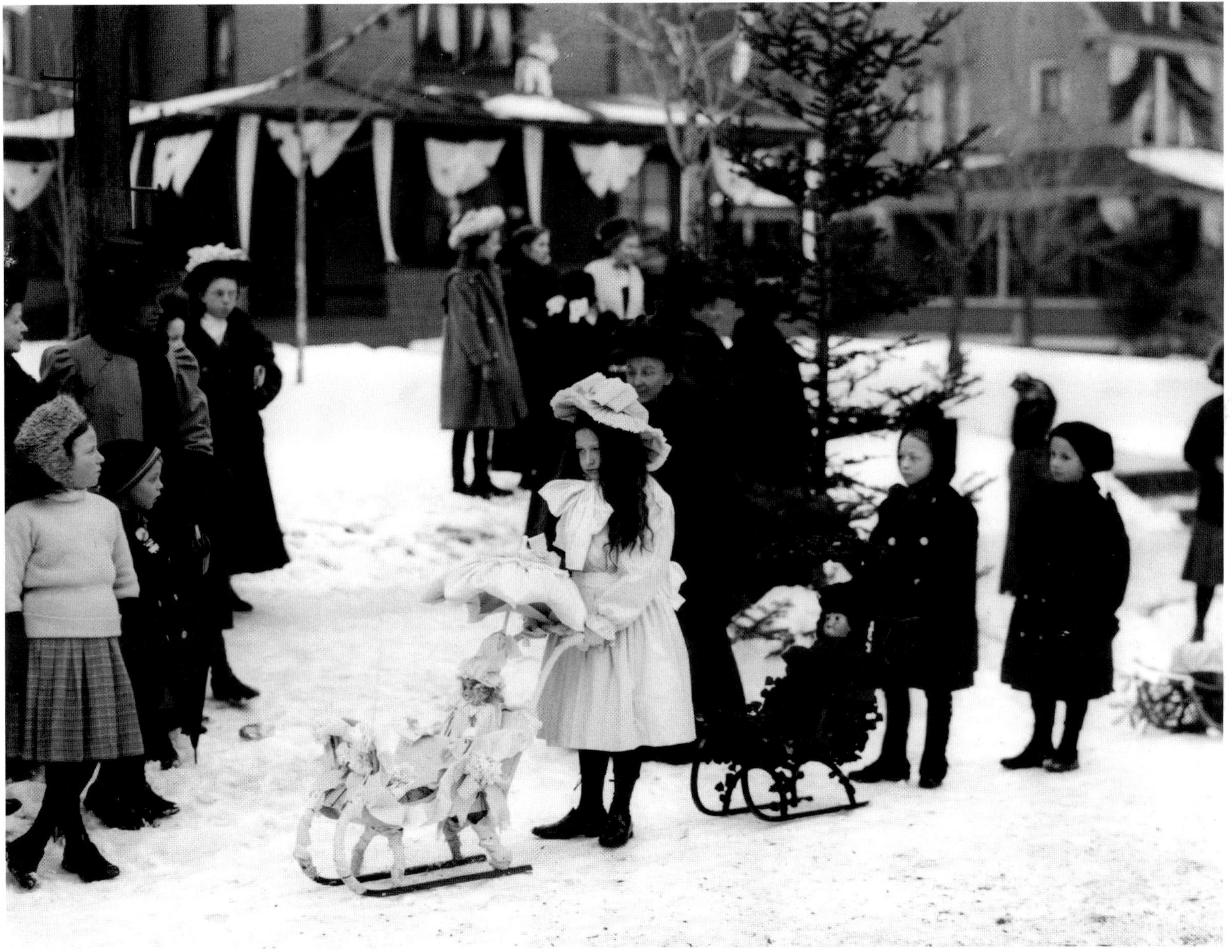

At the 1909 midwinter carnival in Upper Saranac Lake, children parade their dolls in doll sleds. Houses in the background are decorated with bunting. The carnival was first held in 1898 and still flourishes today as a popular annual event.

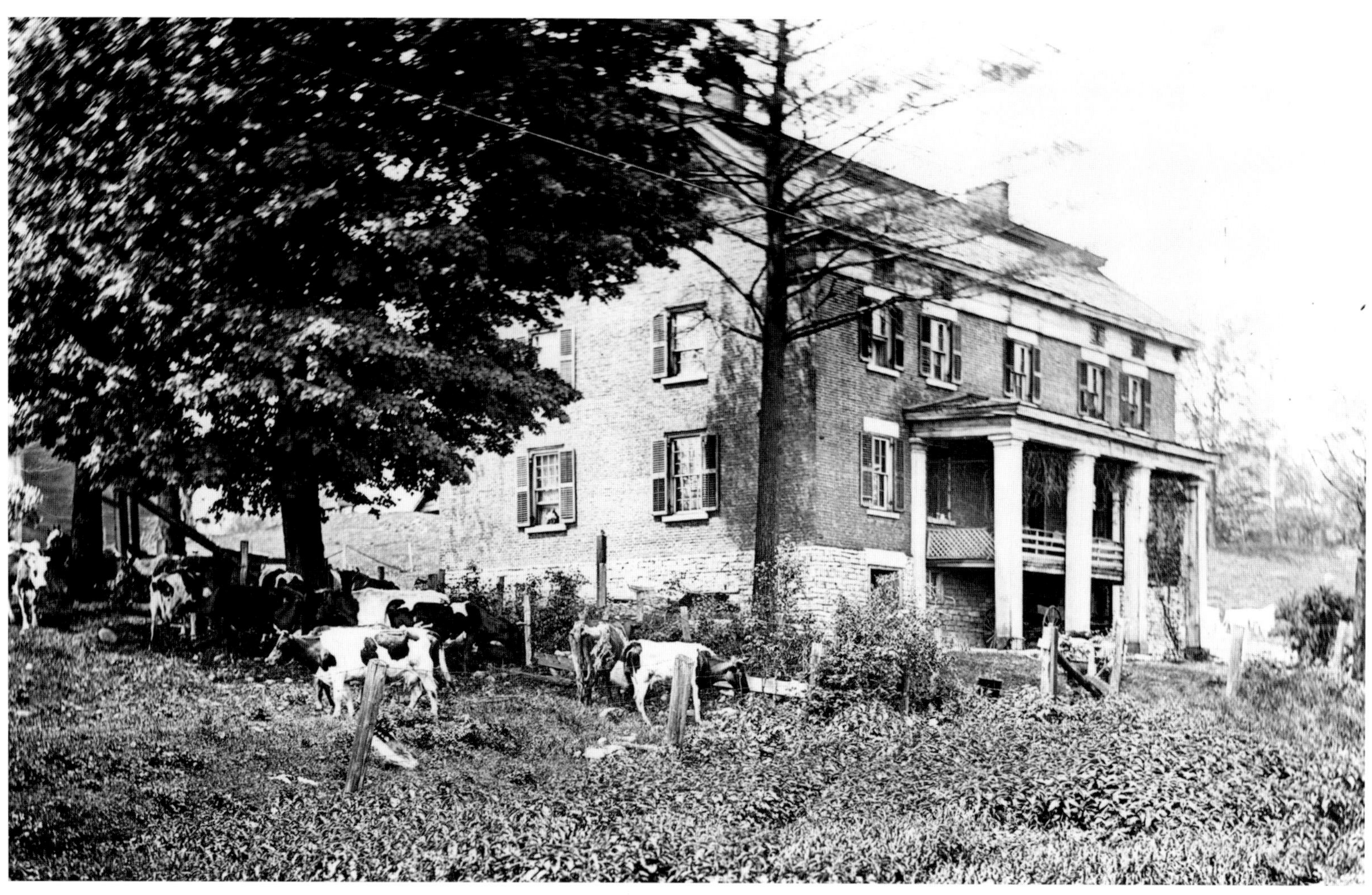

The village of Herkimer sits next to the Mohawk River and Erie Canal. This is farming country in central New York State. Shown with cattle grazing around a large tree, this nineteenth-century farmhouse near Herkimer featured a gambrel roof with chimneys at both end gables and a five-bay façade with a two-story portico and Doric columns supporting the porch roof.

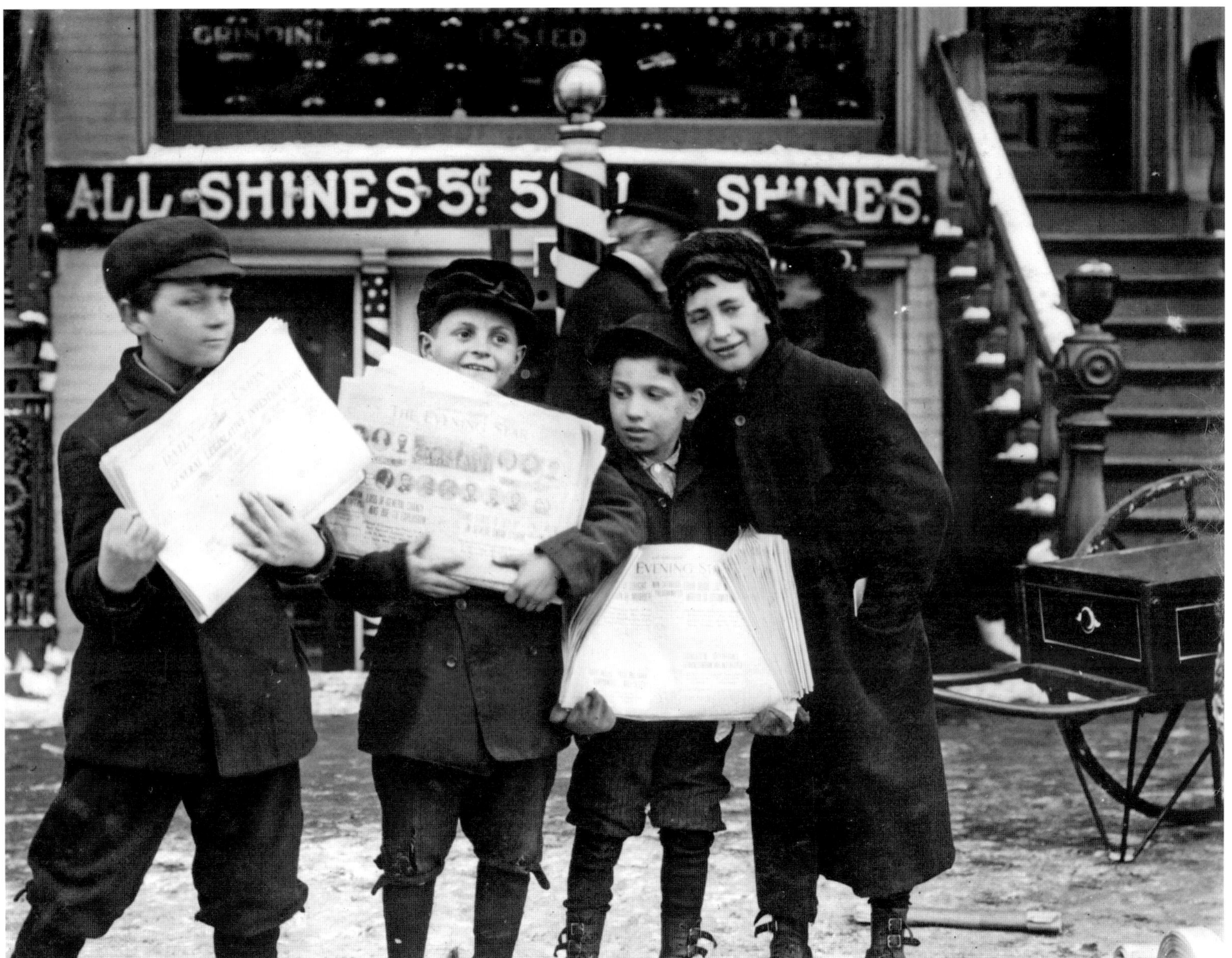

On a wintry day in February 1910, three "newsies" hawk newspapers on the streets of Schenectady. Behind the boys is a barbershop advertising shoe shines for a nickel. Newsies were among the subjects of special focus by photographer Lewis Hine in his work for the National Child Labor Committee.

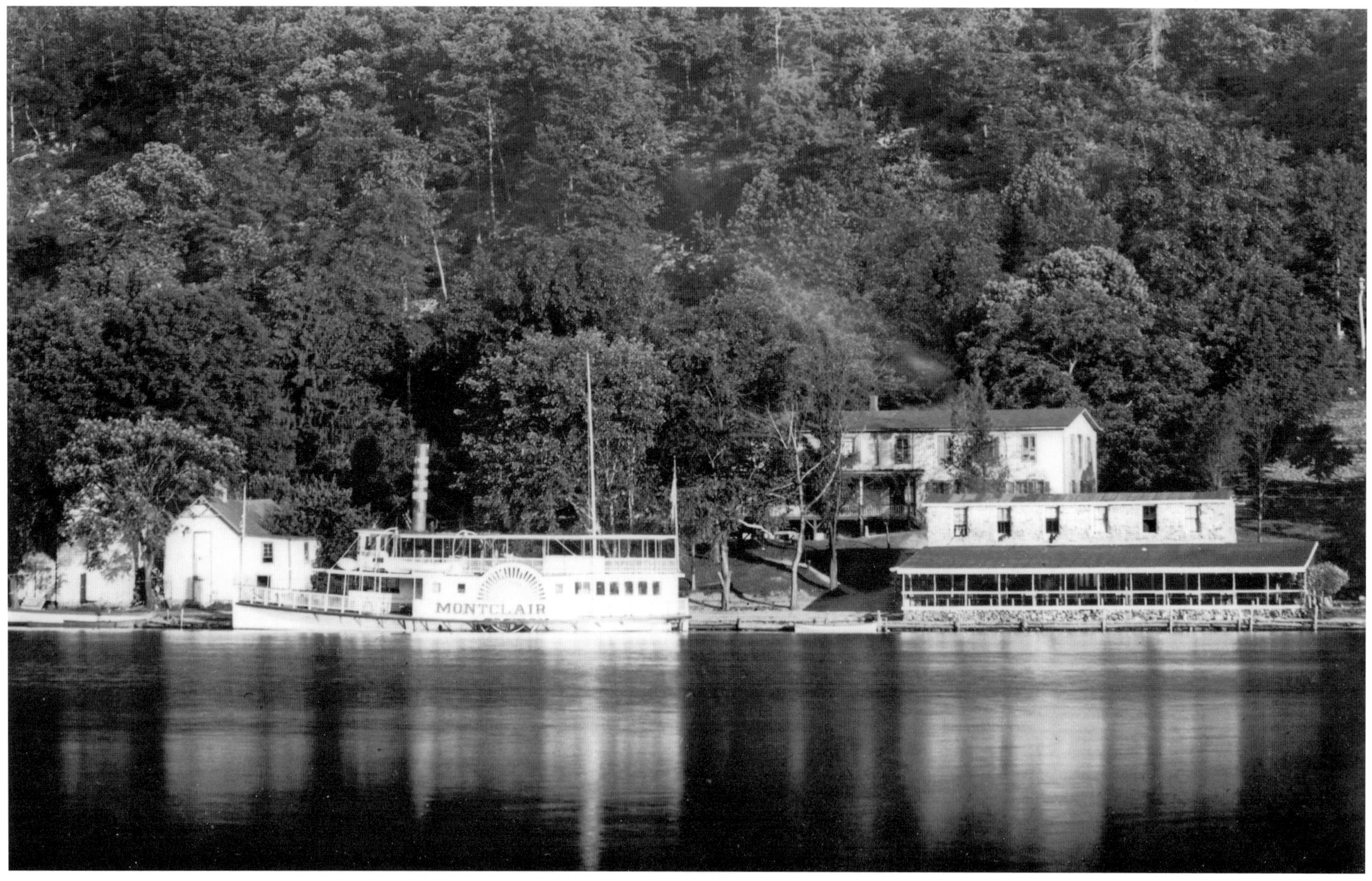

Greenwood Lake at Bellvale Mountain is a village at the north end of a nine-mile-long lake that extends south across the state line. Here in 1910, the village boasted a paddle-wheel tourist boat, the *Montclair,* which provided scenic excursions along the lake. Just 50 miles from New York City, Greenwood Lake remains a resort destination today, with the Appalachian Trail traversing Bellvale Mountain.

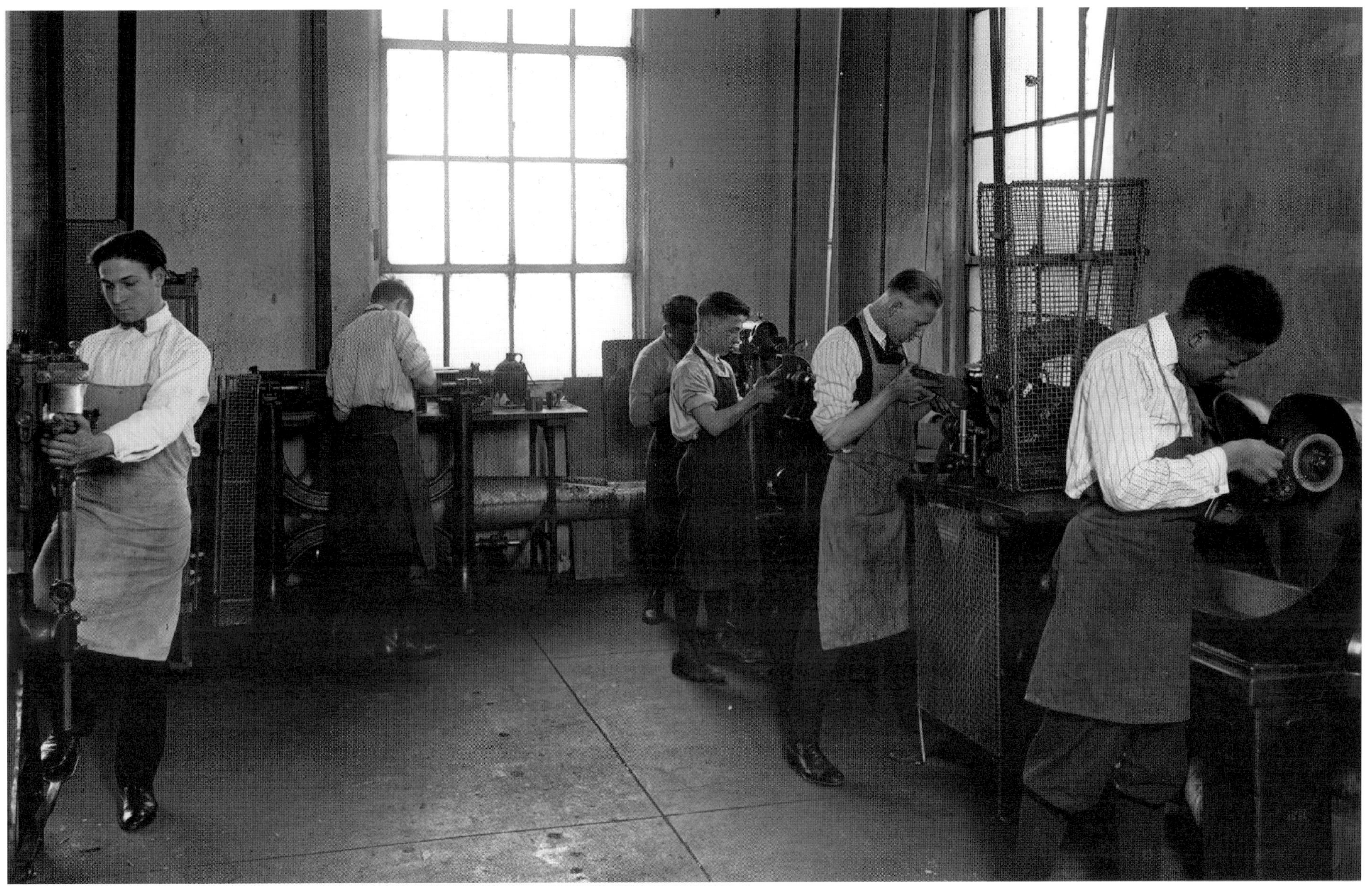

Shown here is a high school industrial arts class in 1910 at the Seneca Day Vocational School in Buffalo. The young men are working at grinders and other machinery.

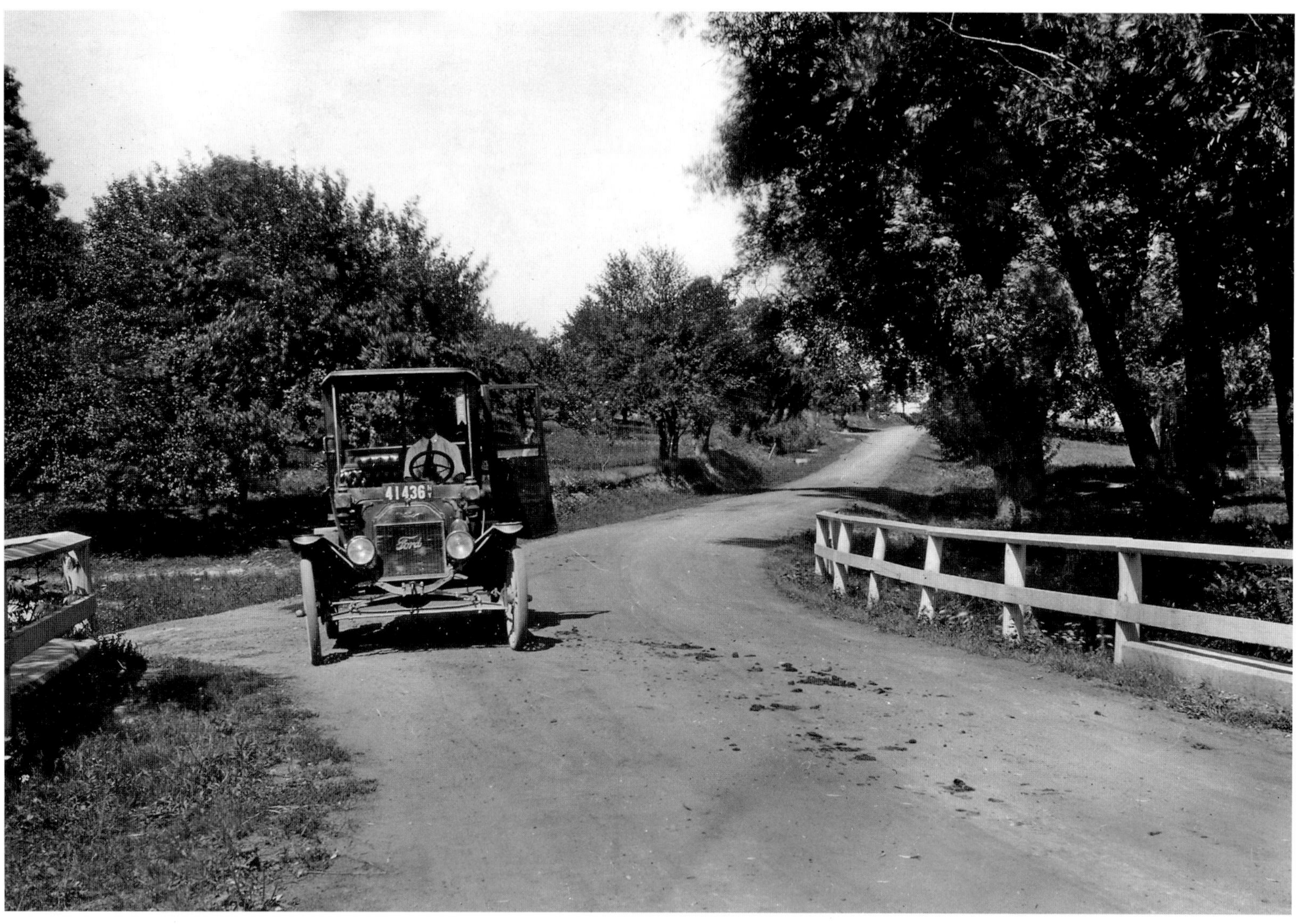

This fellow has pulled over for a photograph on a secondary road near Stone Ridge in August 1911. Stone Ridge is a village in the Shawangunk Mountains south of the Catskills. The automobile is an early Ford sedan.

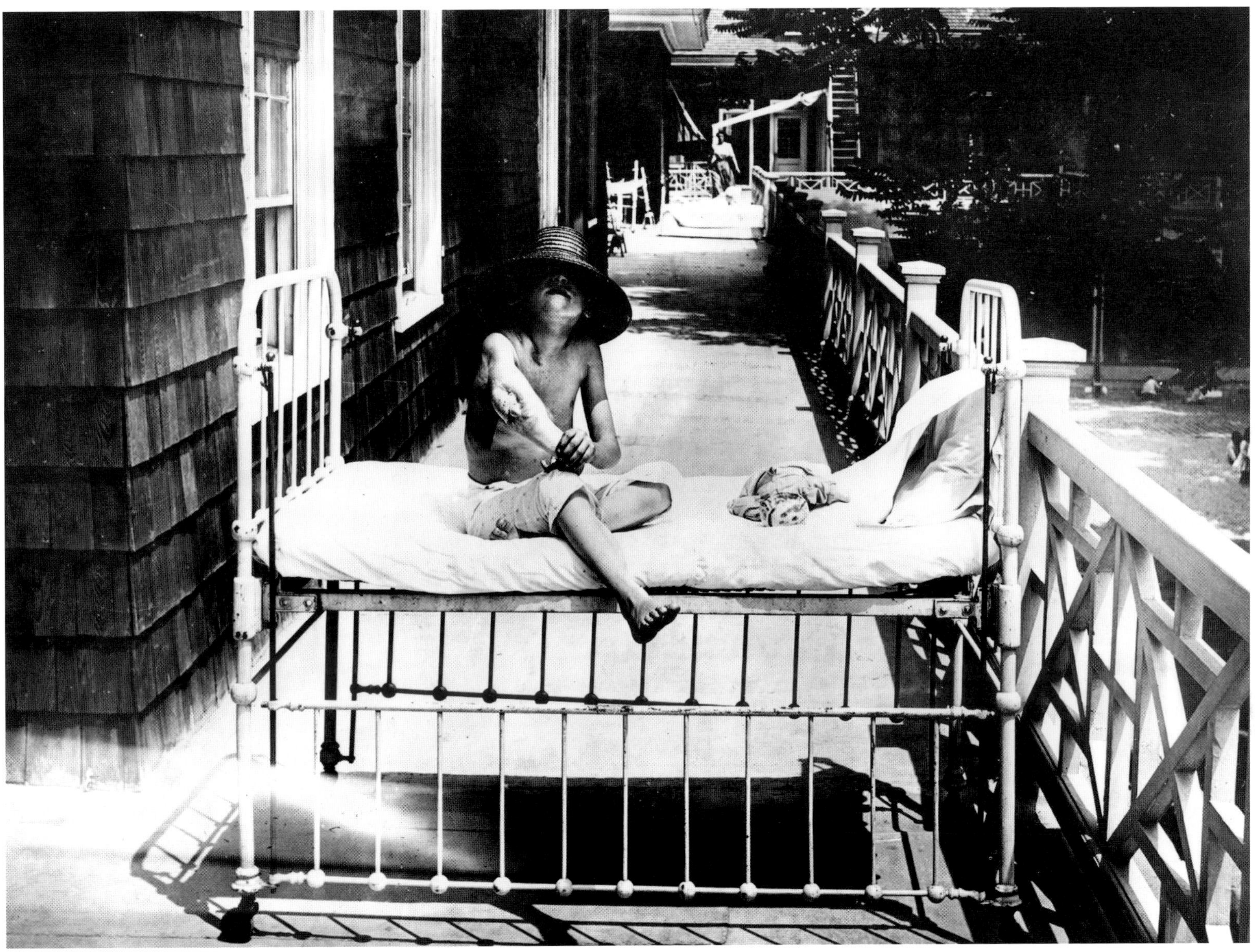

The Sea Breeze Hospital on Coney Island in Brooklyn treated children with surgical tuberculosis, considered incurable at the time. The open-air treatment at Sea Breeze, however, had remarkable success. Sea air, good food (lots of eggs and milk), and salt-water bathing were the formula for conquering the disease. The hospital could hold only 43 patients at a time, so there was a long waiting list. In this image from the early 1900s, a tubercular child displays a seriously infected arm from his hospital bed in the fresh air.

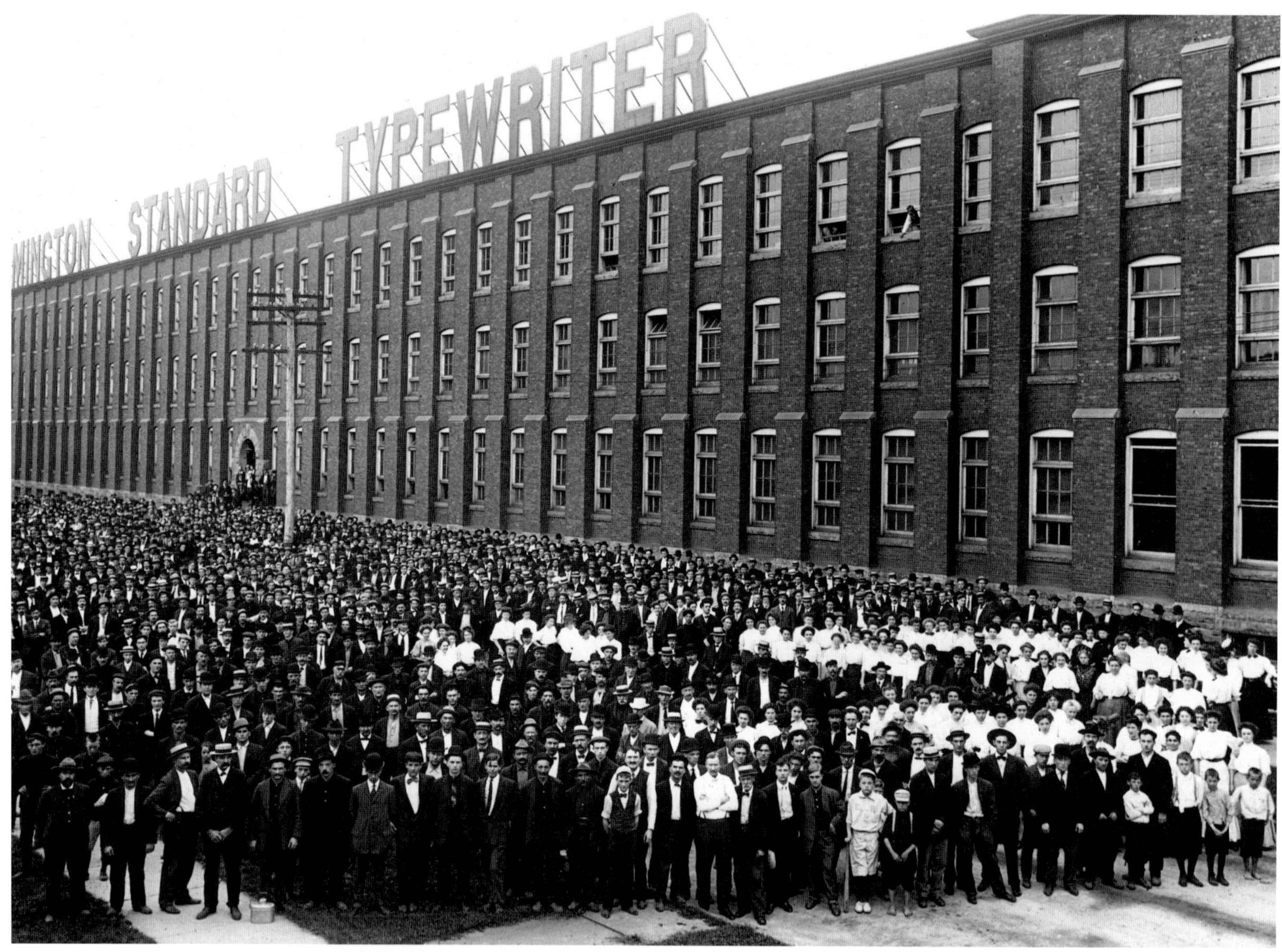

The Remington Arms Company in Ilion, a village on the Erie Canal, was founded by Eliphalet Remington, Jr., who became enormously successful after inventing a superior rifle. He purchased the patent for the first typewriter and began manufacturing Remington typewriters in 1873. By 1911, when this image was recorded, the Remington Standard Typewriter plant was huge, and the employees numbered in the hundreds when they gathered for this picture. Not to be confused with Eliphalet, Frederic Remington of Canton, New York, grew famous as a sculptor and painter of scenes of the American West.

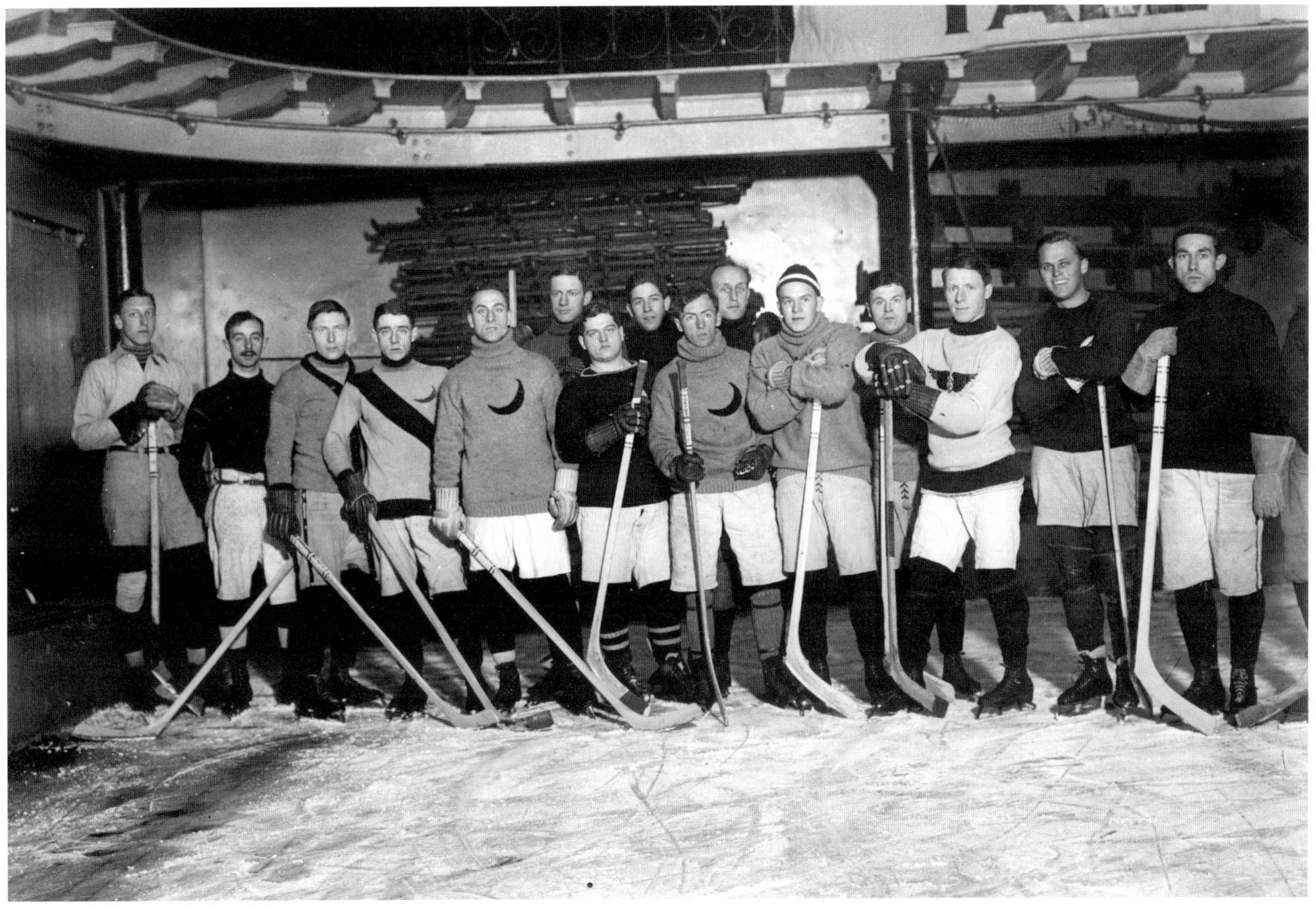

The Crescent Athletic Club of Brooklyn (called "New Mooners") were longtime champions of the New York Amateur Hockey League. They won first place in the league in 1900, 1901, 1902, 1903, 1905, 1906, 1908, and 1911. Their chief competitor was the New York Hockey Club. A couple of their historic games were particularly exciting, including those played on March 9, 1902, and January 20, 1905, at the St. Nicholas Rink. Members of the Crescent Athletic Club pose for a group shot here in 1911.

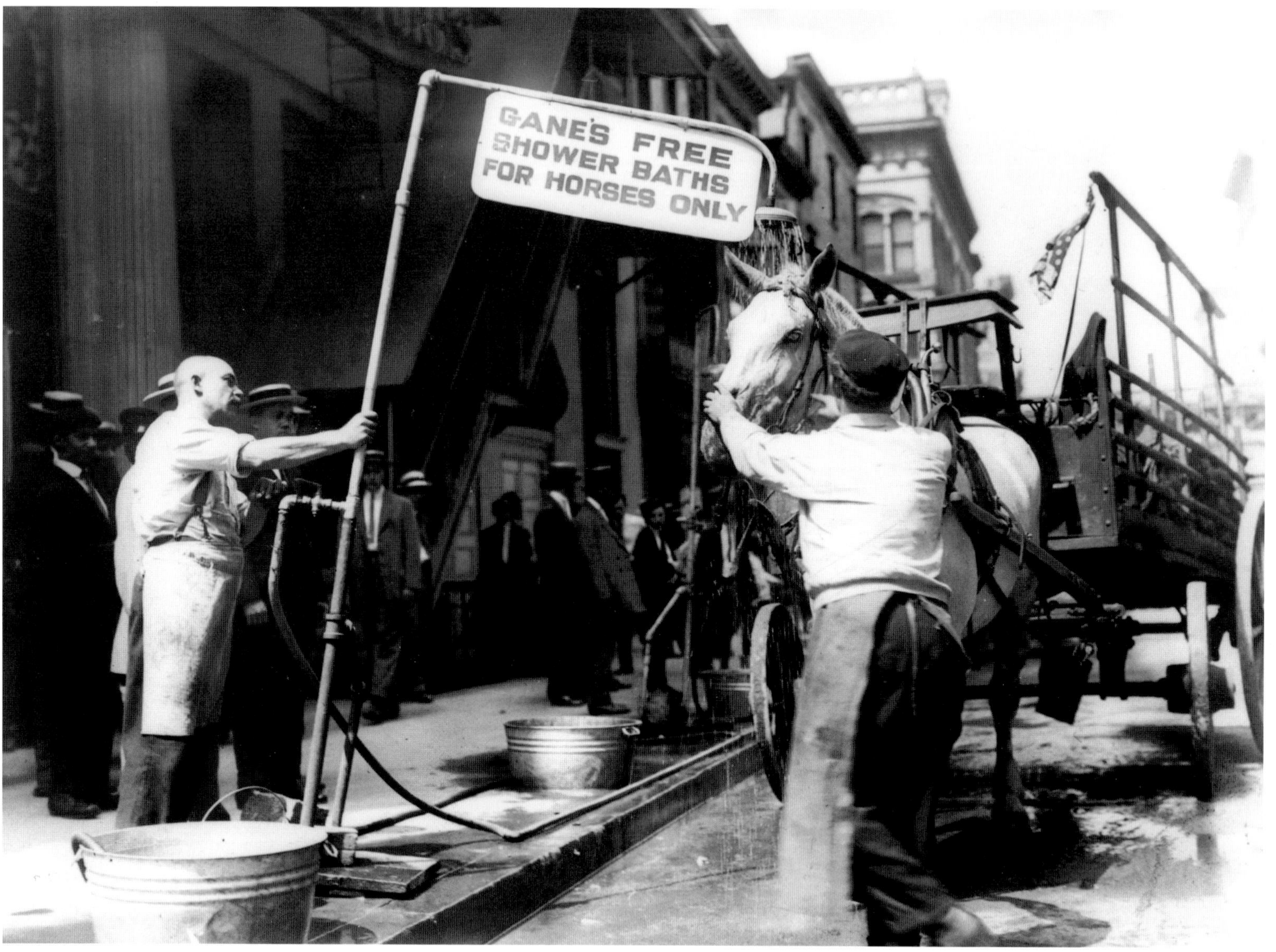

It is August 1911 and the summer is hot. A horse shower connected to a fire hydrant was set up on a street in New York City to provide a cooling shower bath to hard-working horses.

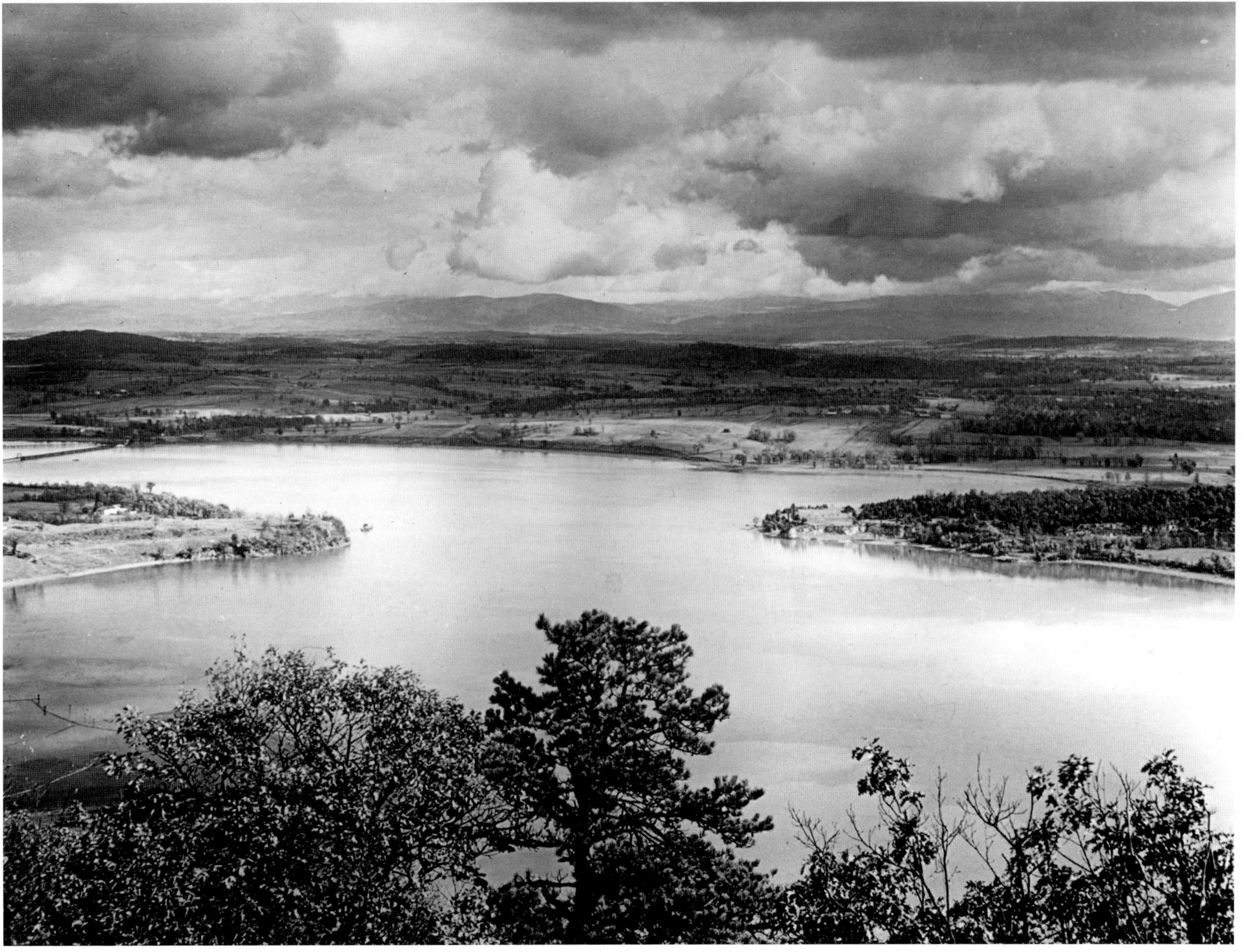

This 1911 panorama from the perspective of Mount Defiance near Ticonderoga in the Adirondacks shows Lake Champlain at one of its narrowest points. The vista faces east toward Vermont. At left is the location of Fort Ticonderoga, and on the peninsula at right stood Fort Independence in Vermont.

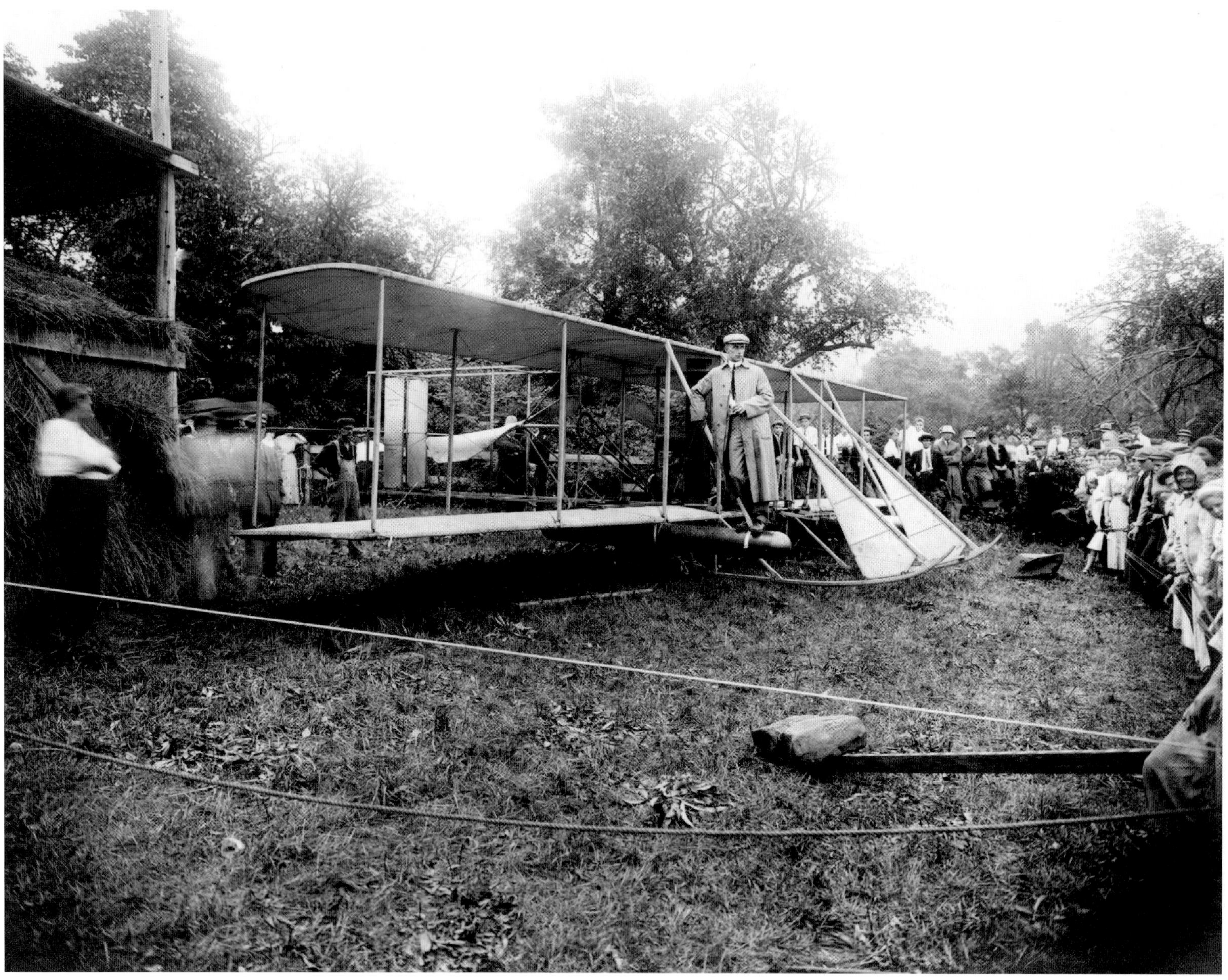

H. N. Atwood prepares for takeoff near Nyack on the west side of the Hudson River in 1911. Besides the paired wings, this early airplane has runners rather than wheels. The design seems to be based on the original Wright Brothers Flyer of 1903, with modifications that include the triangular sails above the front runners. A large crowd has gathered to witness the event.

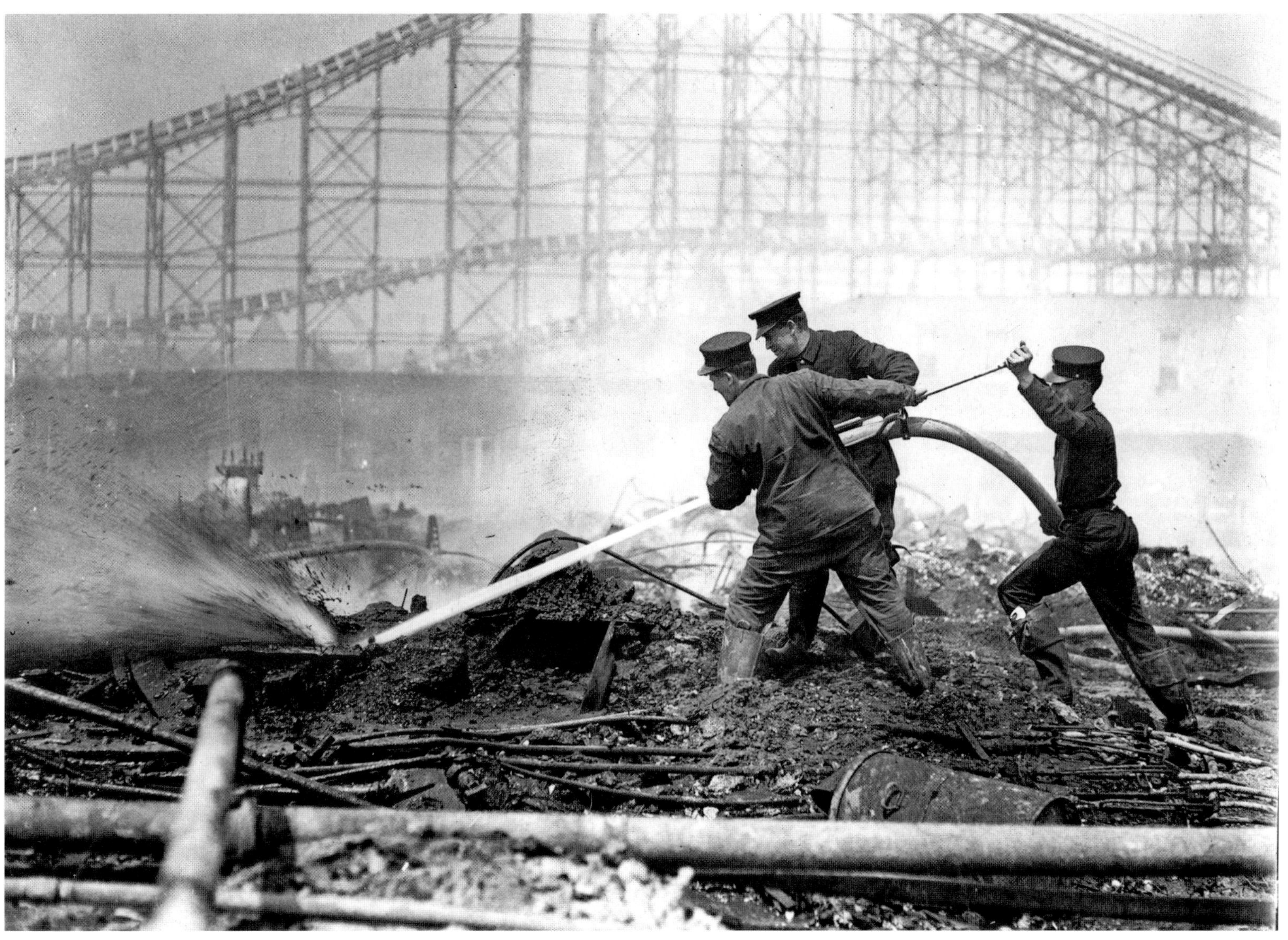

At 2:00 a.m. on May 27, 1911, light bulbs burst in the Hell Gate attraction at Coney Island's Dreamland Amusement Park. The burst bulbs ignited buckets of tar, creating a fire that quickly engulfed the park. Burning for 18 hours, the fire destroyed all of Dreamland except for the roller coaster in the background, which was untouched. Three firemen are shown here extinguishing the final remnants of the historic blaze.

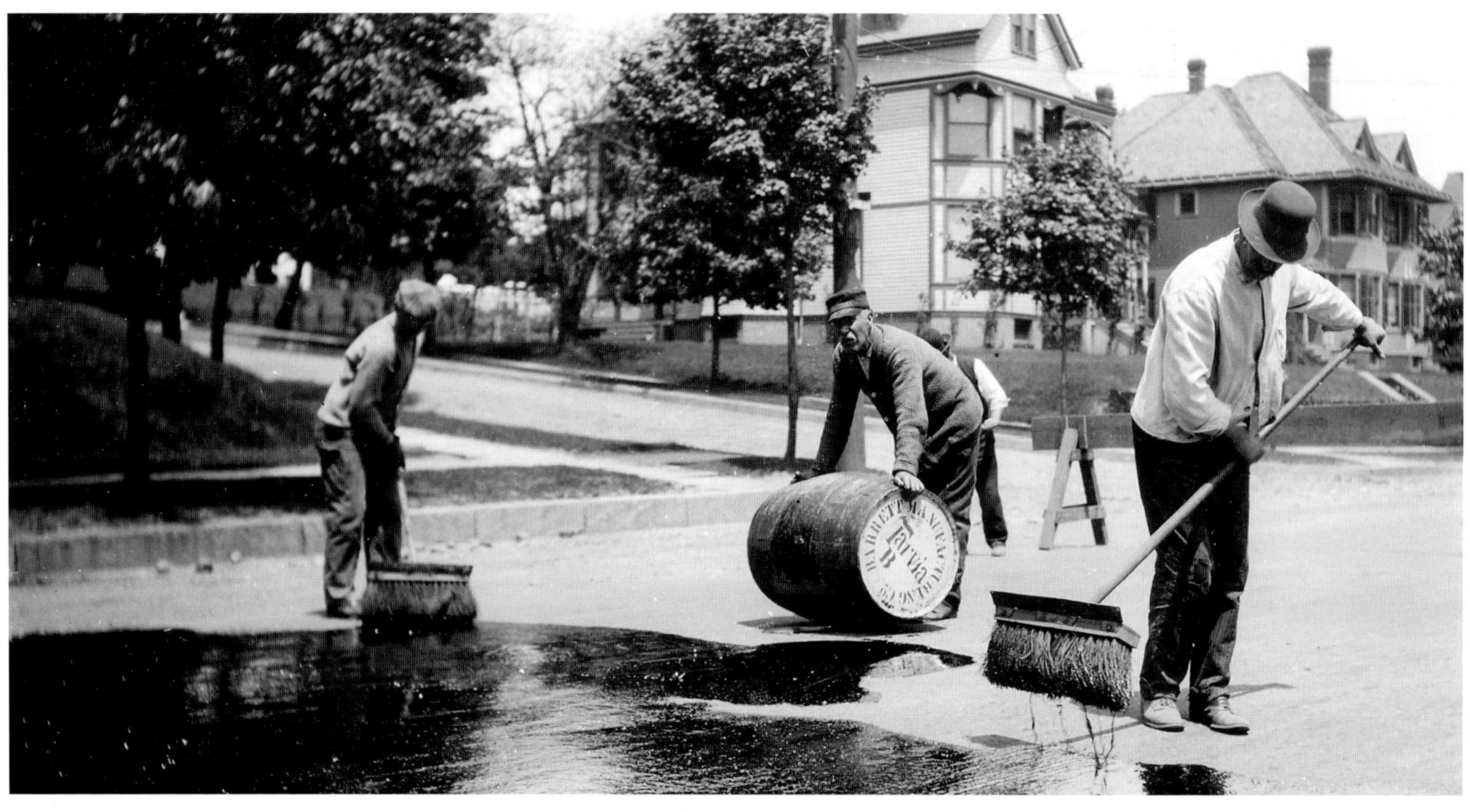

The advent of the automobile gave rise to the need for better roads. In May 1912, a street maintenance crew spreads an experimental material as a sealant on a road in Jamaica, Queens, Long Island. Created by the Barrett Manufacturing Company, Tarvia B did not require heating prior to application, yielding significant cost savings, according to a promotional pamphlet.

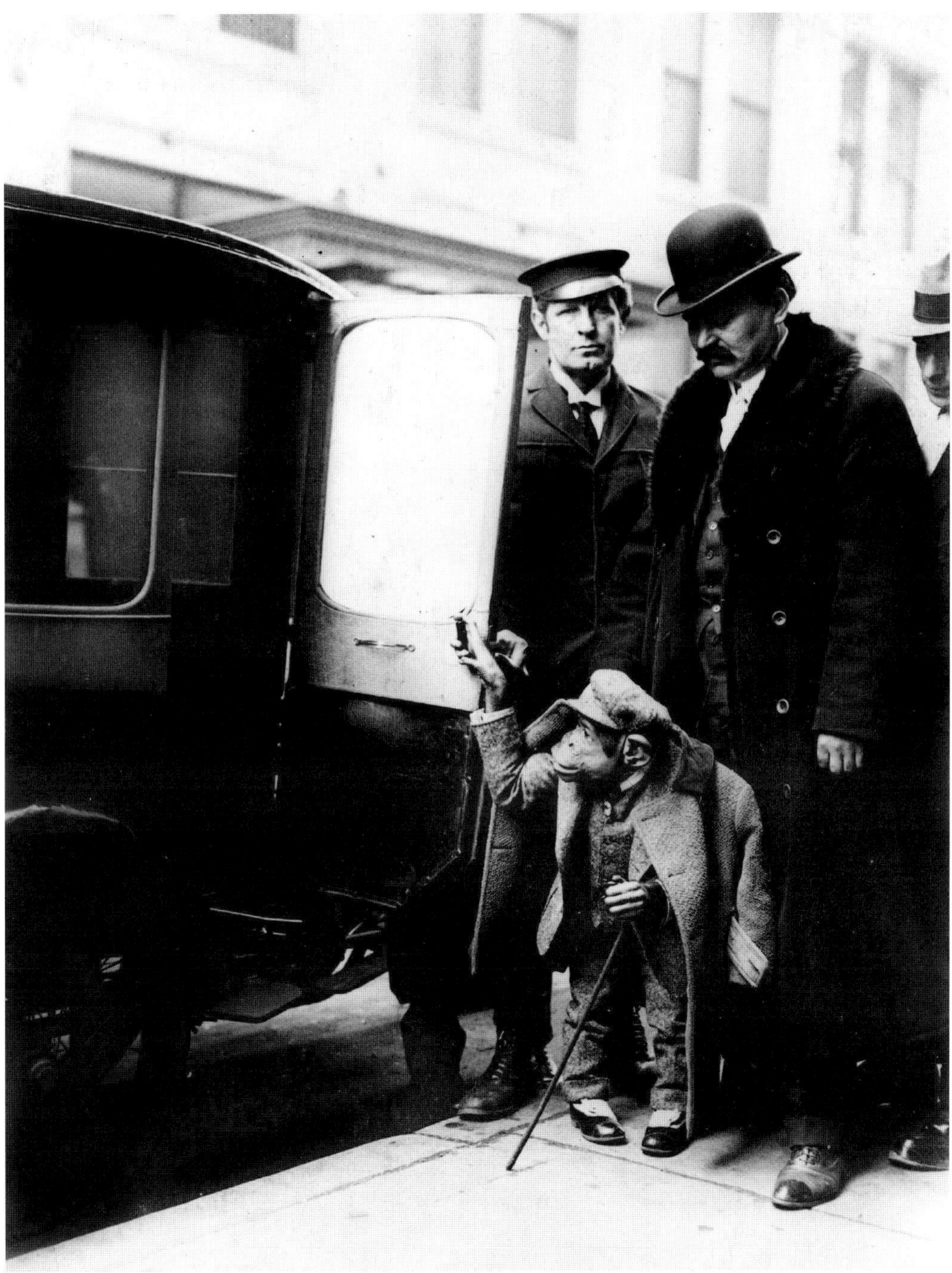

This well-dressed chimpanzee carries a cane and rides in a car. He is attended by a liveried driver and a distinguished gentleman in bowler hat and fur-collared winter coat. The sophisticated primate was spotted around 1910 in New York City near the Hippodrome Theatre at 756 Sixth Avenue, Manhattan, which featured circus acts.

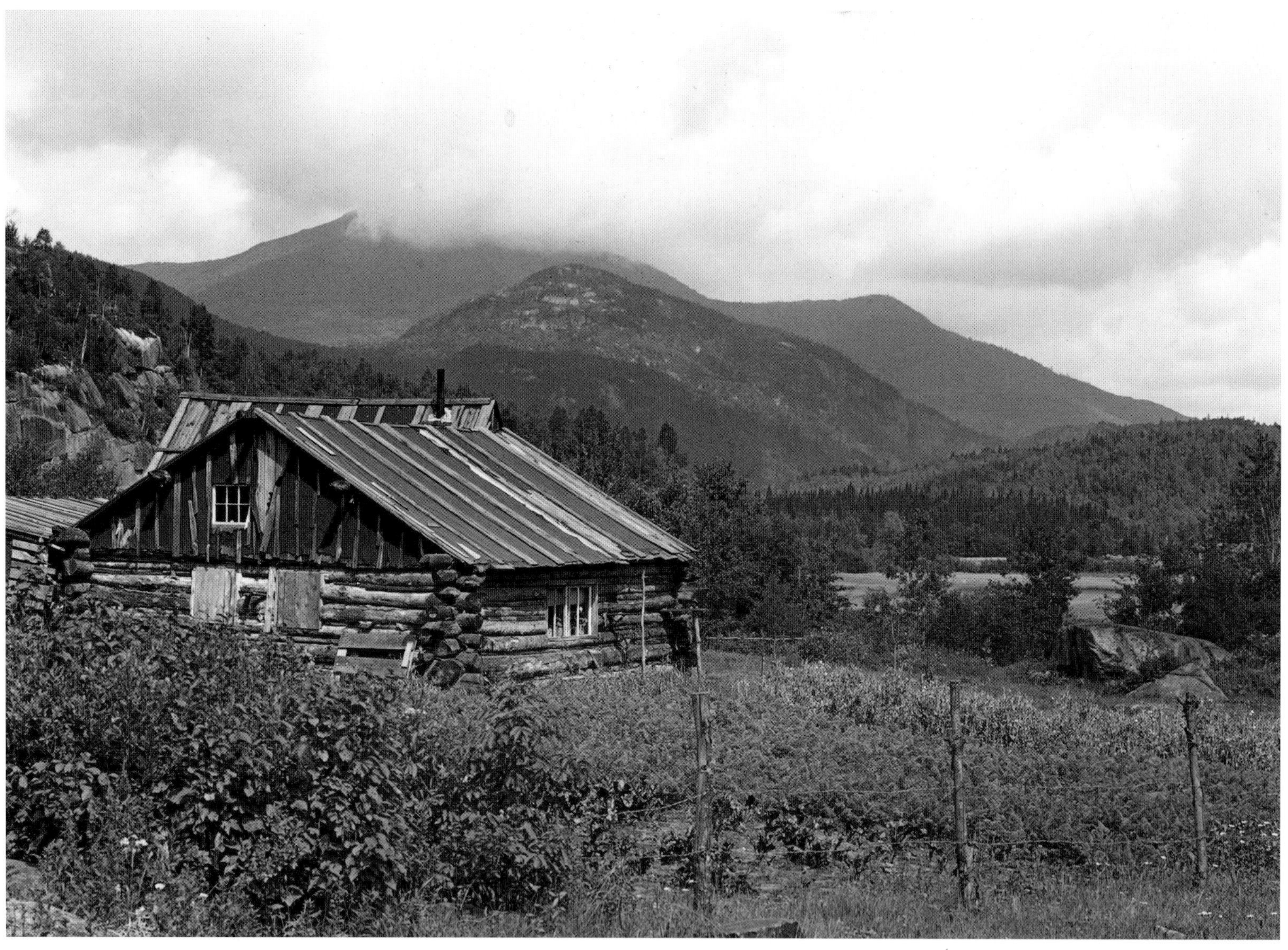

Mighty Whiteface Mountain in the northern Adirondacks is shrouded in clouds in this 1912 image, which faces north from Wilmington Notch in Essex County. In the foreground is an Adirondack-style log cabin. The Adirondack architectural style borrowed from the Swiss chalet style. In the construction of this cabin, whole logs rather than half logs were used.

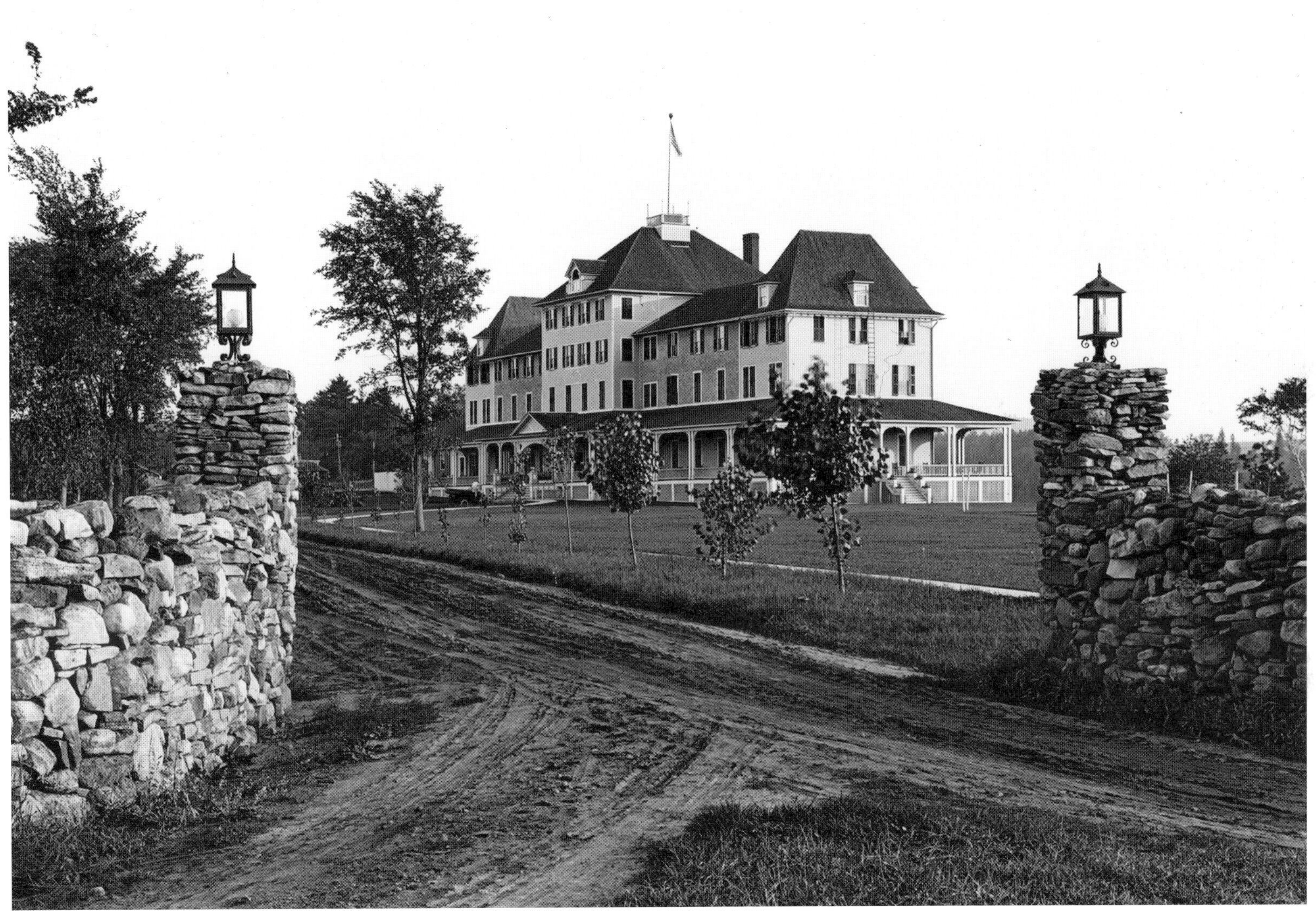

Hotel Ausable Chasm, just two miles outside Keeseville in the Adirondacks, was a large, popular resort hotel where guests came to explore the dramatic Ausable Chasm gorge created 500 million years ago by the Ausable River, whose headwaters start at Mount Marcy. The breathtaking natural phenomenon has been a favorite destination since 1870. And the grand Hotel Ausable Chasm, with its stone entrance wall, its wraparound porch, fine accommodations, and scenic outlook over the chasm was the place to stay until 1954, when it burned to the ground.

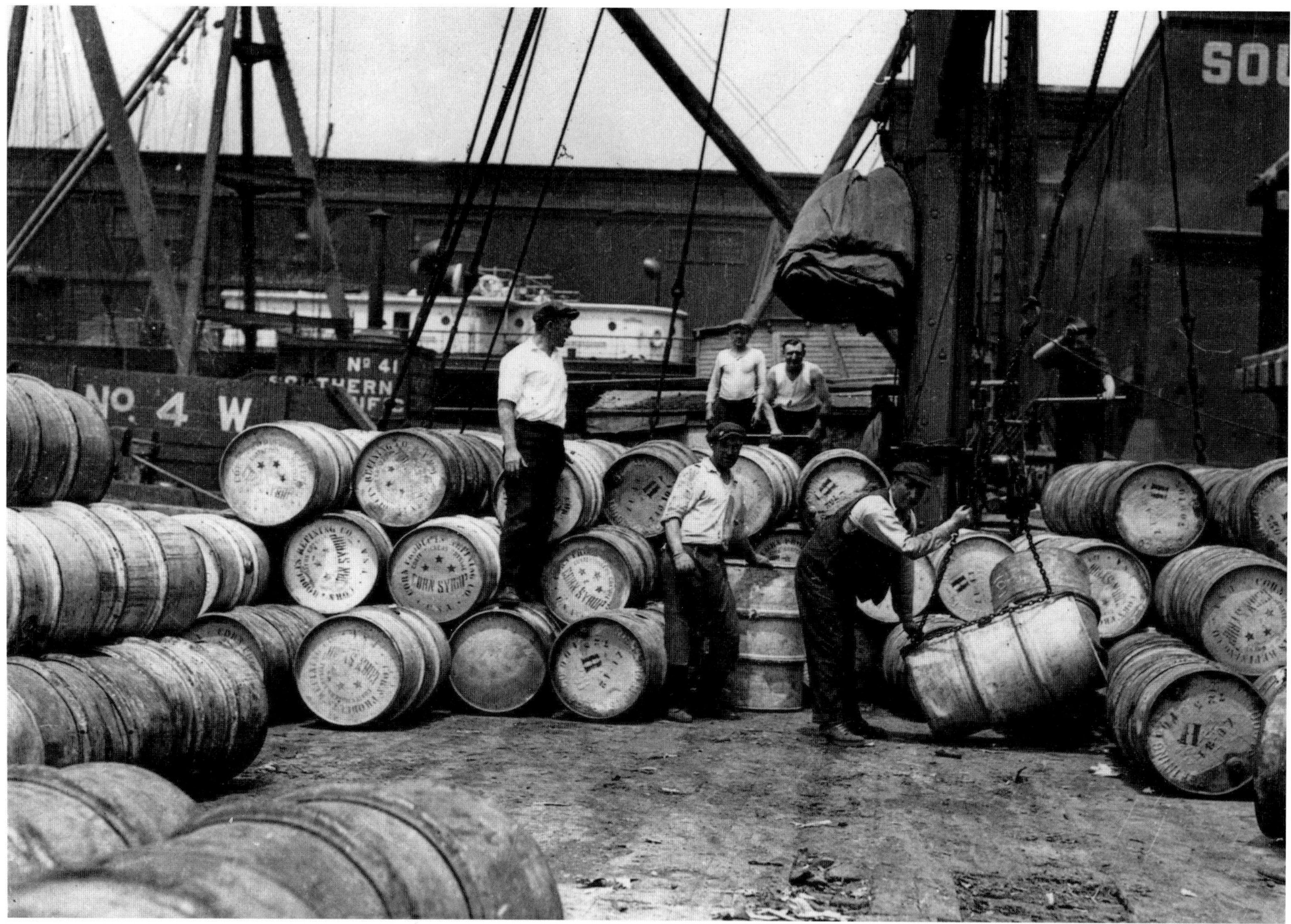

This is a Lewis Wickes Hine image from 1912 depicting stevedores on a New York City dock loading barrels of corn syrup onto a barge on the Hudson River. Raised in Wisconsin, Hine moved to New York City in 1901, rising to become an accomplished member of his profession. His subjects include Ellis Island immigrants, Red Cross relief efforts during World War I, construction of the Empire State Building, and his work for the National Child Labor Committee, examples of which also appear in this section. No longer patronized by the government late in life, Hine died at Dobbs Ferry, New York, in 1940, succumbing to the penury he had spent his life documenting.

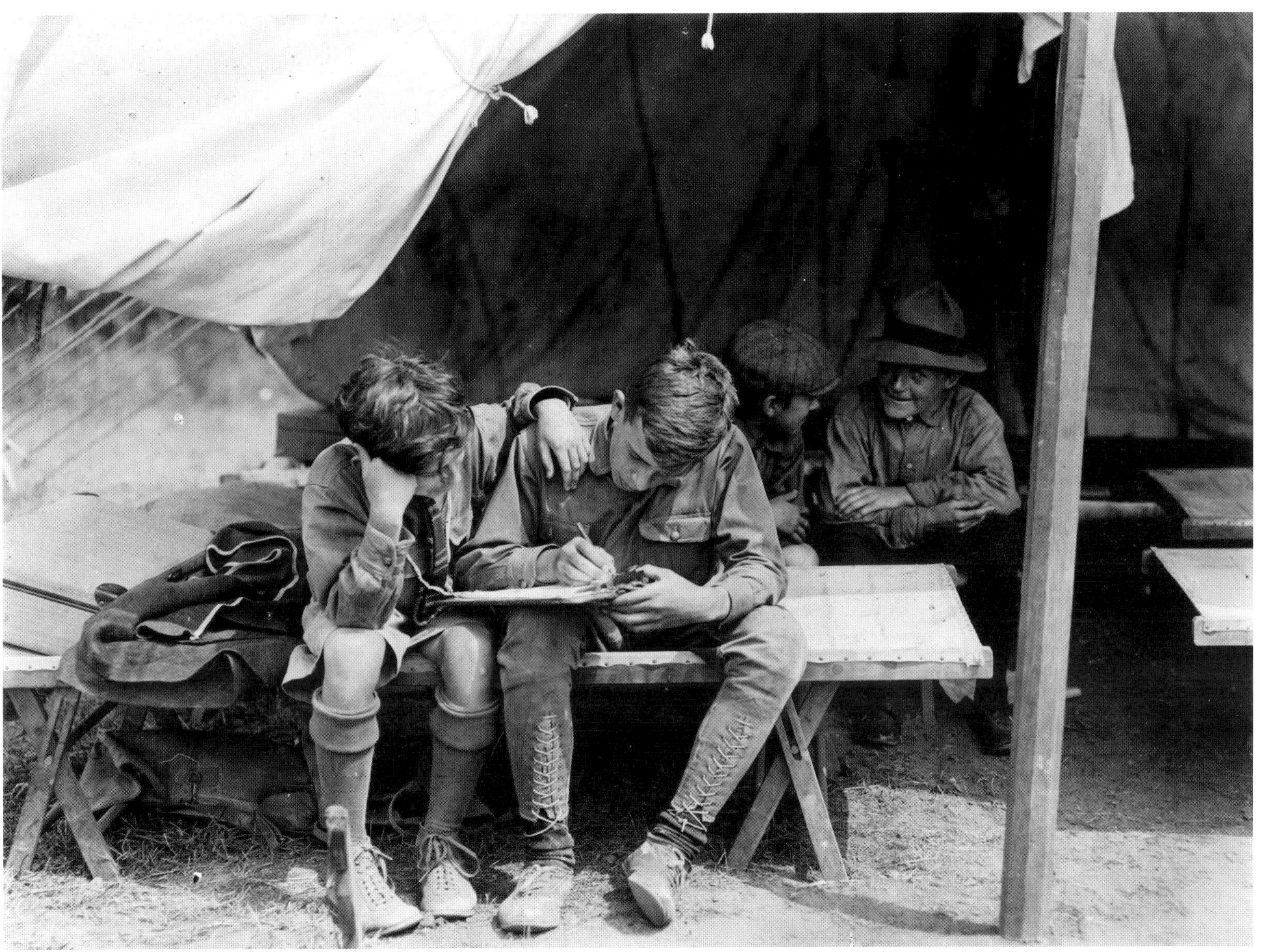

Here in 1912, Boy Scouts are camping on Hunter Island, Pelham Bay, in the Bronx. One boy is writing, perhaps a letter home to his folks. Hunter Island got its name from John Hunter, a wealthy auctioneer and farmer who once owned the island before the city of Bronx bought it. The Boy Scouts of America was founded only two years before this image was recorded.

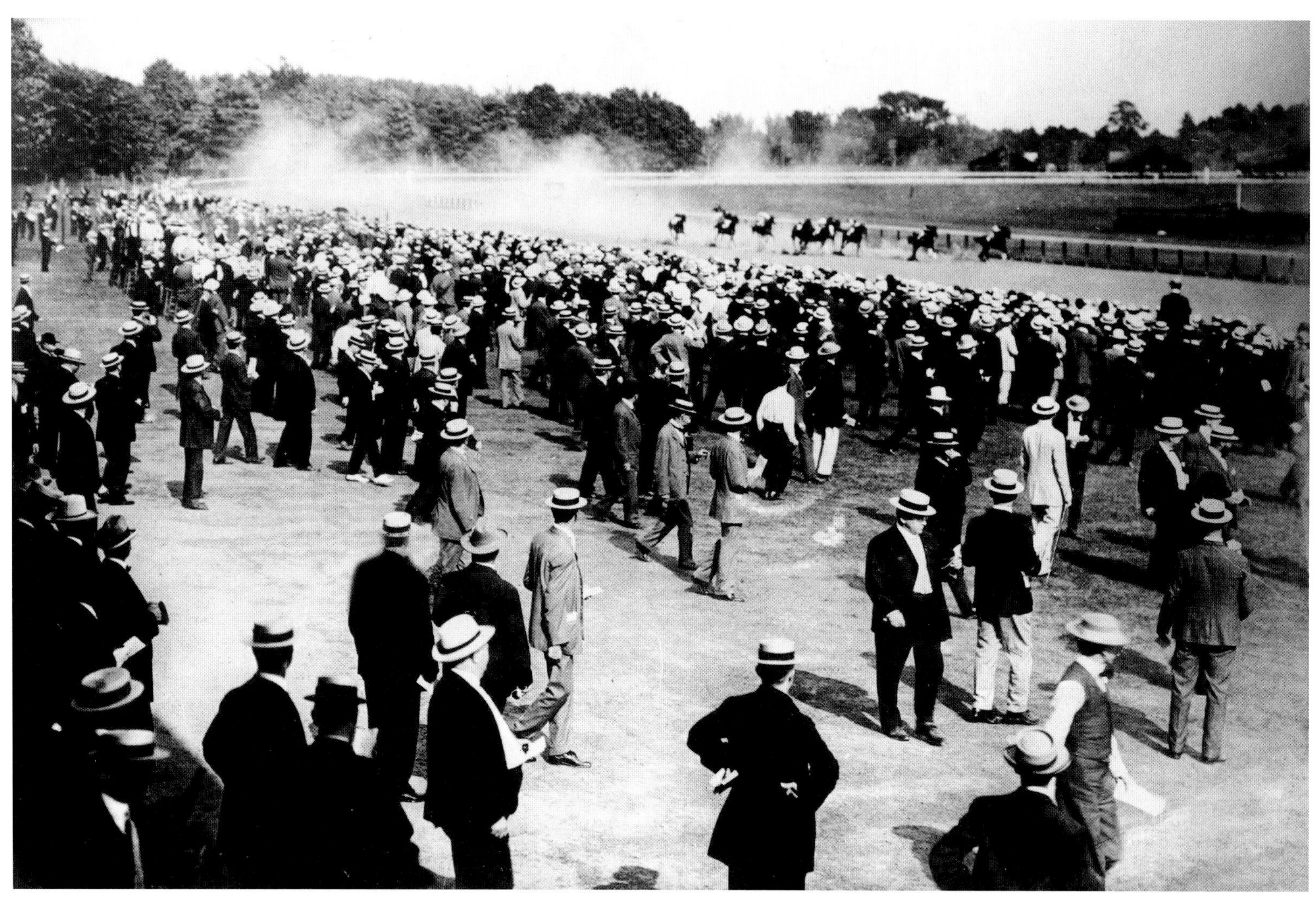

July and August are horse-racing months at the Saratoga Springs Race Course. Here in July 1913, crowds gather at the track as horses race by, raising dust as they pass. Saratoga's racetrack is the oldest continuously operating course in the United States, dating to 1863. The town of Saratoga Springs grew up around the mineral springs abundant here and once featured the Grand Union Hotel, in its heyday the largest hotel in the world. It was razed in 1953 to make way for a supermarket.

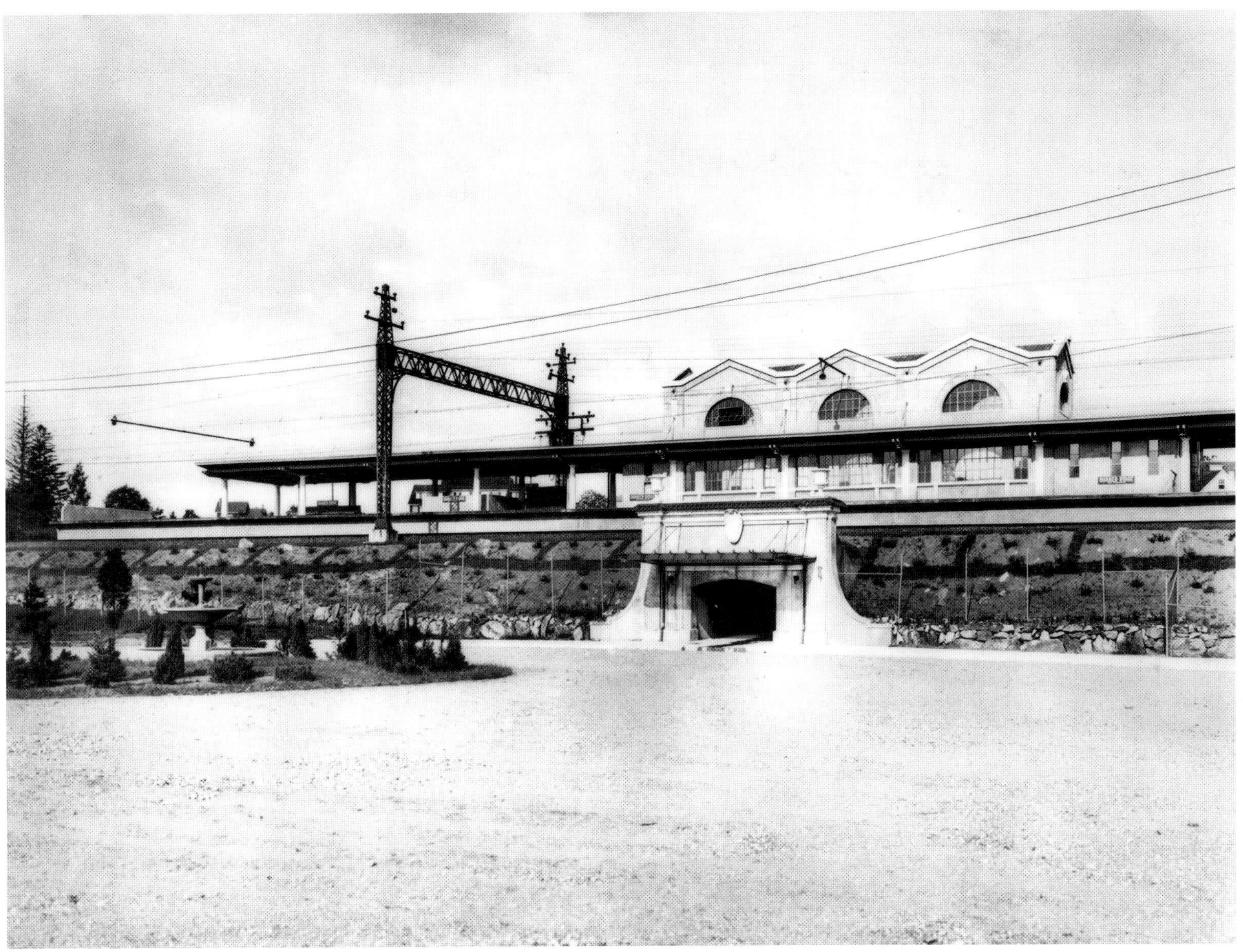

Here in 1913 is the Quaker Ridge railroad station in New Rochelle on the Long Island Sound in Westchester County. When the New York and New Haven Railroad opened a line with a stop in New Rochelle, it became famous as a summer resort and also as a residential community for New Yorkers who could afford to live there. The Quaker Ridge station is a stop on the New York, Westchester, and Boston Railroad line.

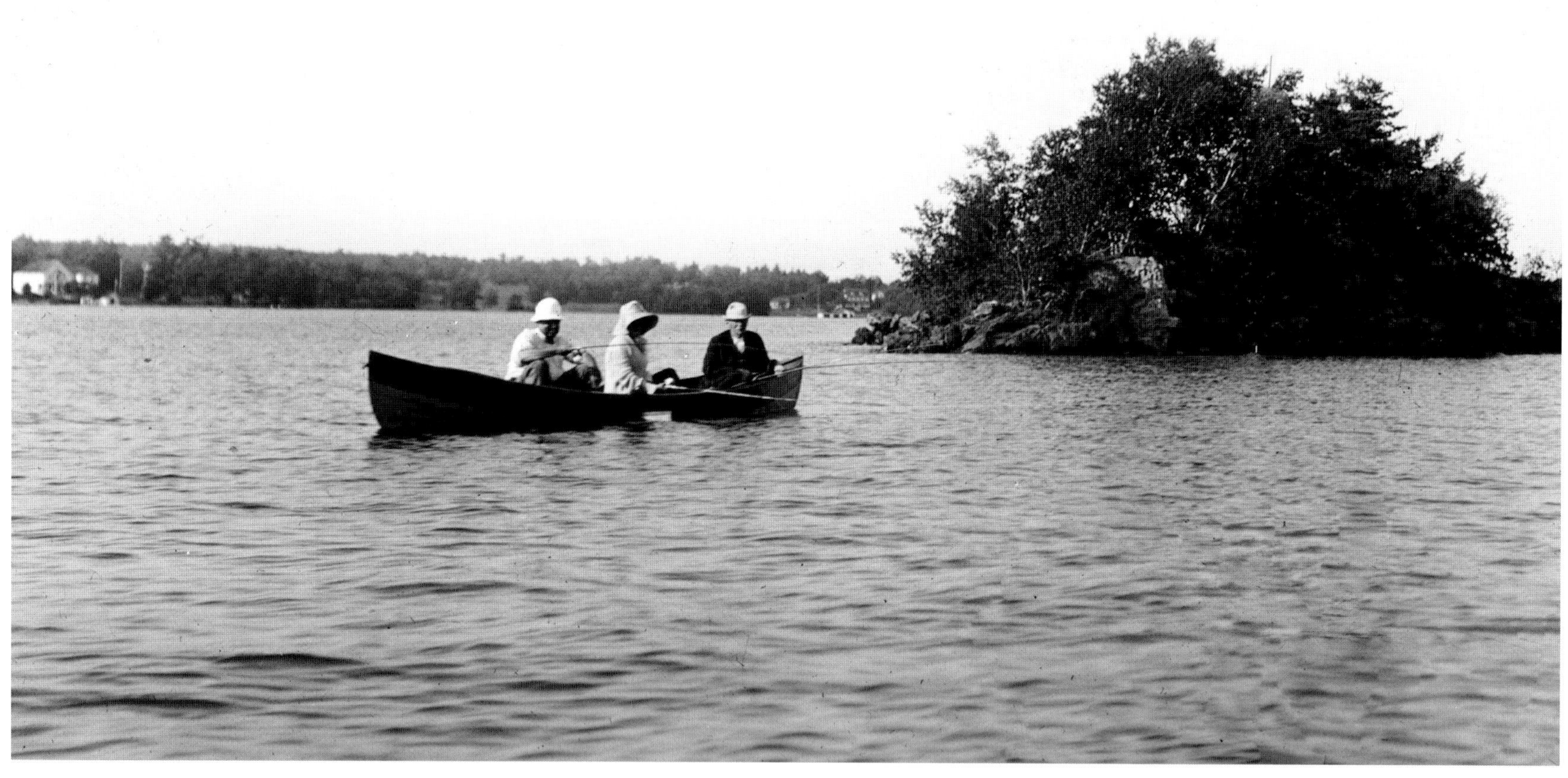

Three people in a small boat are fishing in the St. Lawrence River in the Thousand Islands in 1914. The St. Lawrence receives fresh water from Lake Ontario, which collects overflow from the other Great Lakes and carries it to the Atlantic Ocean. The U.S.-Canadian boundary runs roughly down the middle of the river, dividing the islands somewhat equally between the United States and Canada. At the turn of the century, one of the islands became home to Singer Castle, owned by Singer sewing machine company president Frederick Bourne.

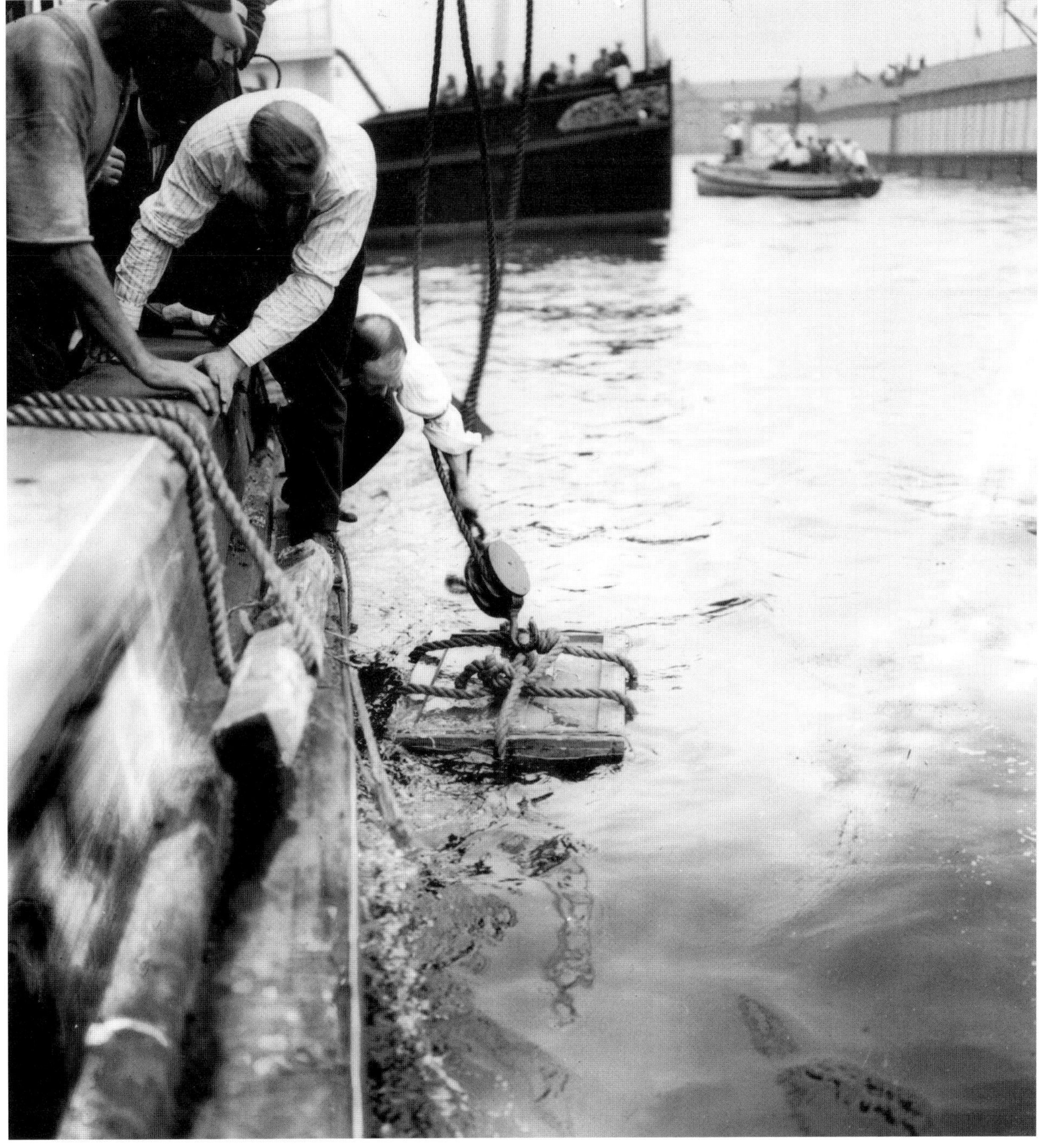

In 1914, Harry Houdini (1874–1926), world-famous escapologist, was tied up and put into a packing crate along with 600 pounds of iron weights and lowered into New York Harbor. He escaped in 2 minutes and 55 seconds. In 1918, he became the sensation at New York City's Hippodrome when he made a ten-thousand-pound elephant disappear from a brightly lit stage. Houdini also owned a brownstone in Harlem. The well-known photographer Carl Dietz recorded this image.

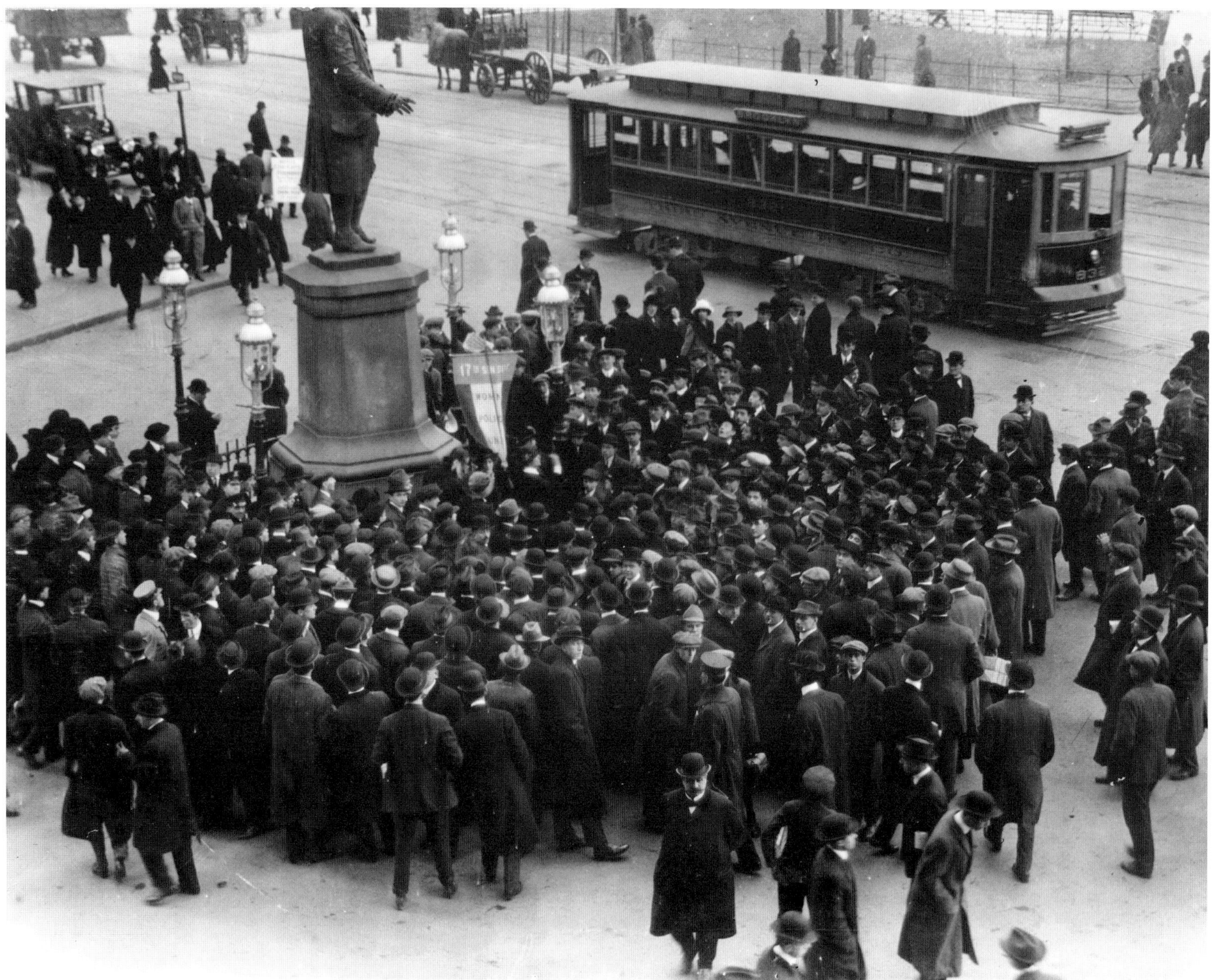

A suffrage demonstration on Park Row, a street in lower Manhattan in the financial district, is under way in 1913. The Nineteenth Amendment to the U.S. Constitution, giving women the right to vote, would not become law until 1920.

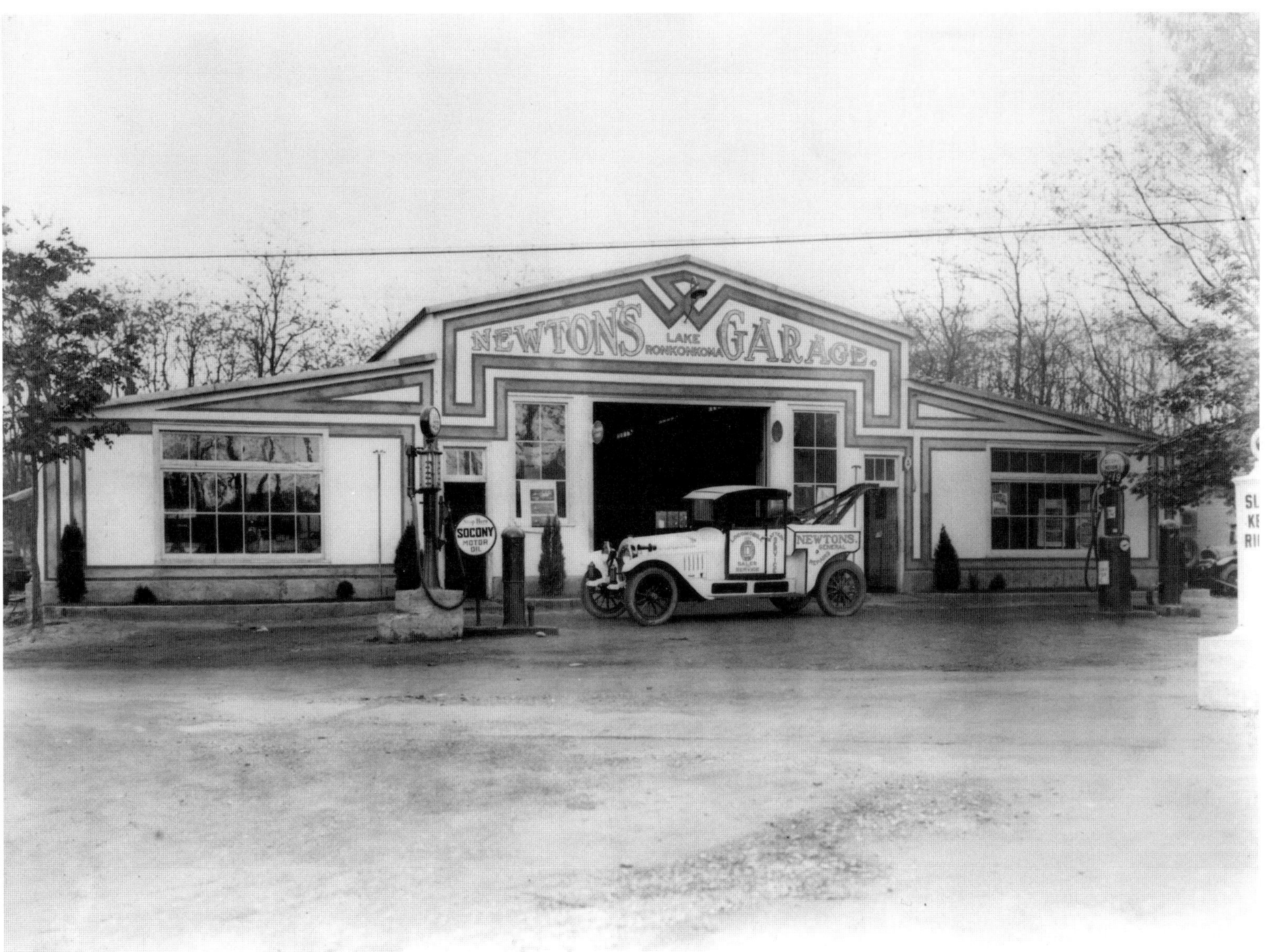

Newton's Garage did business in the village beside Lake Ronkonkoma—a large, oval-shaped lake one hundred feet deep in places, the largest on Long Island. The area was a well-known and fashionable summer resort during the era. Early filling stations typically featured whimsical architecture, and this garage is no exception. Columns flank the center entrance, large windows fill the façades of the side wings, and fancy geometric trimwork covers the face of the structure. Newton's "Locomobile" is parked proudly in front, ready for the next service call.

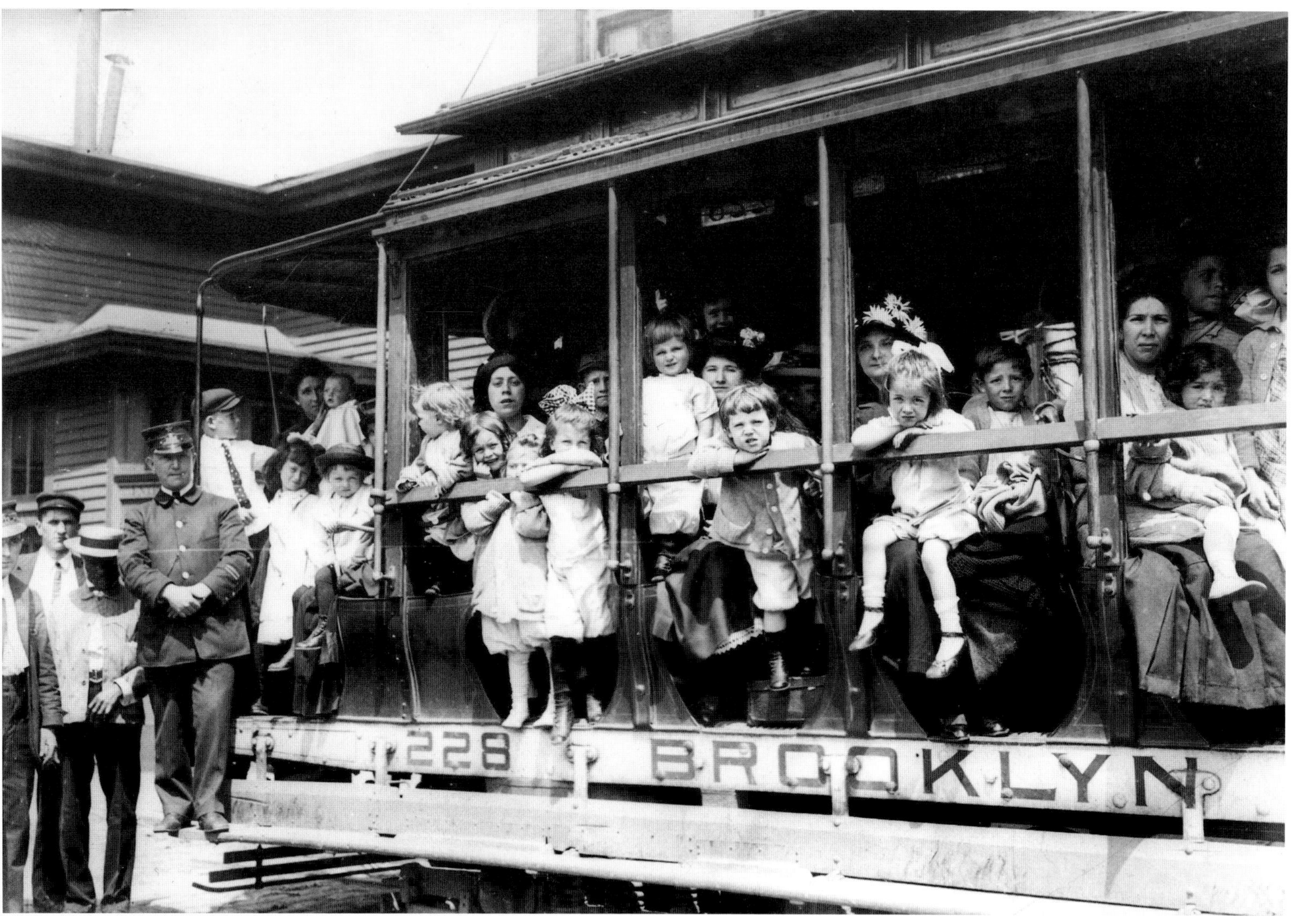

On June 2, 1913, mothers take their children on a Brooklyn trolley for a fresh-air outing. Fresh sea air was readily available—Brooklyn is located at the western end of Long Island and is surrounded by water on three sides. Early on a city in its own right, Brooklyn was joined with Queens, the Bronx, Staten Island, and Manhattan to become one of the five boroughs of New York City in 1898.

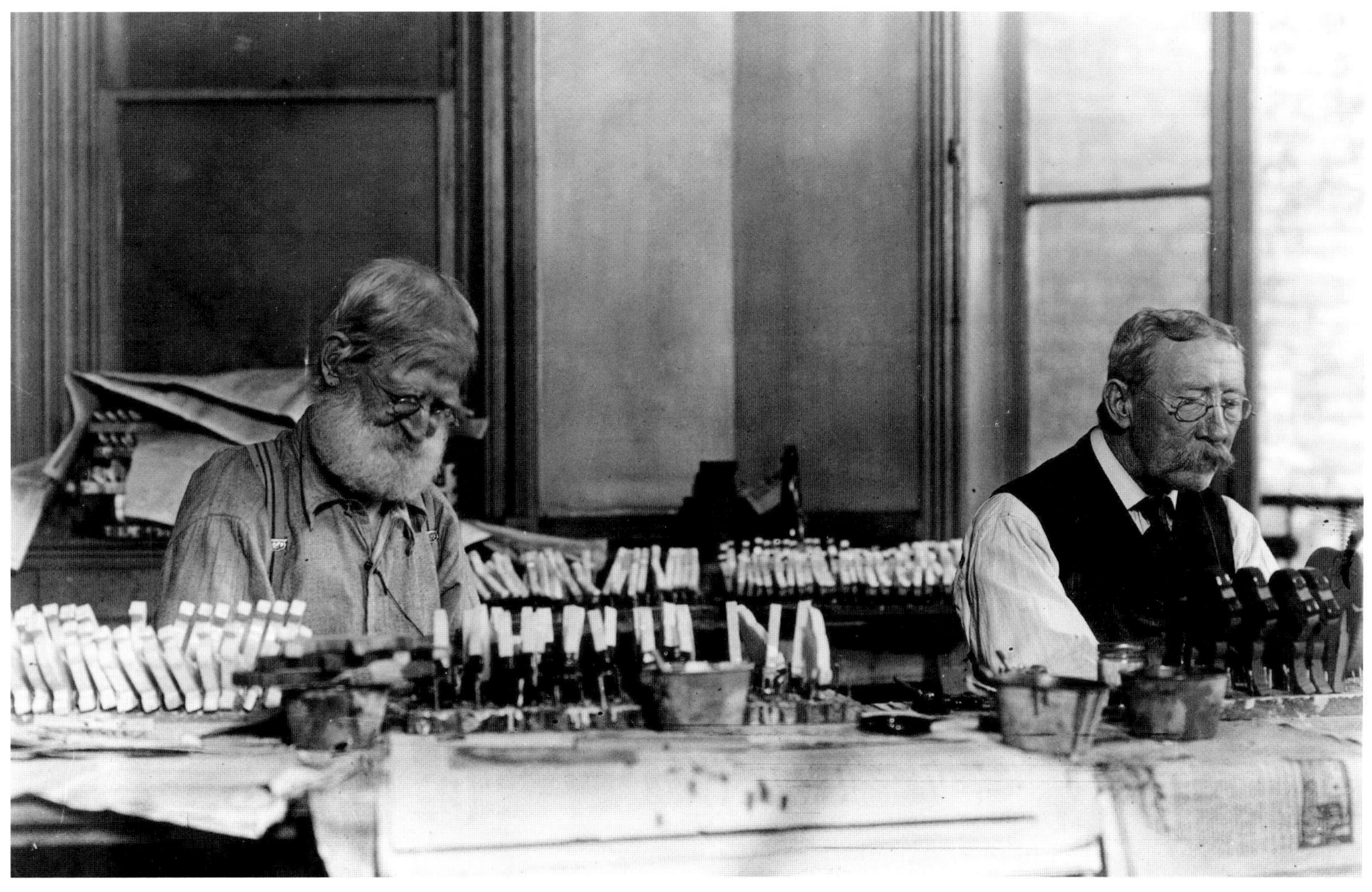

Two elderly men assemble handmade toys in a toy workshop in 1915, probably in New York City. New York's oldest toy store, FAO Schwarz, opened its doors in the city in 1870, its fame renewed in recent times in the movie *Home Alone 2.*

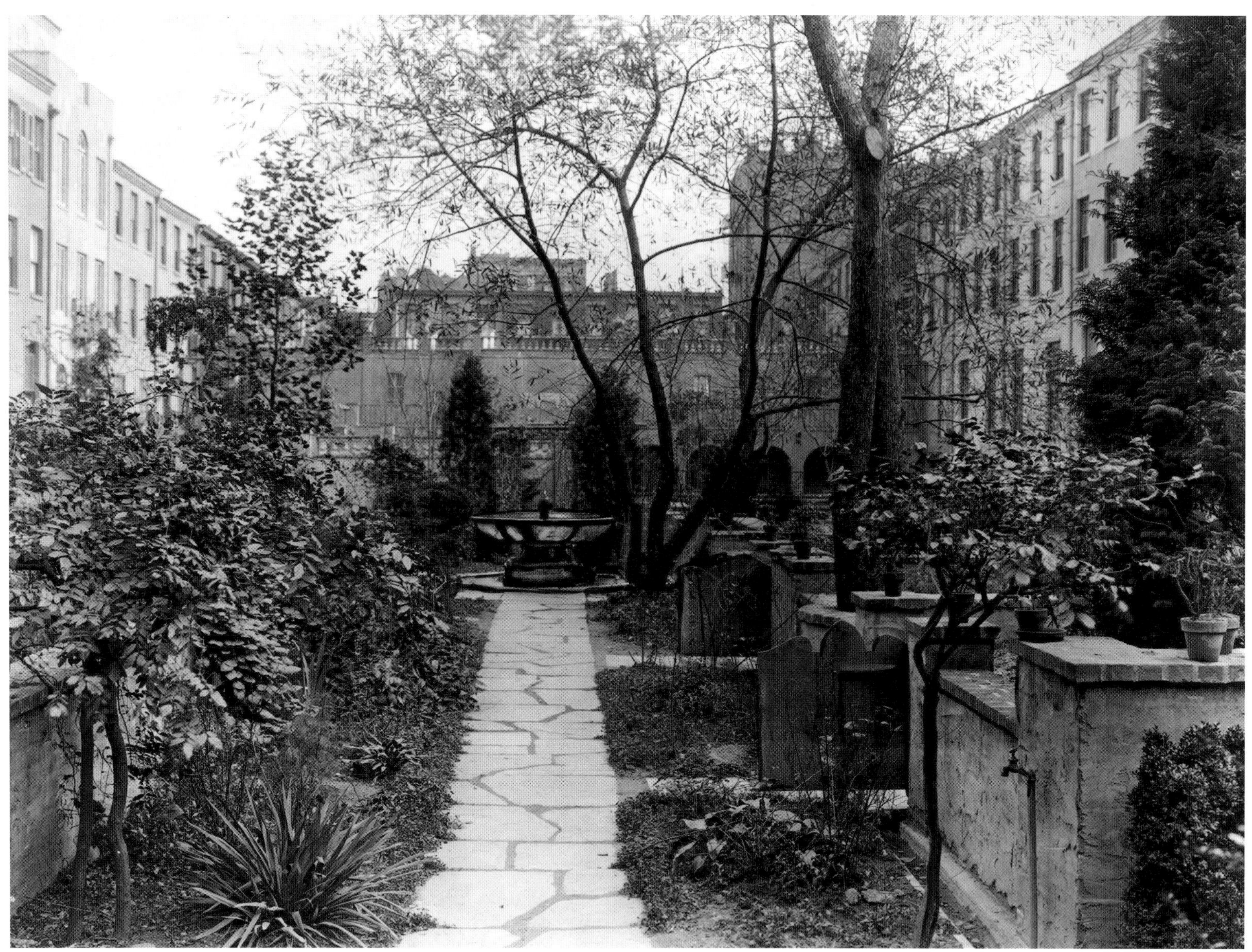

The Turtle Bay neighborhood in Manhattan extends from 43rd to 53rd Street and from Lexington Avenue to the East River. At least it did when this photograph was taken early in the twentieth century. Today, the United Nations building stands where the bay itself once existed. A 40-acre tract that was once Turtle Bay Farm has evolved into an urban neighborhood of tree-lined streets and small-town sensations.

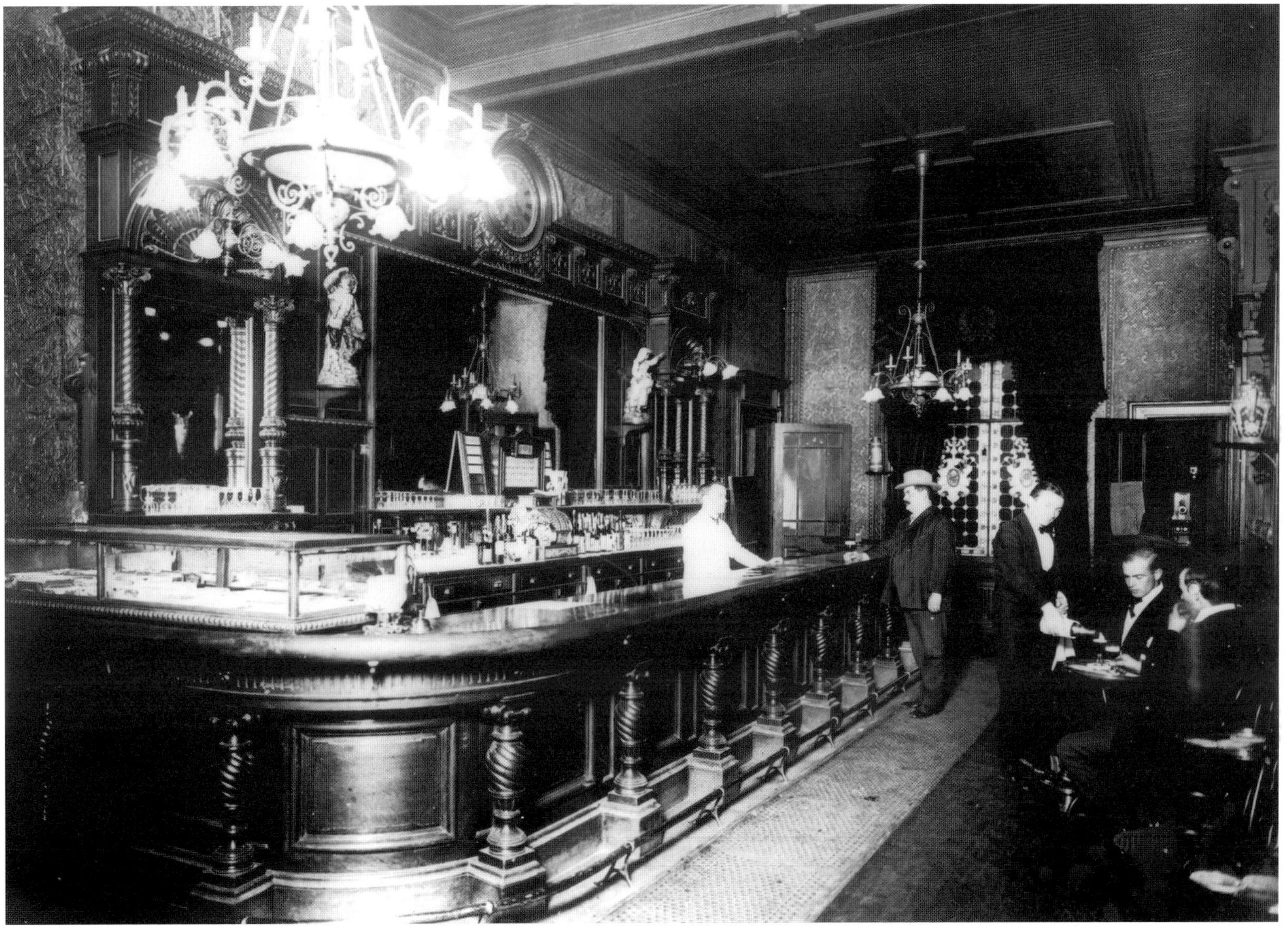

Here is the elegant barroom of the Arion Society Club, located on Park Avenue at 59th Street in Manhattan and photographed in 1915. Arion was organized in 1854 as a professional music and poetry club, named for the Greek poet and musician who lived and performed around 700 b.c. A long, heavy, carved-wood bar is shown, partly supported by wood columns incorporating a spiral motif, which is repeated in the mirrored back bar. Enormous Victorian chandeliers illuminate the space. Manhattan is home to more than a few bars dating to the nineteenth century, including the Ear on Spring Street, New Town on 18th, and McSorley's on East 7th.

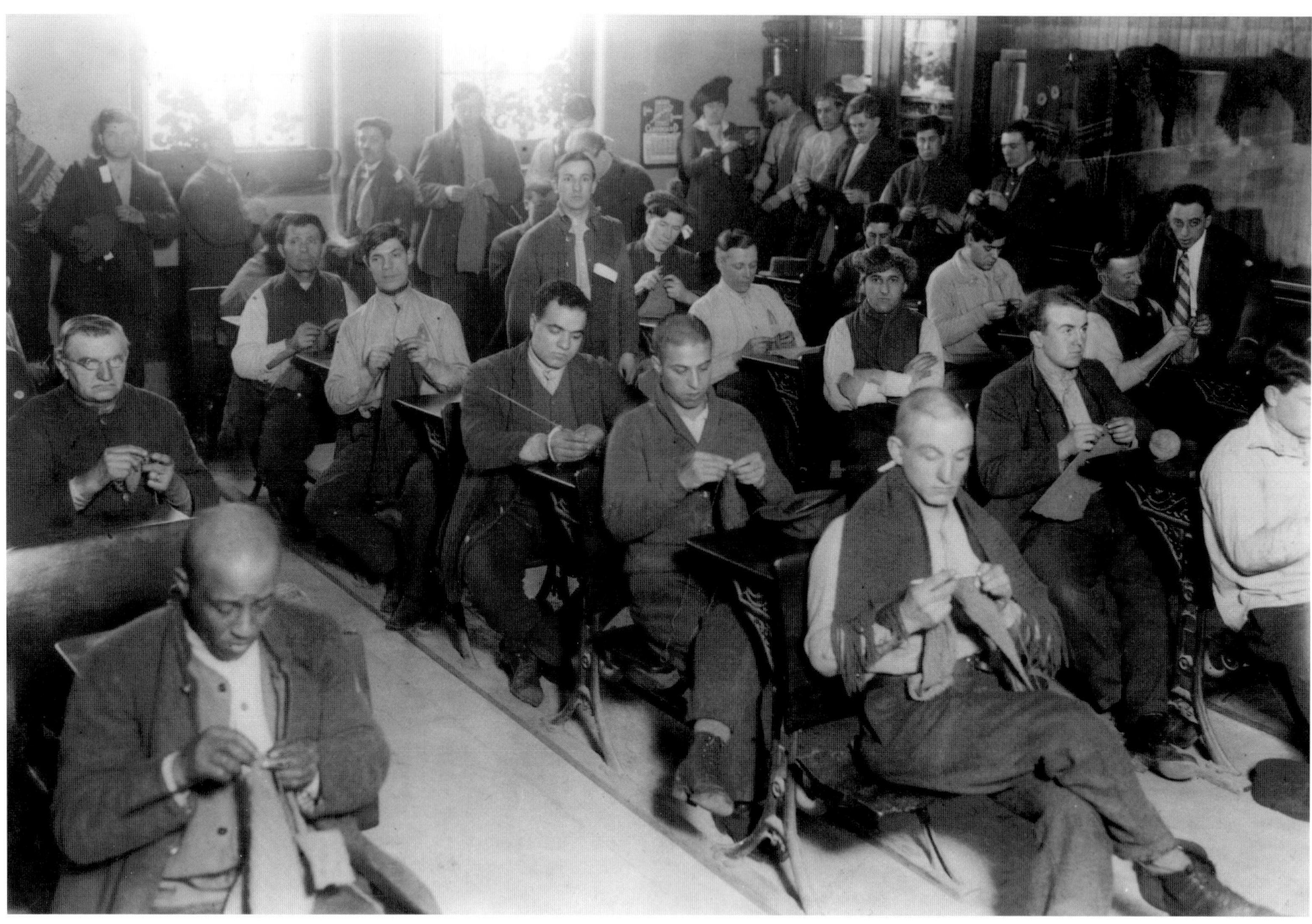

Sing Sing Correctional Facility is a maximum-security prison in Ossining on the banks of the Hudson River. The prison started in 1825 and today holds 1,700 inmates. In this 1915 image, prisoners sit in a classroom learning how to knit. The name "Sing Sing" comes from the Indian tribe Sinck Sinck, from whom the land was purchased. The words mean "stone upon stone," an appropriate appellation for the prison, which was built with marble excavated by prisoners from a nearby quarry.

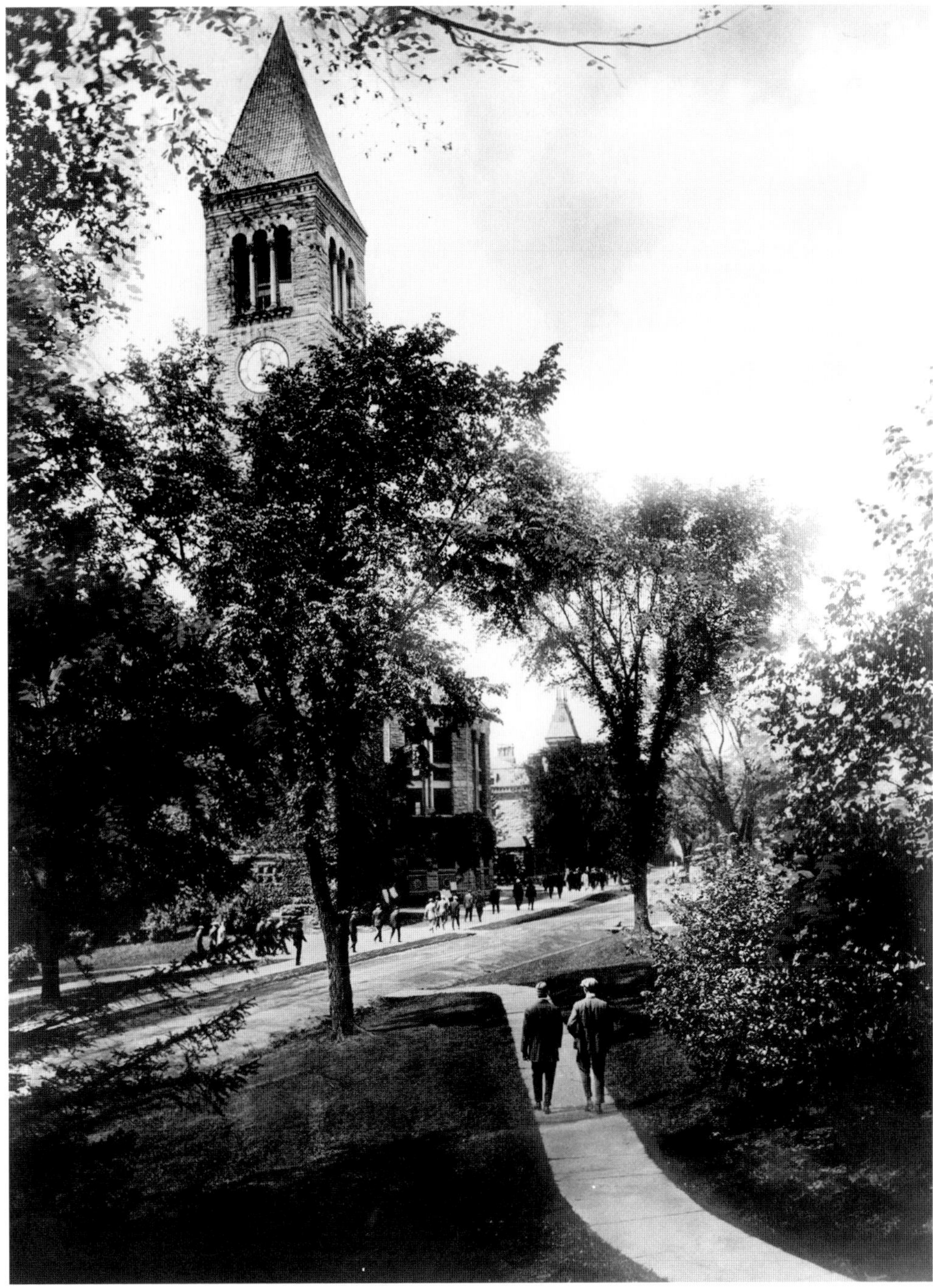

The most iconic building on the Cornell University campus in Ithaca is the Jennie McGraw Tower, built in 1891 and shown here on June 4, 1915. The 173-foot-tall tower was designed by architect William Henry Miller, a Cornell alumnus. It stands adjacent Uris Library. Inside are the 1875 Seth Thomas clock with a 14-foot pendulum and 21 bells that not only mark the hours but also are played three times a day during the school year.

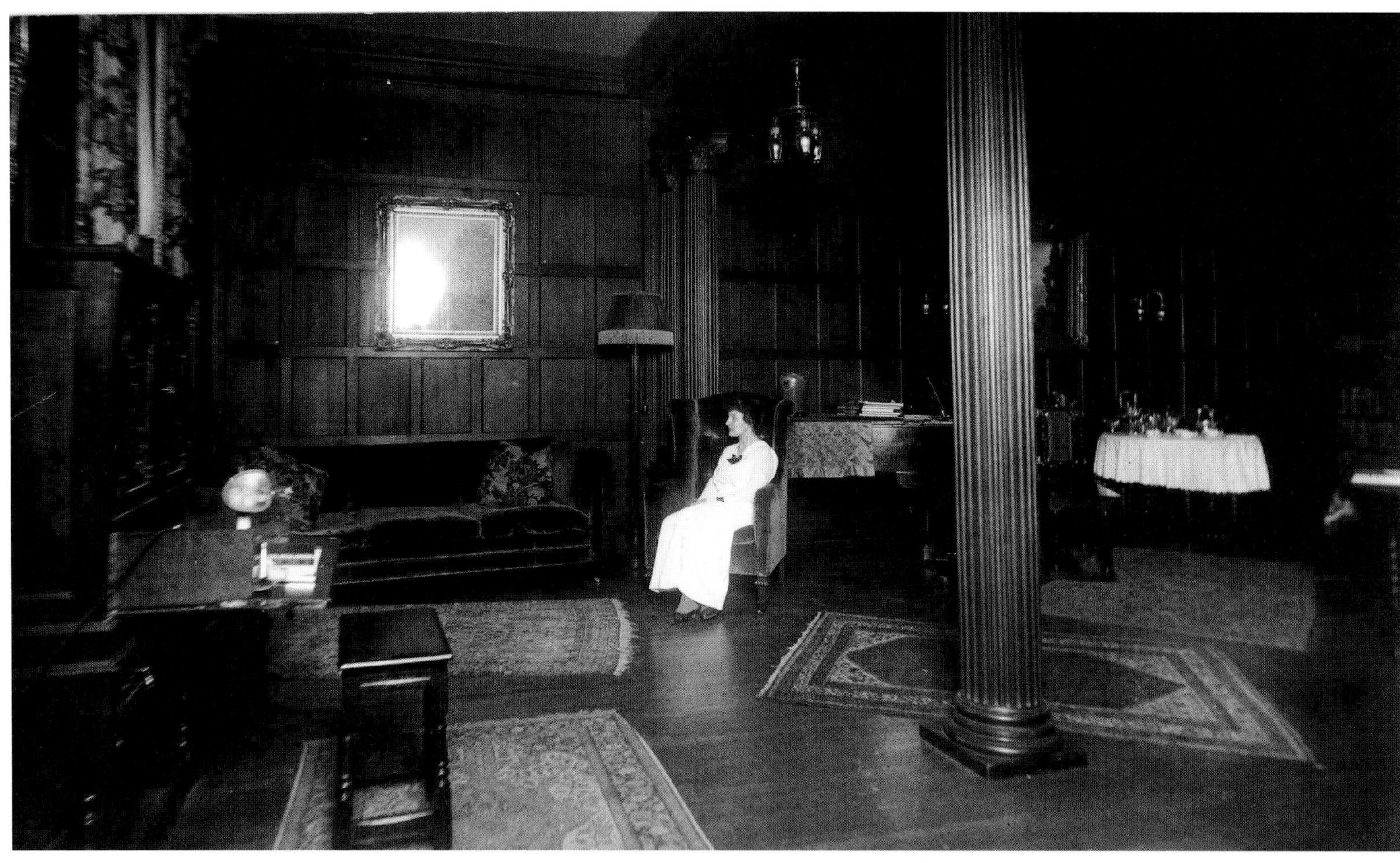

The senior parlor, pictured here in 1915, was opened at Vassar College in Poughkeepsie in 1895, with members of the senior class of 1895 contributing many articles of value and unique interest to their room. The parlor was designed in Colonial style with draperies in green and yellow, mahogany furniture, and Bocara rugs. On the walls are paintings by Corot and Millet, and in the background is a tearoom. Sitting for her photograph, one of the seniors relaxes in an easy chair.

Wine, Women, Want, and War

(1917–1930)

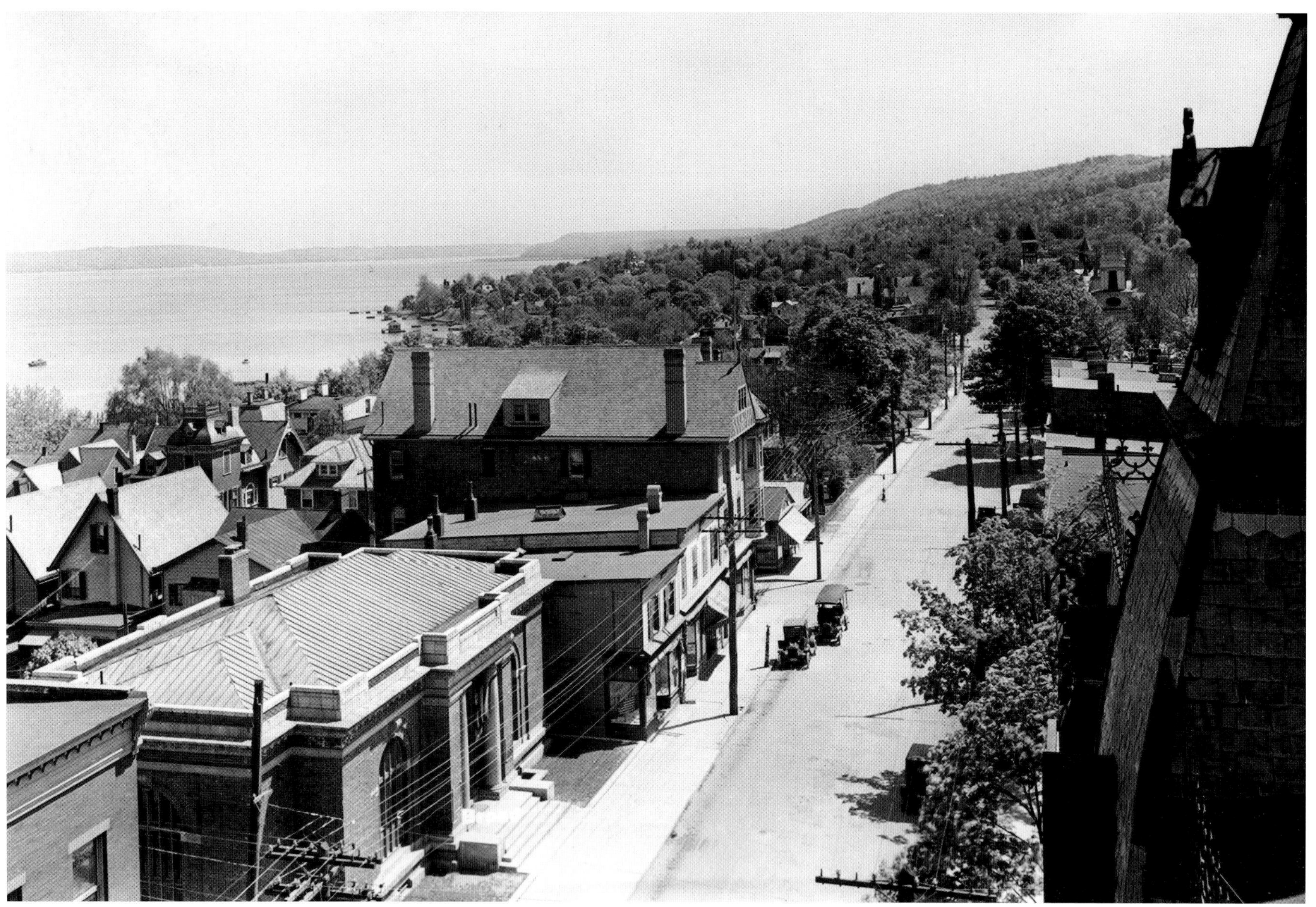

A view down South Broadway in Nyack as it appeared in 1917. The image was recorded from the Burke Building, part of its Second Empire–style mansard roof appearing at right. The Hudson River flows at left, and on a clear day, New York City would be visible in the distance.

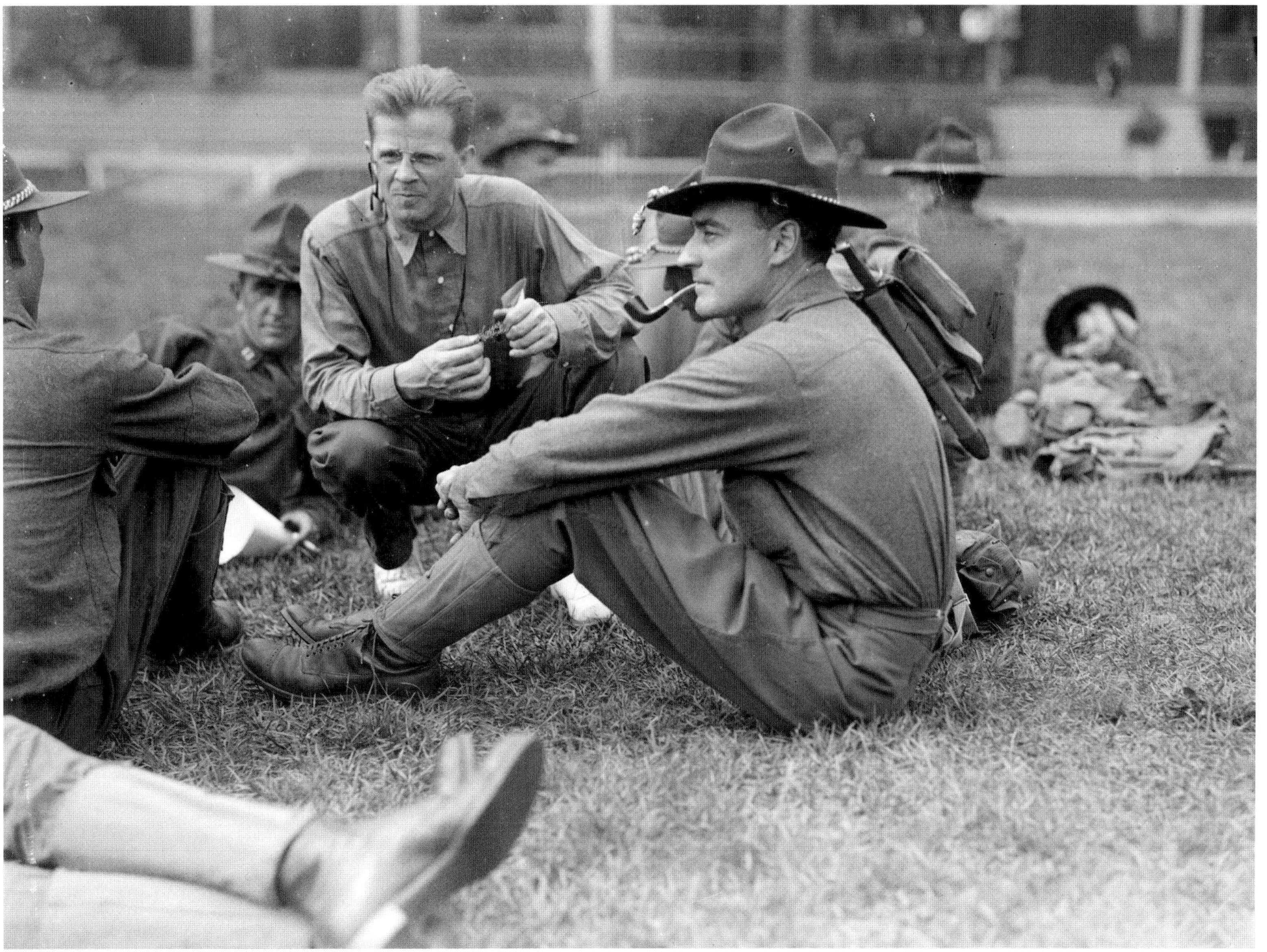

At the start of the First World War in 1914, the United States worried that it might be drawn into the conflict. At the time, the Army was small and the National Guard was insufficient for the prospects of fighting in Europe. To swell the ranks and the number of officers able to lead men into battle, conscription was instituted and a National Army Officer Candidate School was established in 1917 in Plattsburgh on Lake Champlain. In this image, officers-in-training relax on the school grounds.

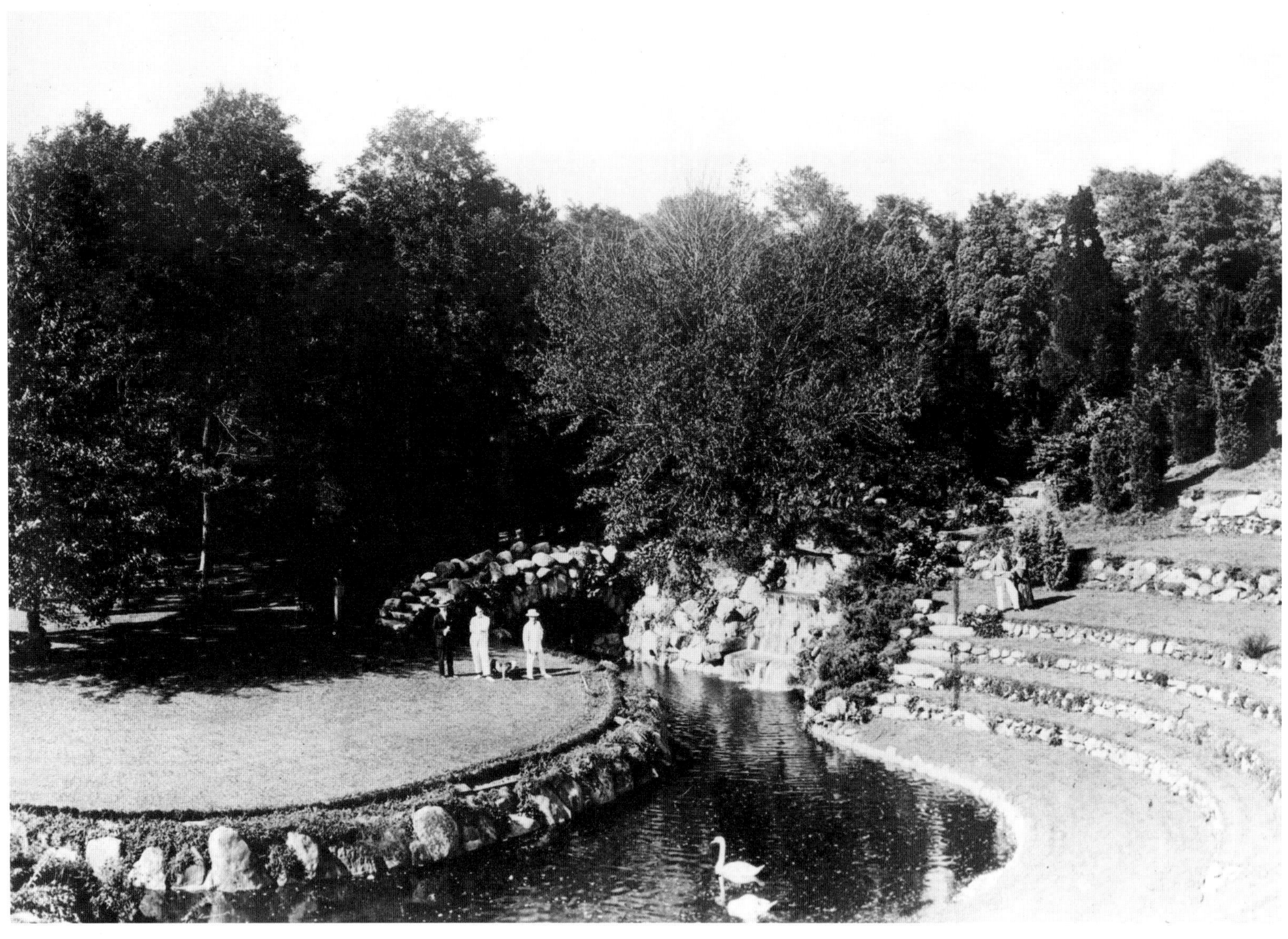

A pageant promoting efforts of the American Red Cross in World War I was held on October 5, 1917, at Rosemary Open Air Amphitheatre in Huntington, Long Island. About 500 people were invited. Preceding the pageant was a concert by Lieutenant John Philip Sousa and his band of 230 enlisted men, and a dramatic masque was presented by a large contingent of famous stage actors from New York City, including Ethel Barrymore. The photograph shows the presentation group (at center) at a dress rehearsal.

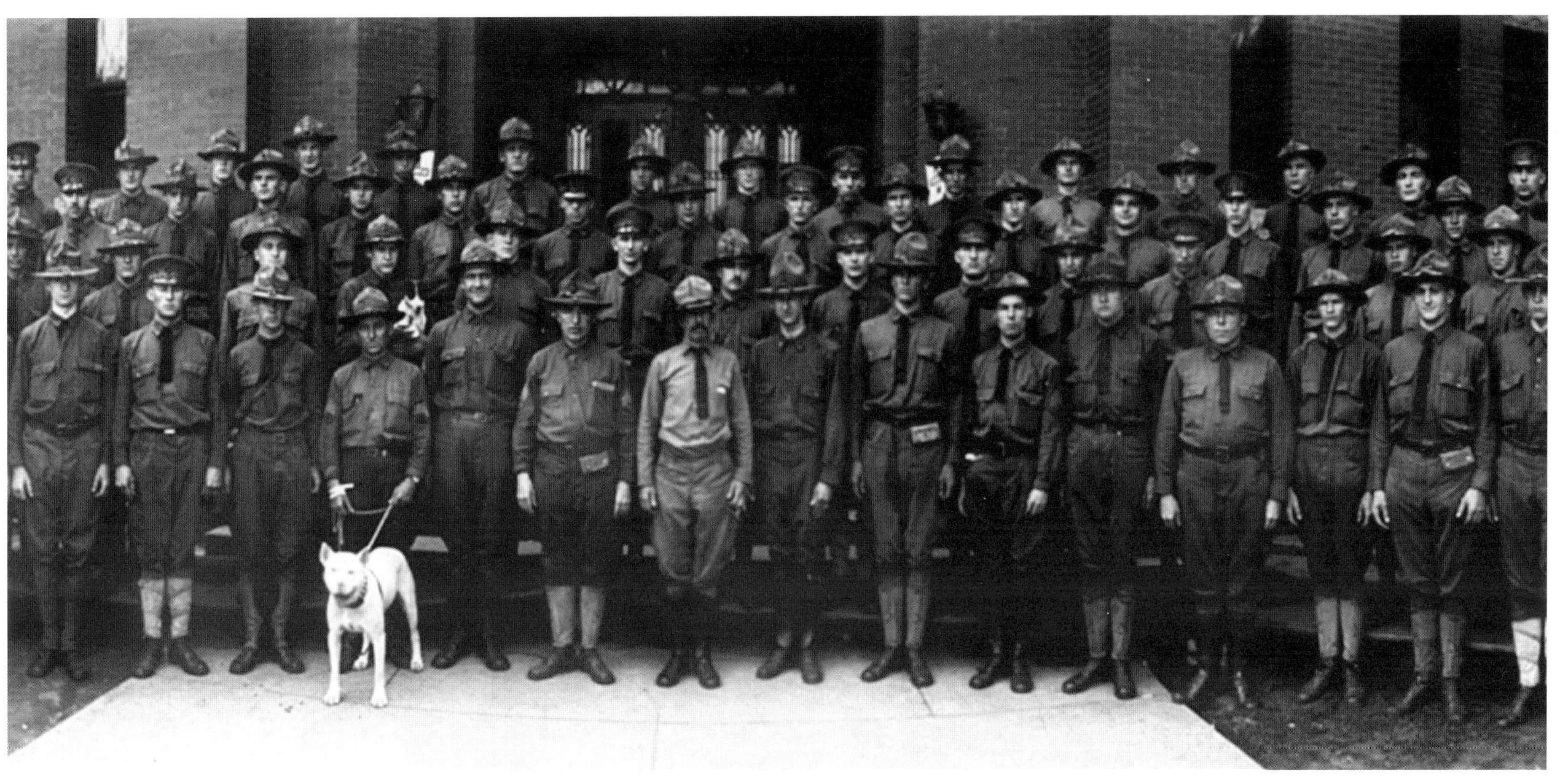

The First Ambulance Company of the New York National Guard poses with their mascot before departing for Spartanburg, South Carolina, in August 1917. There they will attend a training camp before being sent overseas. When the U.S. Congress declared war against Germany on April 6, 1917, the country was able to mobilize quickly.

In April 1918, renowned Hollywood motion-picture actor Douglas Fairbanks, from the base of George Washington's bronze statue, exhorts the crowd at Wall Street in lower Manhattan to buy war bonds. The monumental statue stands at the top of the steps to Federal Hall National Memorial, an imposing marble building in Greek Doric style completed in 1842. It was here in 1789, in the original Federal Hall, that George Washington took the oath of office as the first president of the new republic.

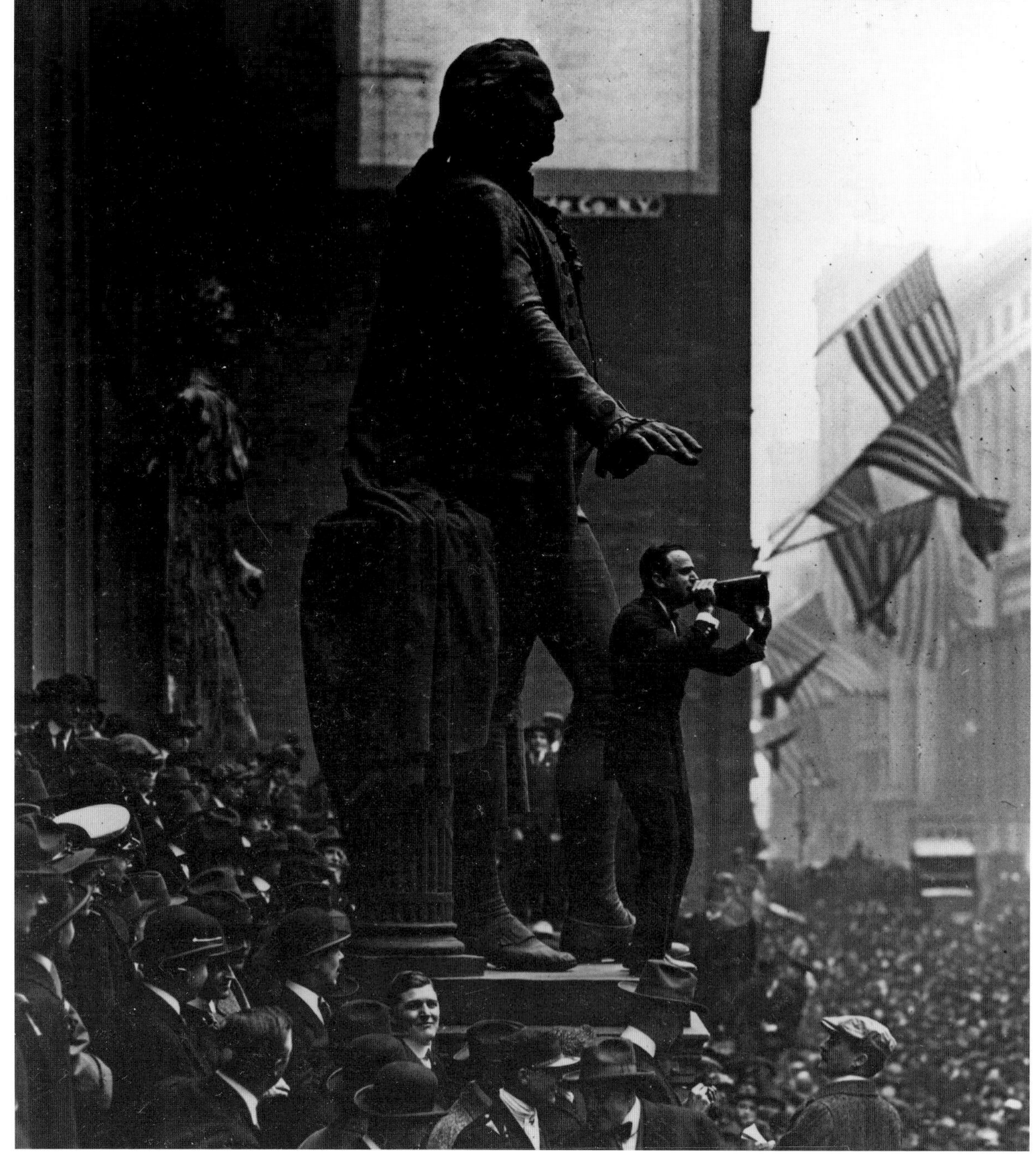

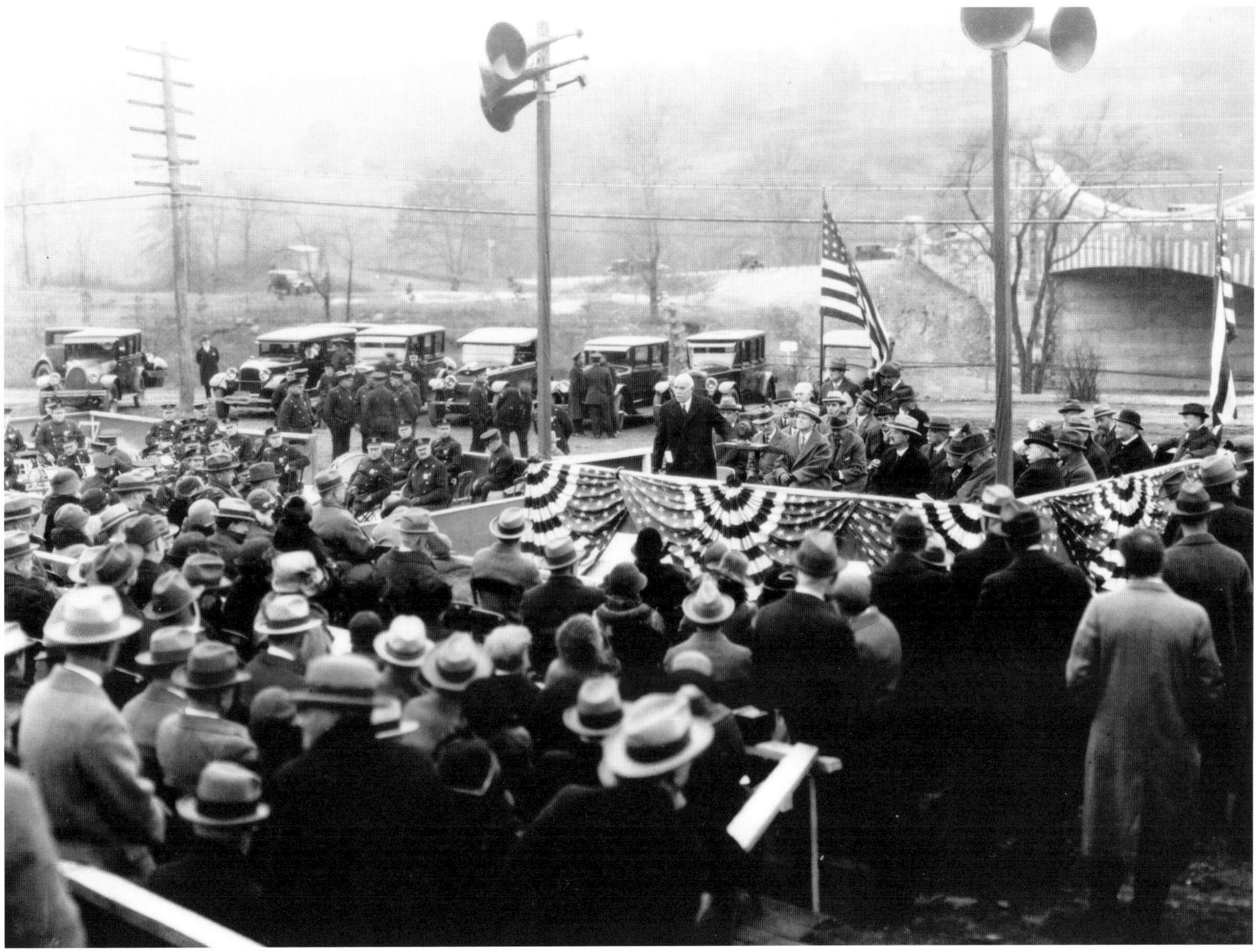

In White Plains, loudspeakers, the Stars and Stripes, and patriotic bunting showcase a platform with speakers and seated guests—all of whom are facing a crowd of onlookers, suggesting a political rally sometime around the 1920s. The United States Post Office issued a stamp in 1926 to commemorate the sesquicentennial of the Battle of White Plains on October 28, 1776. Today the souvenir sheet is a prized collector's item.

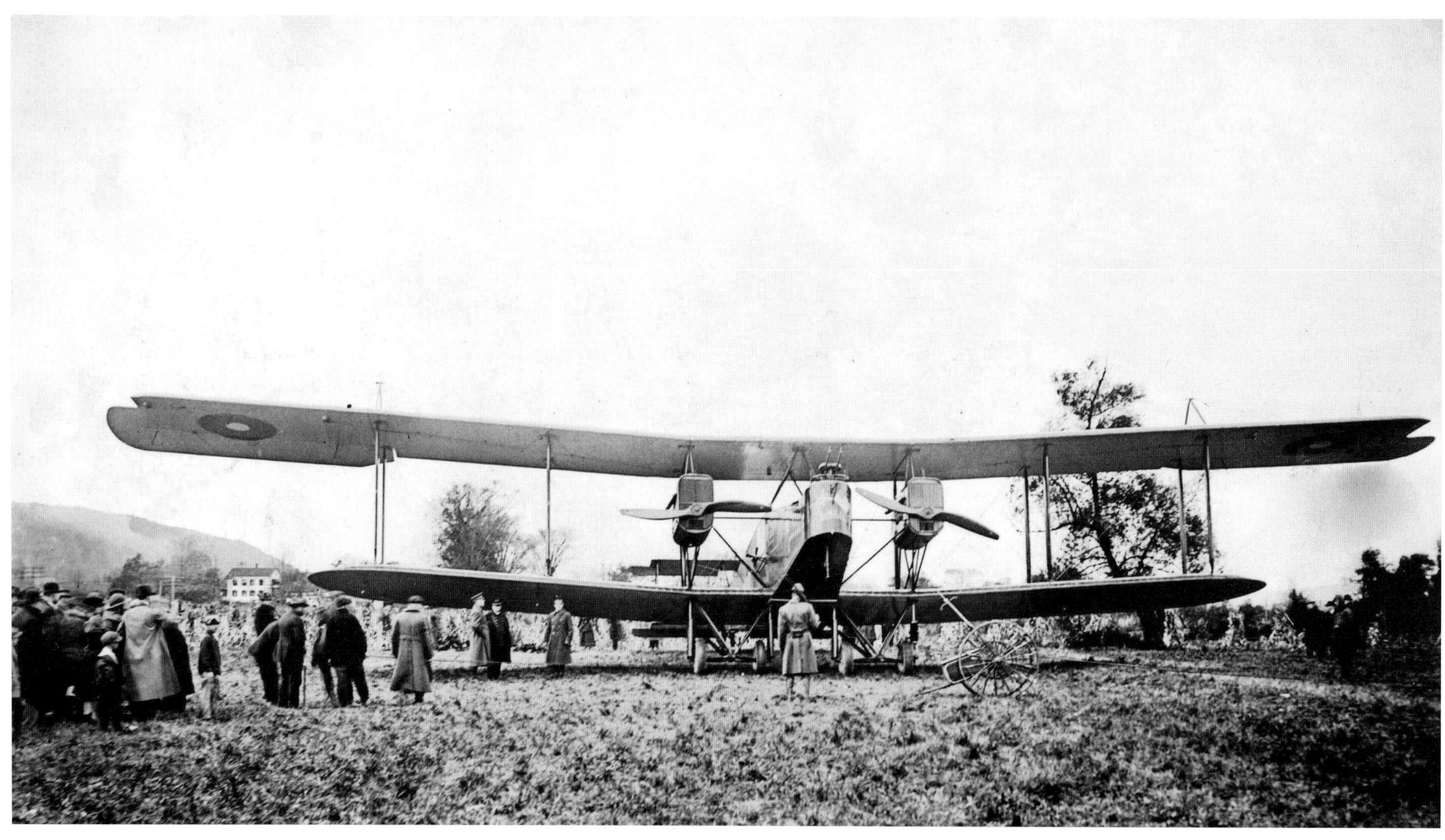

During the First World War, aircraft were first used as fighter planes and bombers. American bombers of the time were too vulnerable to interception by fighter planes in daylight, so night-bombing planes were developed. The Langley Night Bombing Airplane utilized concepts devised by the aviation pioneer Samuel Pierpont Langley (1834–1906). It was a two-engine biplane as shown in this October 15, 1918, photograph made in Frankfort, New York, a town on the Mohawk River east of Utica.

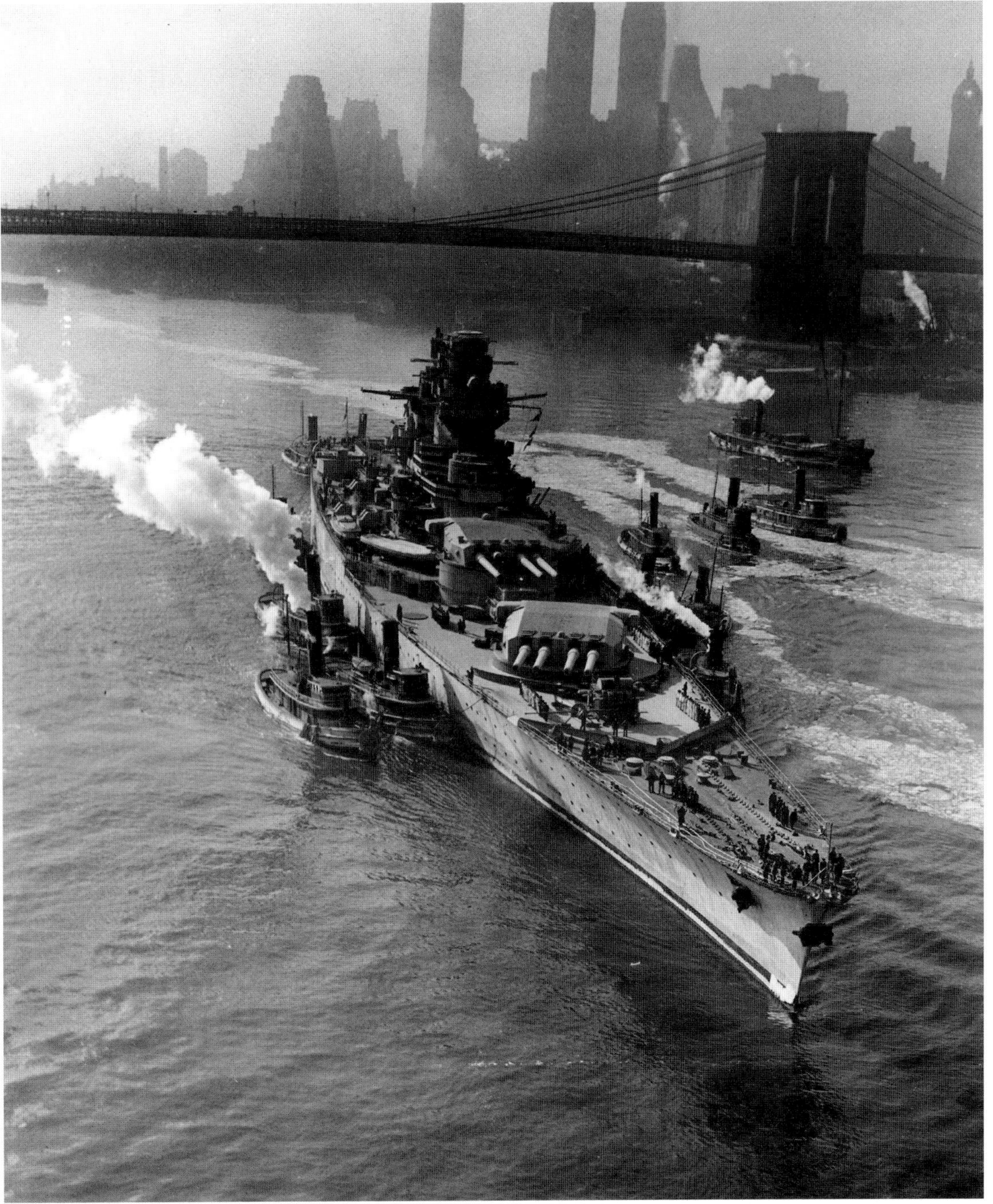

In the early 1920s, tugboats escort a United States Navy battleship up the East River. The war had ended a few years earlier, on November 11, 1918. In the background are the Brooklyn Bridge and the Manhattan skyline.

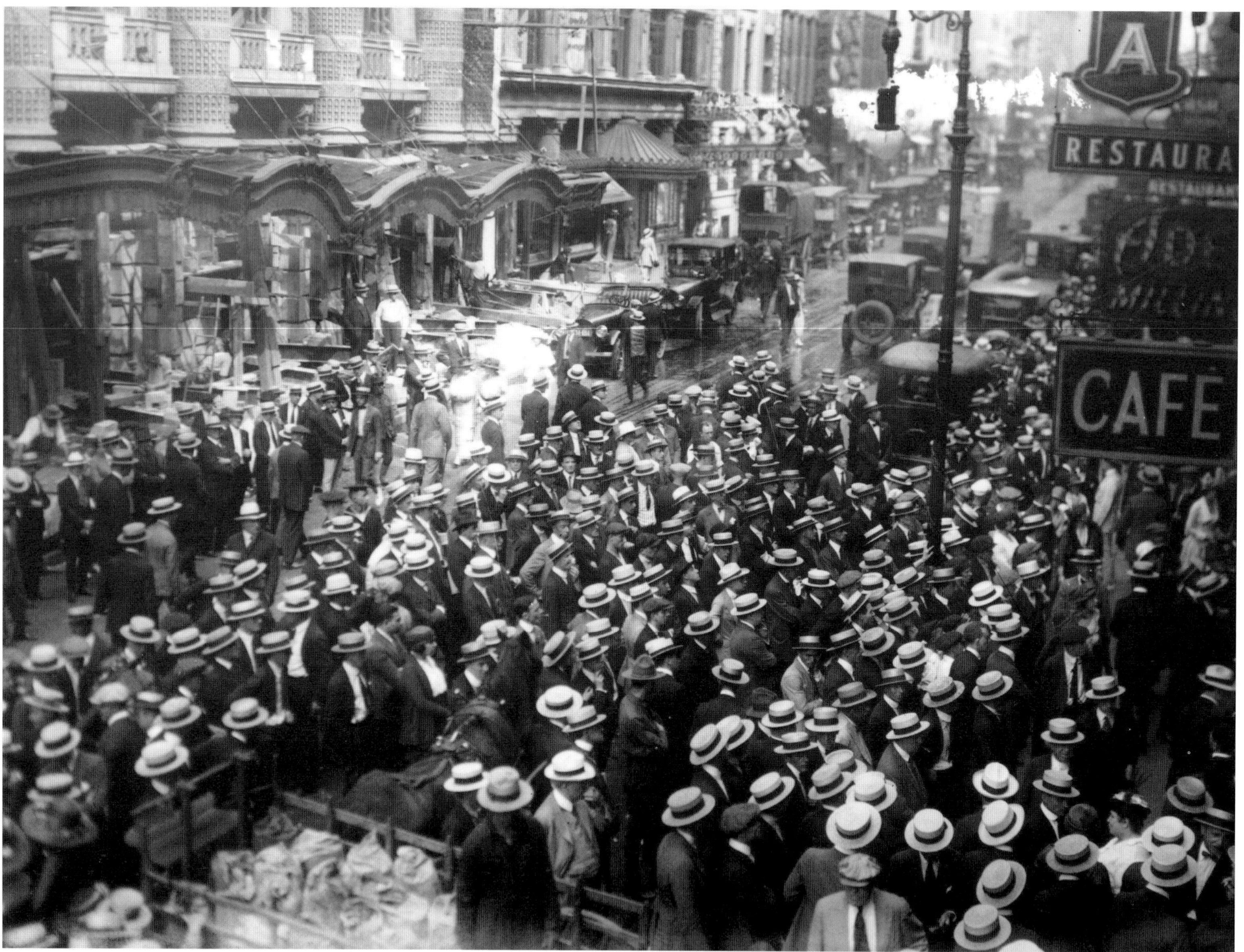

The first strike in the history of American theater occurred in New York City in August 1919. Actors objected to paying for their own costumes, rehearsing hours on end without pay, and being fired without notice. Stagehands honored the strike, and that closed down all theatrical productions in the country. The crowd in this 1919 image is demonstrating on 45th Street in Manhattan.

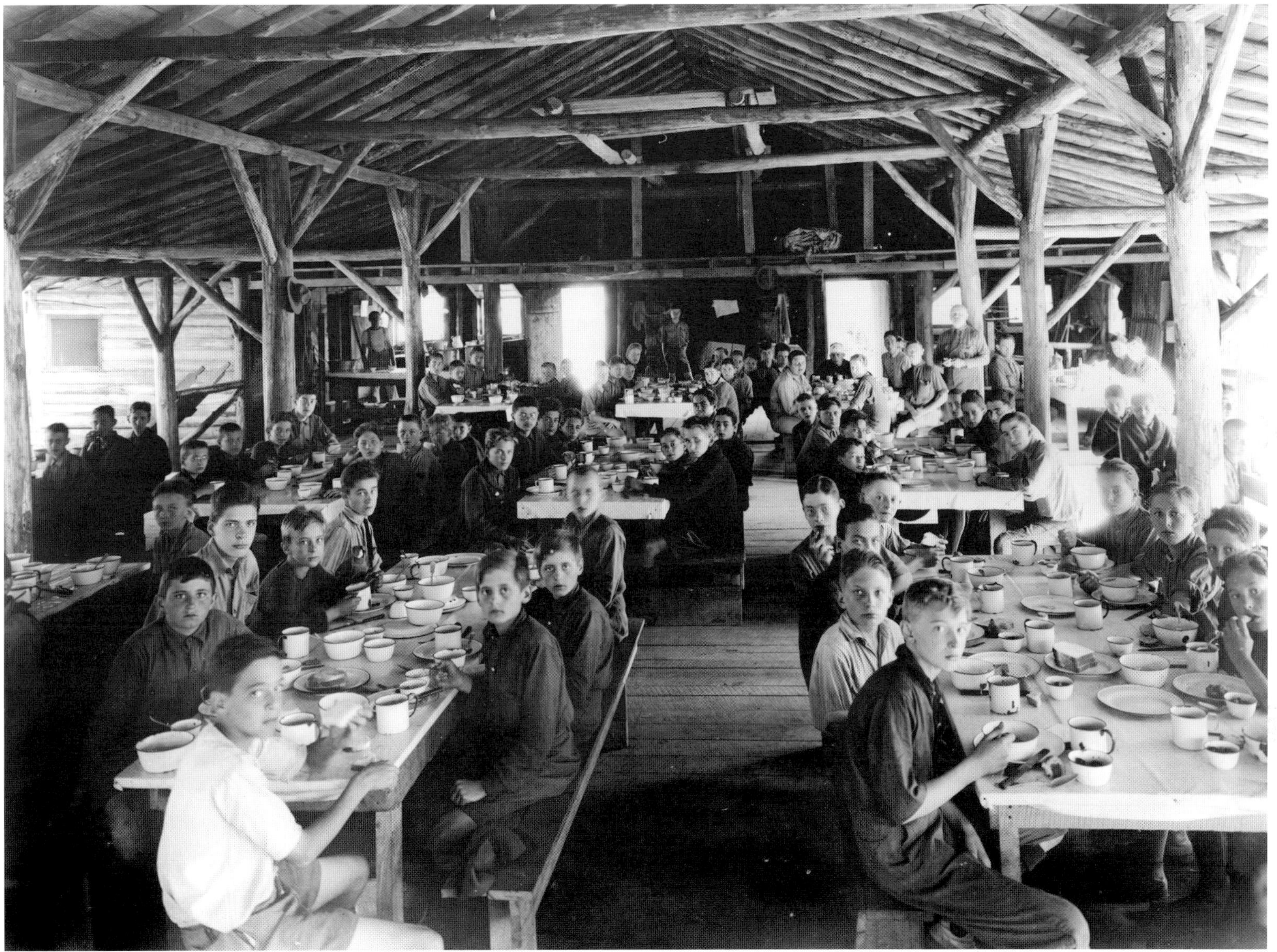

Camp Ranachqua is located on Lake Nianque near Narrowsburg on the Delaware River and is the principal Boy Scout camp serving the Hudson Valley. This image, made August 8, 1919, shows campers in the dining hall eating a meal served family-style. Swimming, sailing, hiking, handicrafts, marksmanship, archery, scouting skills, and more are provided at this outstanding 12,000-acre summer camp that still operates today.

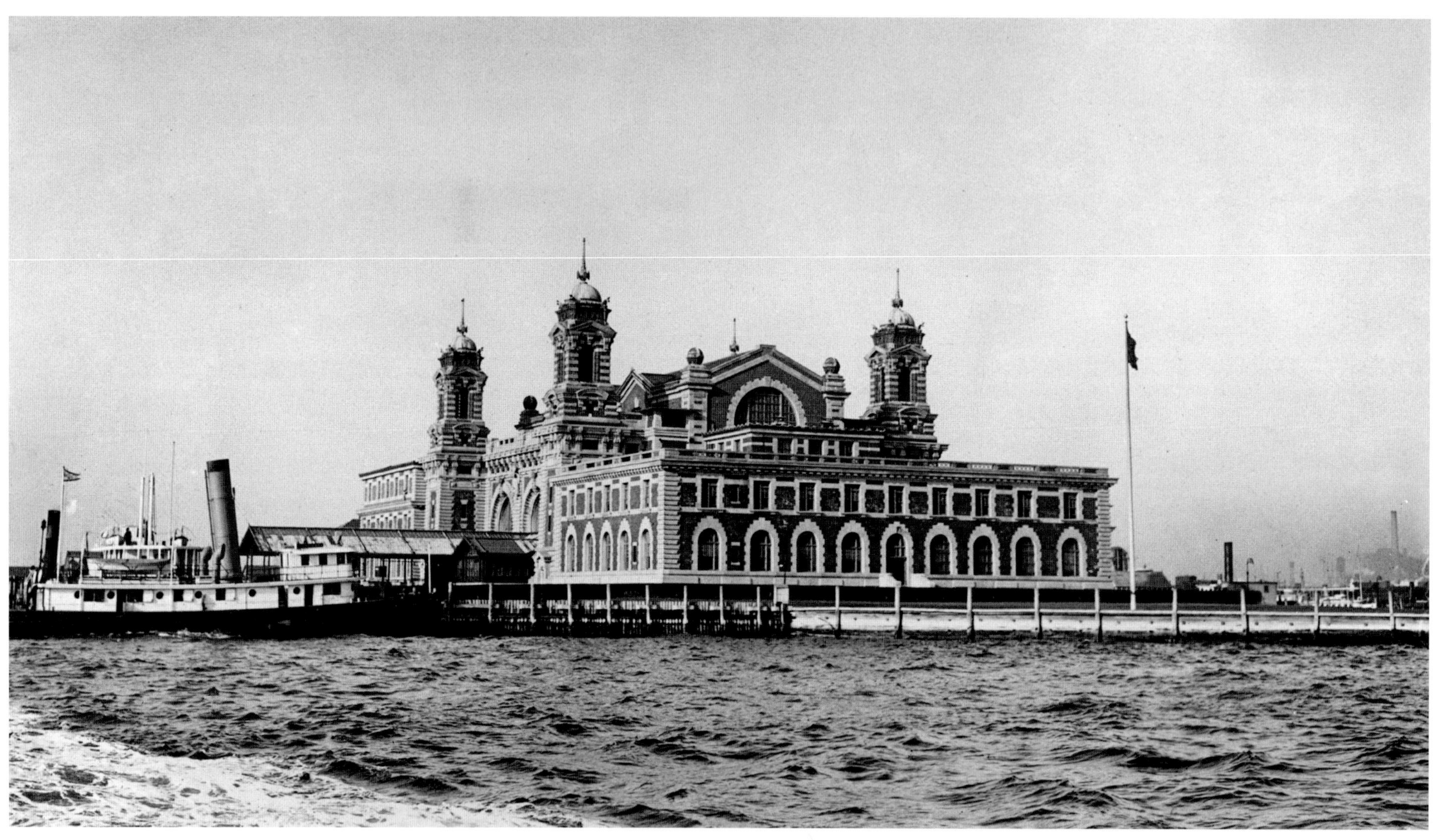

Opening on December 17, 1900, the first building that twentieth-century immigrants to America saw was this impressive structure on Ellis Island in New York Harbor. Designed in French Renaissance Revival style, the grand facility is a brick-and-limestone structure with three triumphal arches at the entrance and impressive towers at the corners of the façade. Between 1892 and 1954, more than 12 million immigrants passed through Ellis Island, many of them through this building. Since 1990, the facility has been open to the public as the Ellis Island Immigration Museum.

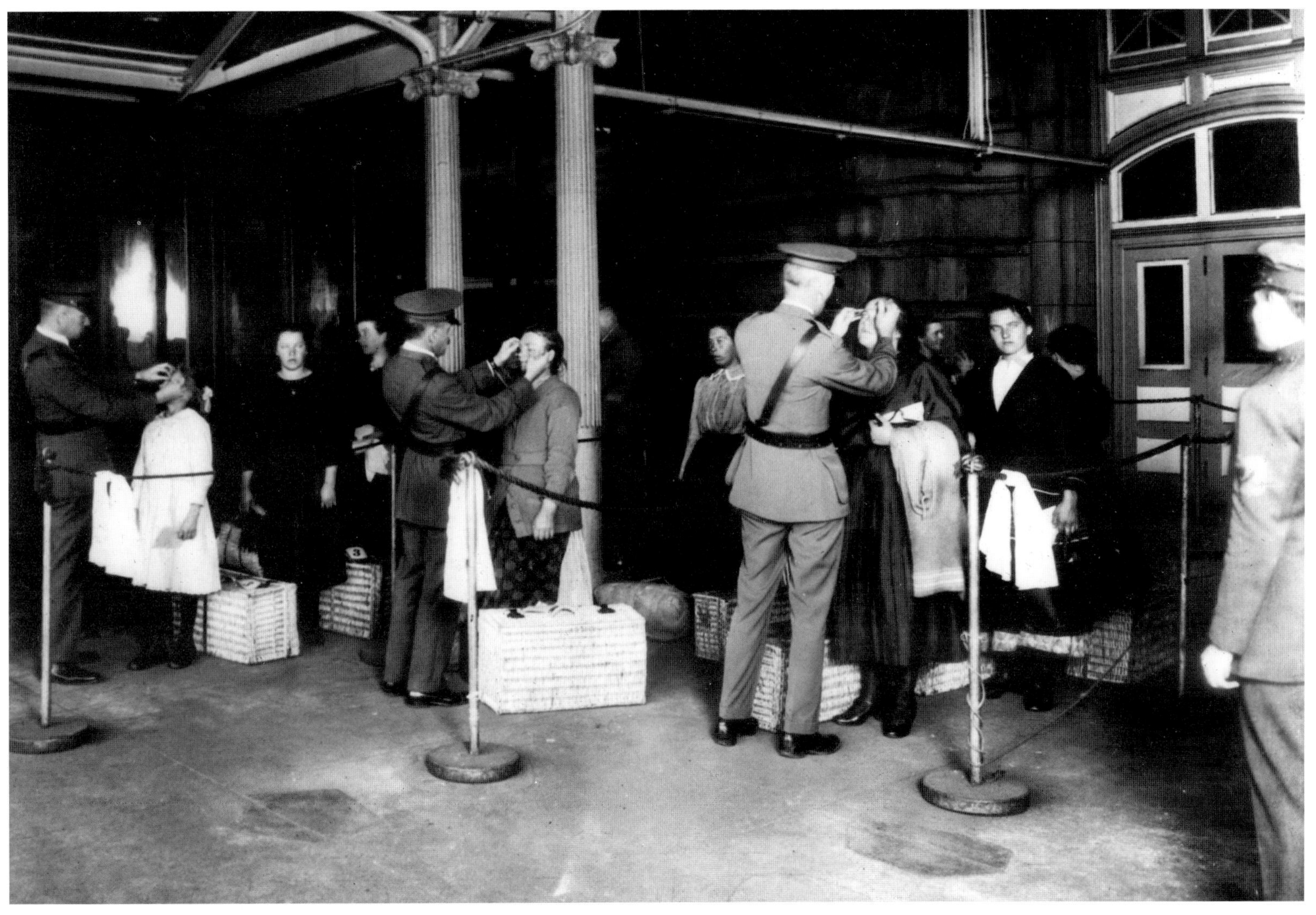

At Ellis Island, immigrants climbed the front steps of the grand Main Building to the great, echoing Registry Room, where they faced legal and medical inspections, like those being administered in this photograph from 1923.

The National Park Bank on Broadway between Ann and Fulton streets in Manhattan was under construction between 1901 and 1904. The Second Empire–style structure, richly decorated in granite and limestone, was designed by architect Donn Barber. A giant arched window on the façade provided a flood of light in the high-ceilinged banking room. Labor-saving devices considered novel and modern at the beginning of the twentieth century included telephones, pneumatic tubes, electric elevators, dumbwaiters, and a refrigerating plant to provide ice water throughout the building.

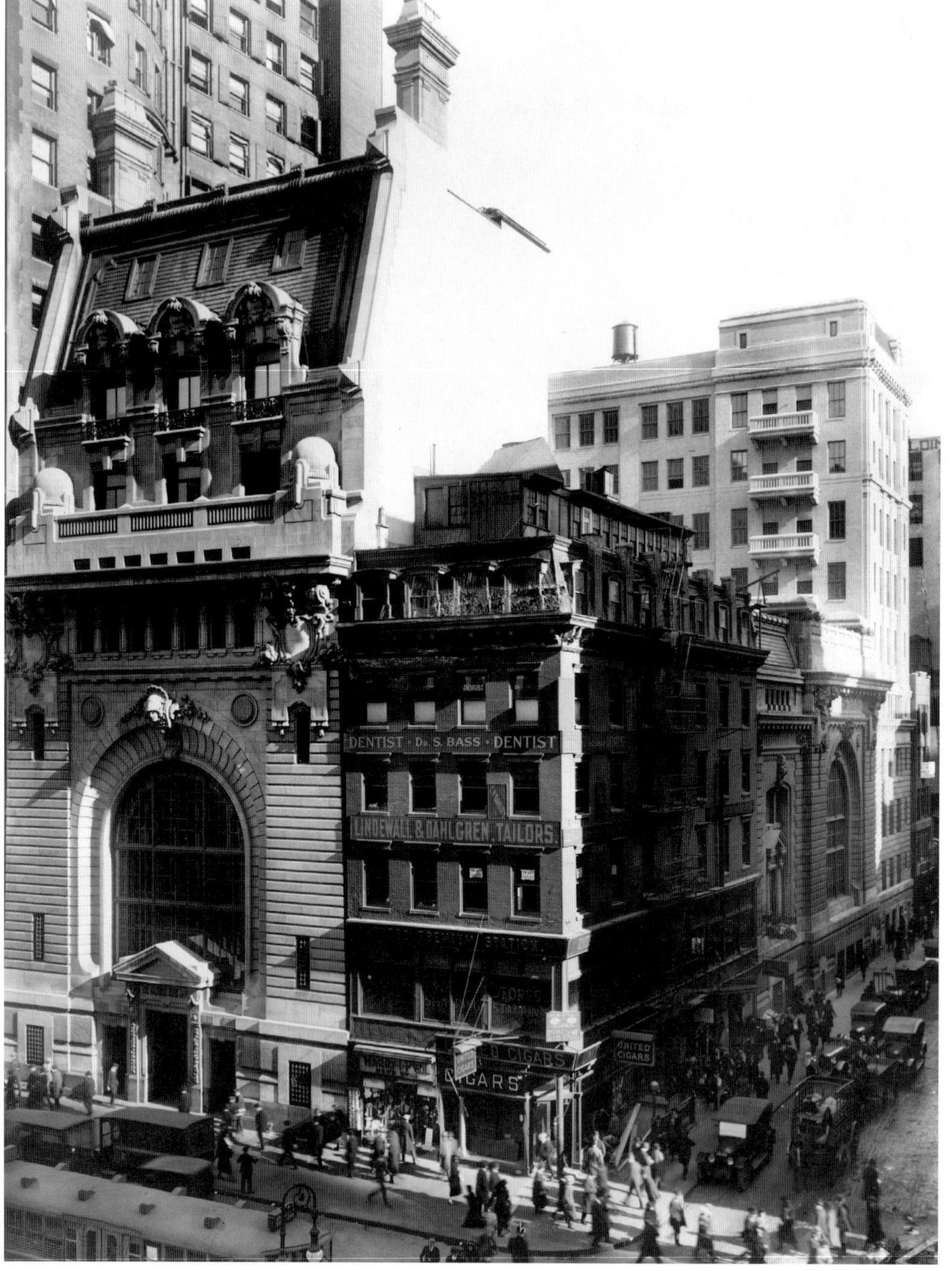

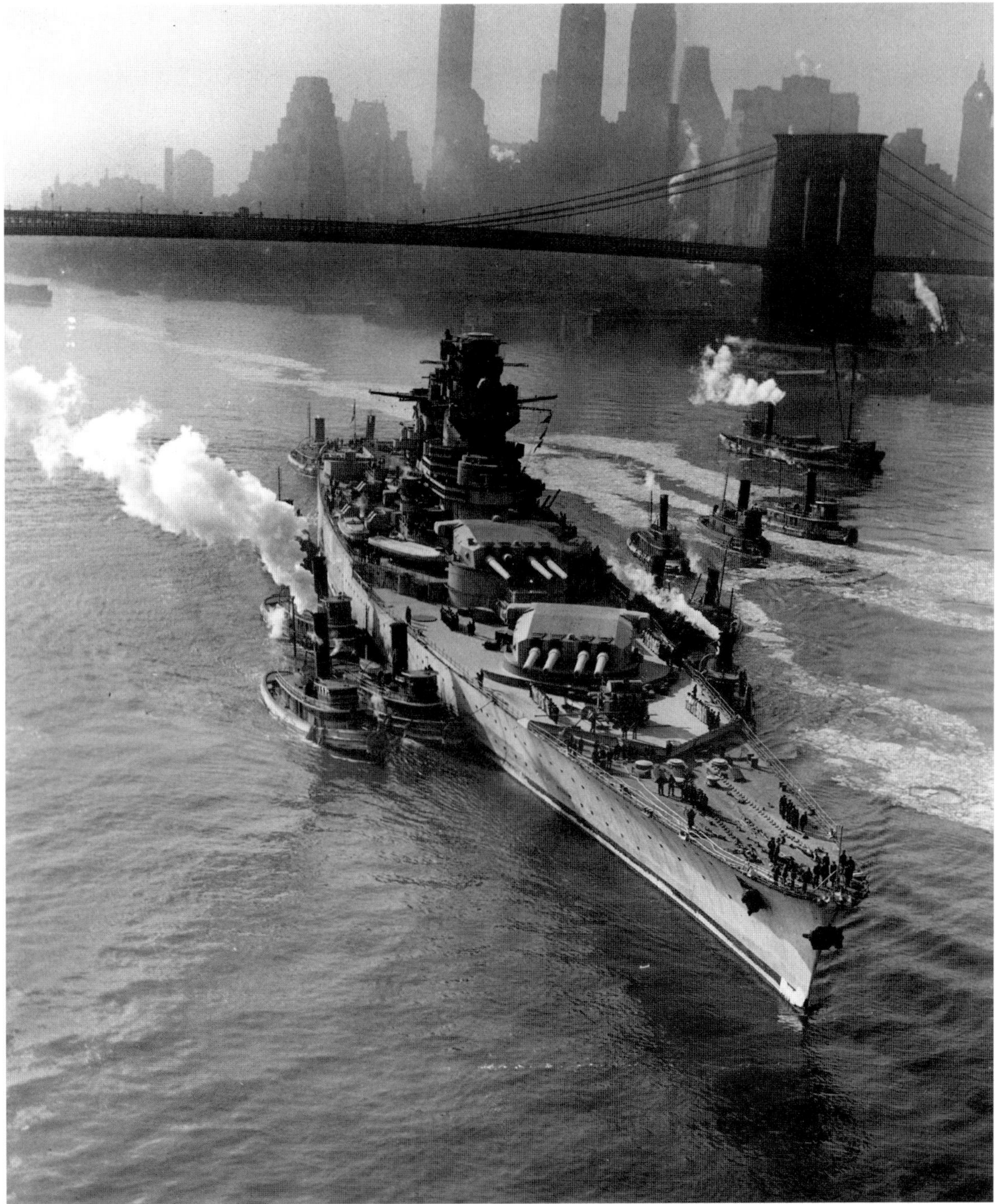

In the early 1920s, tugboats escort a United States Navy battleship up the East River. The war had ended a few years earlier, on November 11, 1918. In the background are the Brooklyn Bridge and the Manhattan skyline.

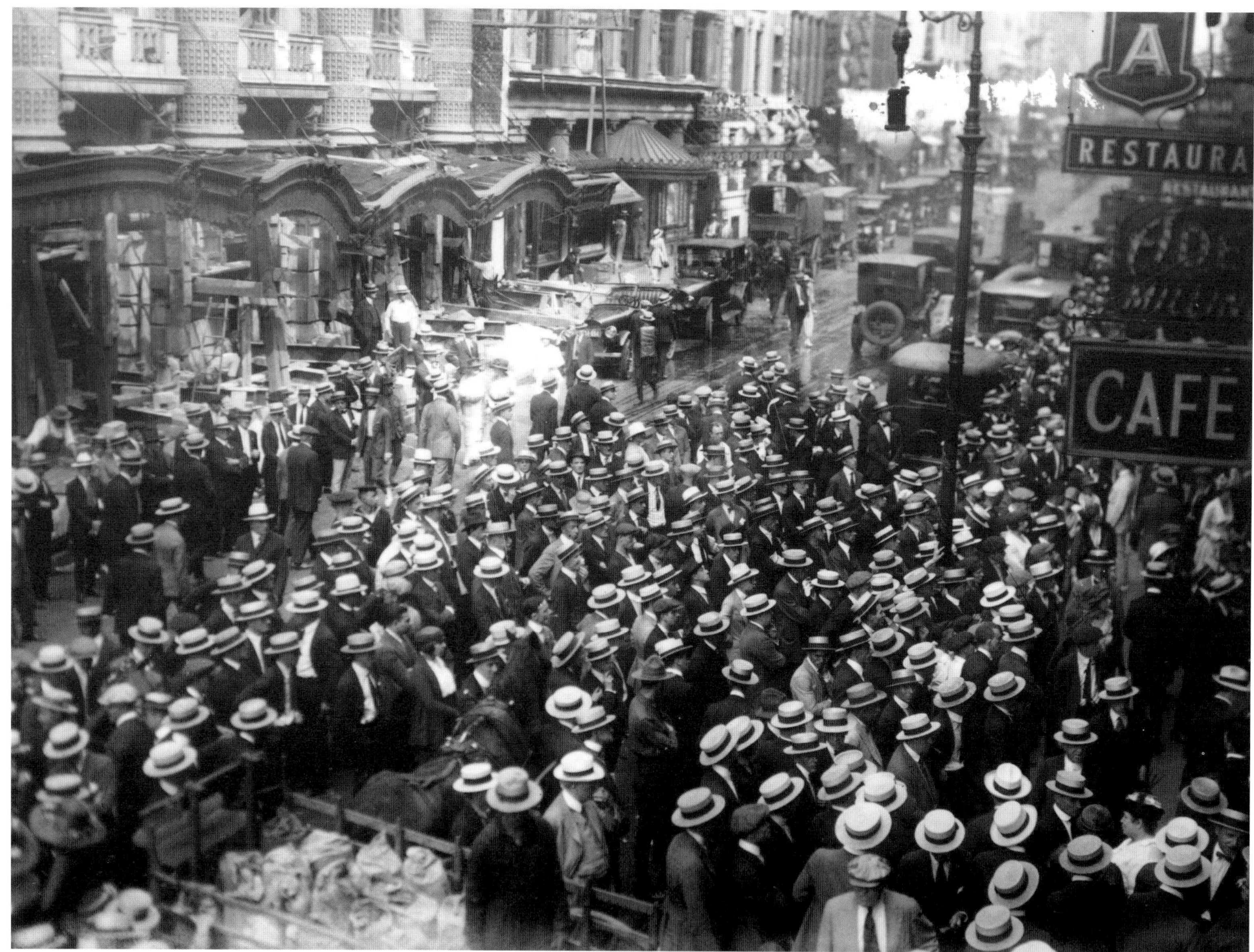

The first strike in the history of American theater occurred in New York City in August 1919. Actors objected to paying for their own costumes, rehearsing hours on end without pay, and being fired without notice. Stagehands honored the strike, and that closed down all theatrical productions in the country. The crowd in this 1919 image is demonstrating on 45th Street in Manhattan.

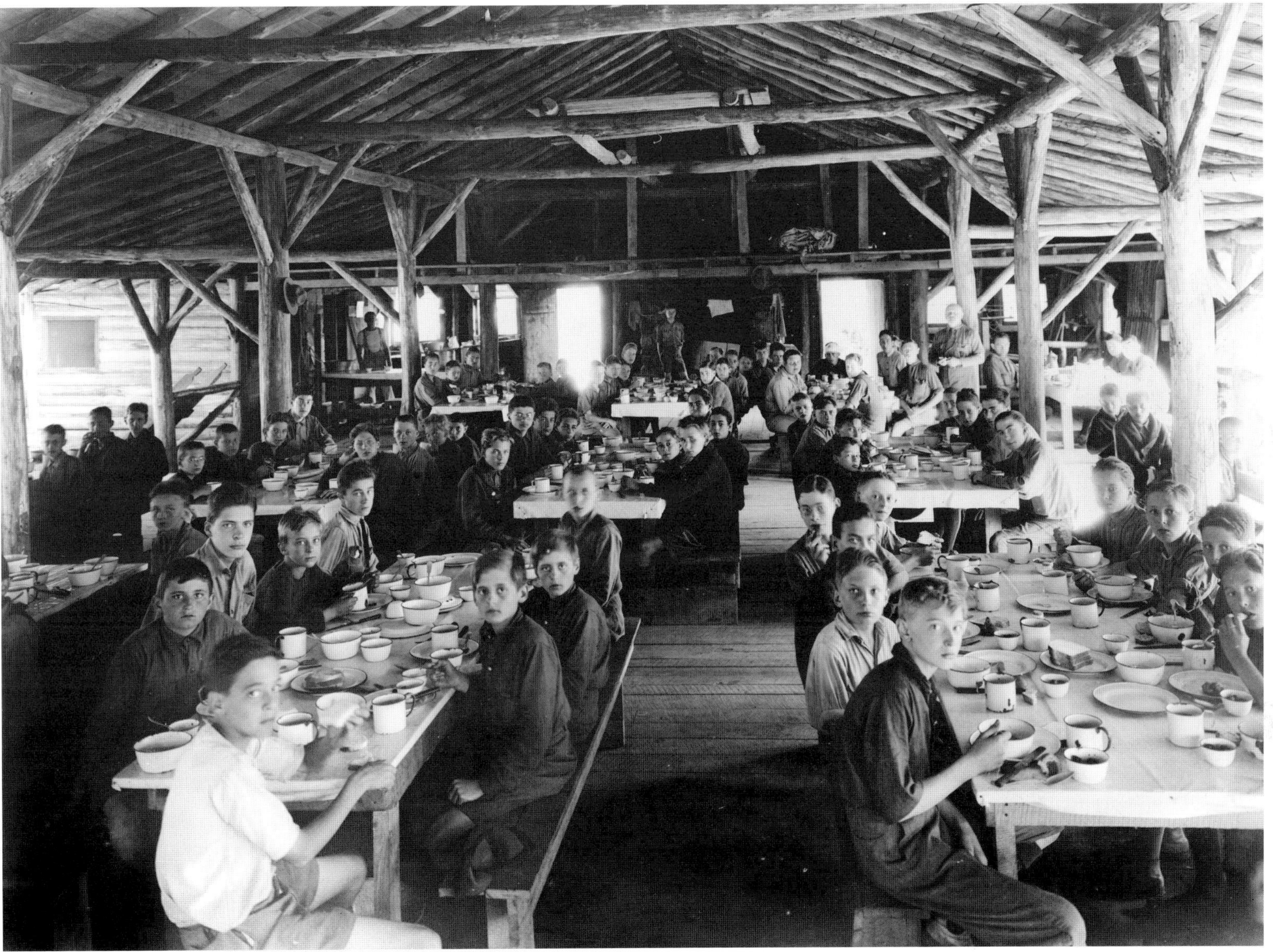

Camp Ranachqua is located on Lake Nianque near Narrowsburg on the Delaware River and is the principal Boy Scout camp serving the Hudson Valley. This image, made August 8, 1919, shows campers in the dining hall eating a meal served family-style. Swimming, sailing, hiking, handicrafts, marksmanship, archery, scouting skills, and more are provided at this outstanding 12,000-acre summer camp that still operates today.

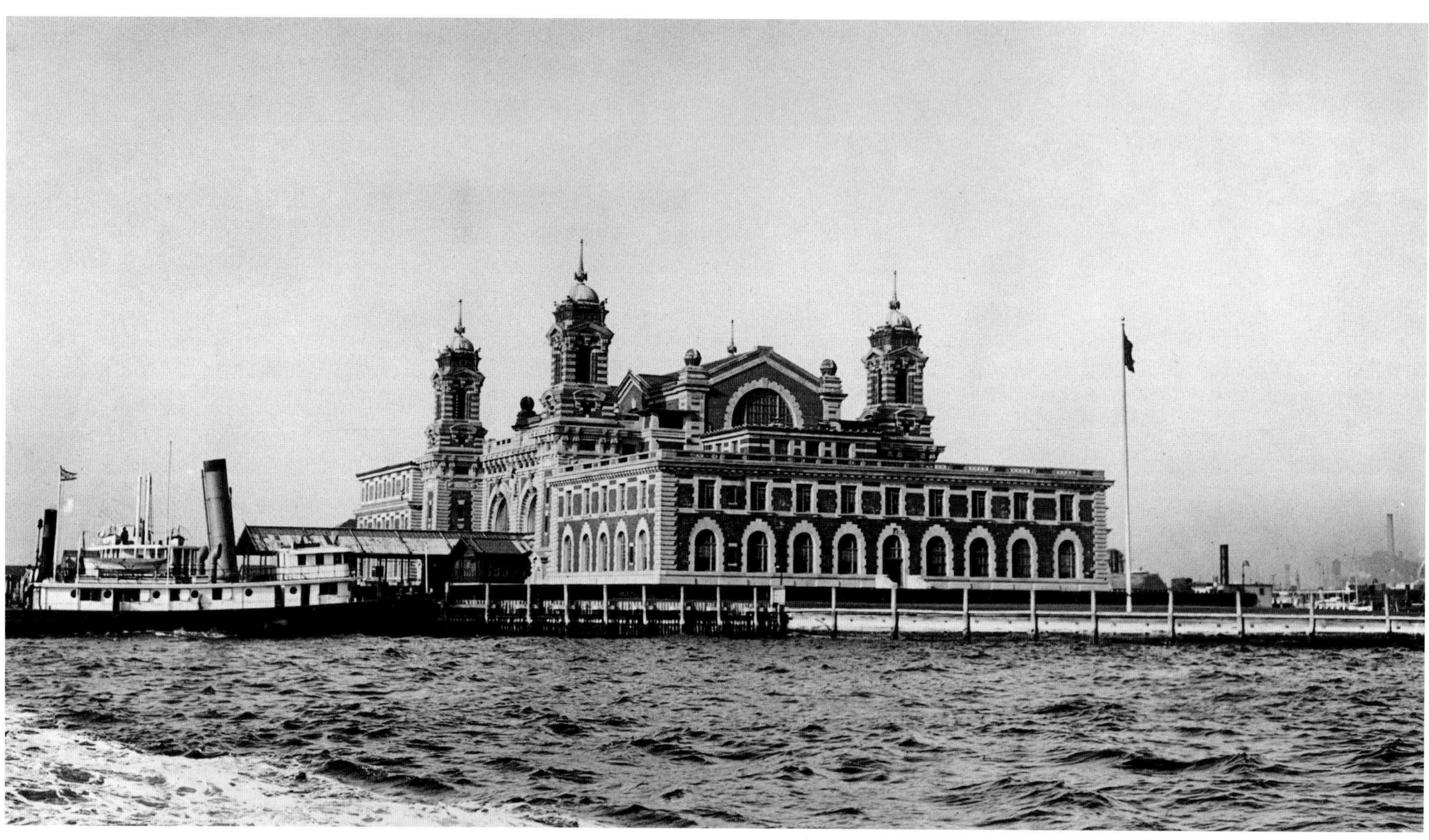

Opening on December 17, 1900, the first building that twentieth-century immigrants to America saw was this impressive structure on Ellis Island in New York Harbor. Designed in French Renaissance Revival style, the grand facility is a brick-and-limestone structure with three triumphal arches at the entrance and impressive towers at the corners of the façade. Between 1892 and 1954, more than 12 million immigrants passed through Ellis Island, many of them through this building. Since 1990, the facility has been open to the public as the Ellis Island Immigration Museum.

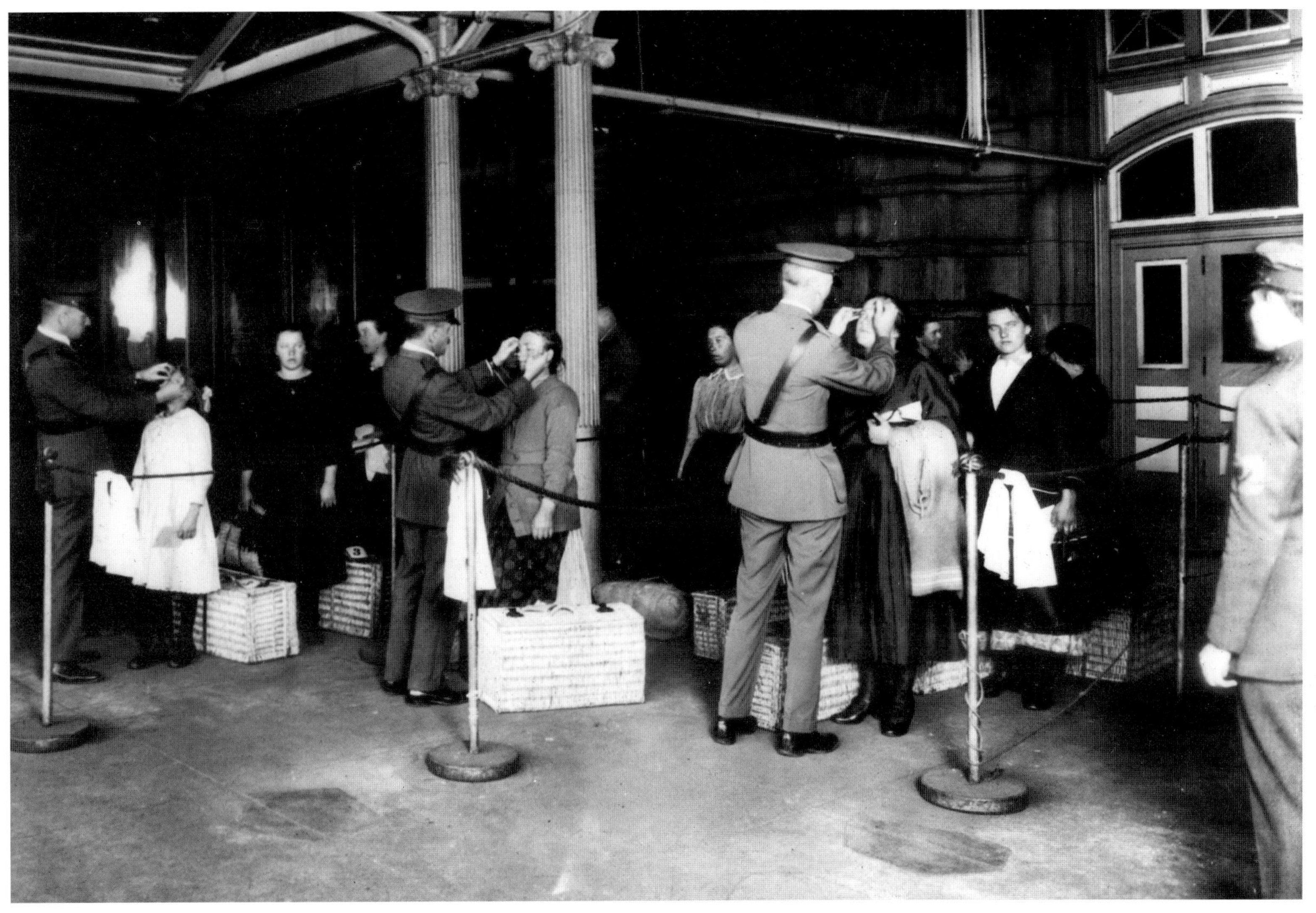

At Ellis Island, immigrants climbed the front steps of the grand Main Building to the great, echoing Registry Room, where they faced legal and medical inspections, like those being administered in this photograph from 1923.

The National Park Bank on Broadway between Ann and Fulton streets in Manhattan was under construction between 1901 and 1904. The Second Empire–style structure, richly decorated in granite and limestone, was designed by architect Donn Barber. A giant arched window on the façade provided a flood of light in the high-ceilinged banking room. Labor-saving devices considered novel and modern at the beginning of the twentieth century included telephones, pneumatic tubes, electric elevators, dumbwaiters, and a refrigerating plant to provide ice water throughout the building.

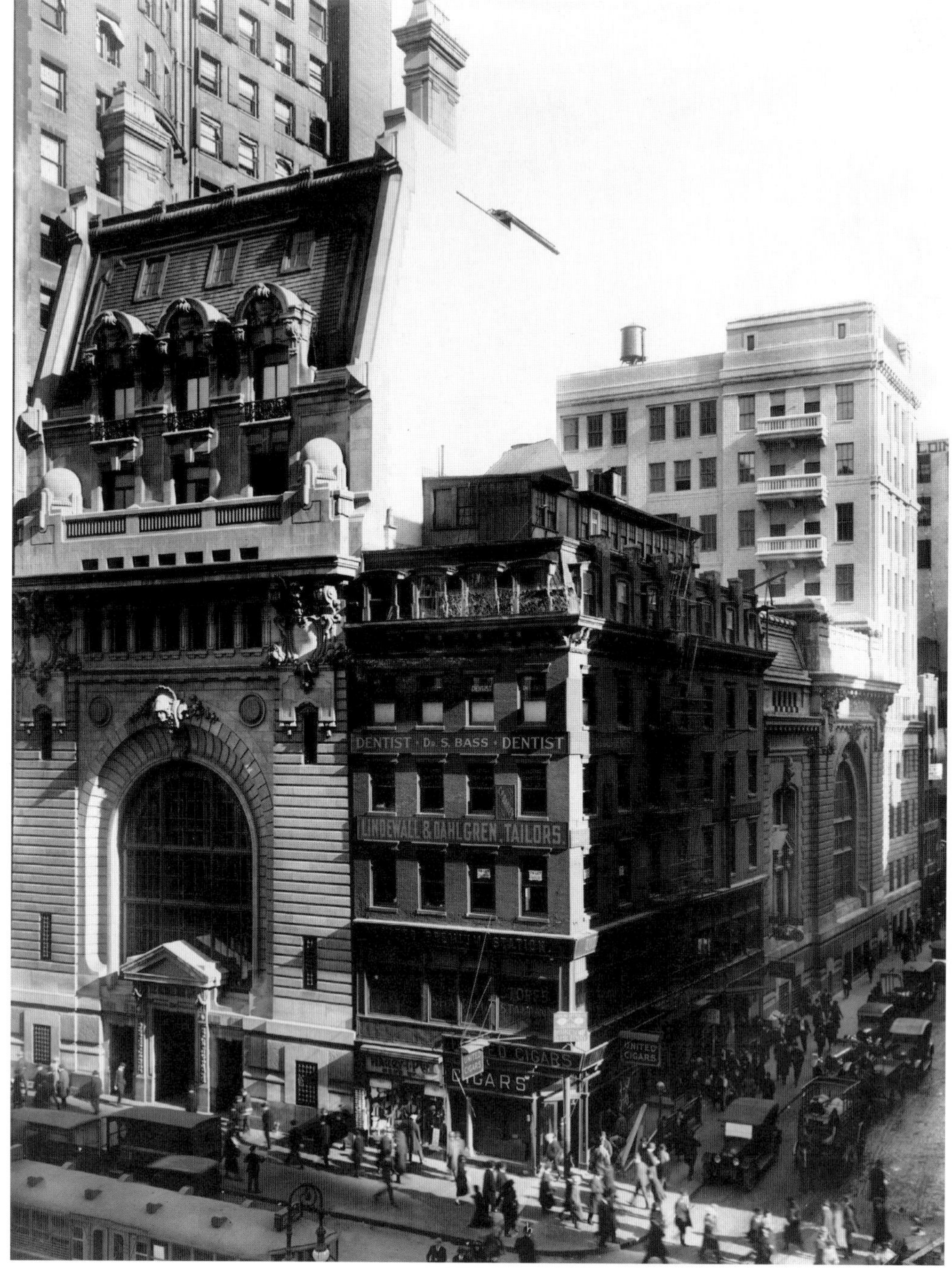

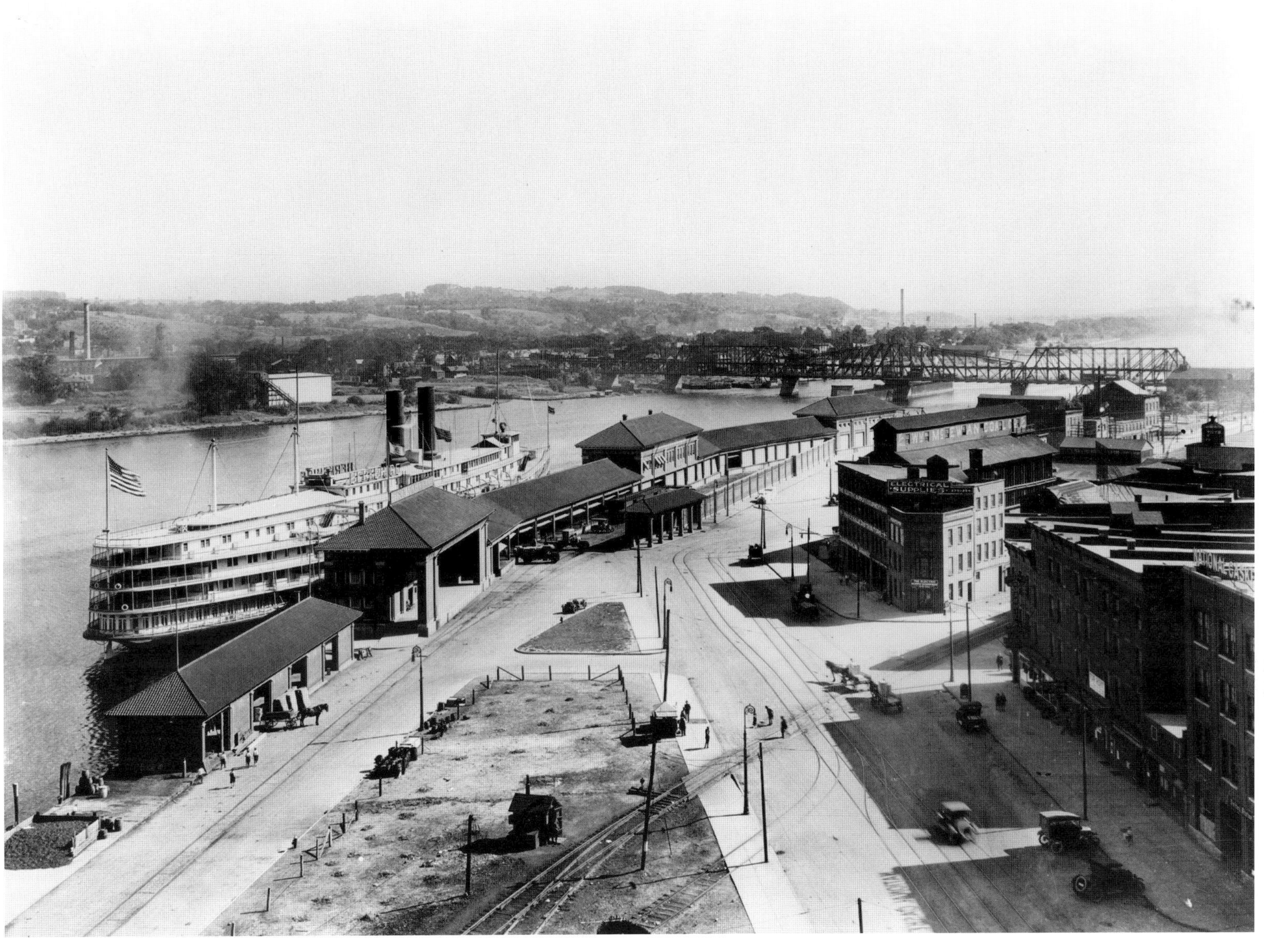

Here is a bird's-eye view of the Albany wharf along the Hudson River as it appeared in 1921. A large passenger steamship, the *Berkshire,* is moored wharfside. The bridge in the background crosses the Hudson to the town of Rensselaer, across the river from Albany. Very little of what appears in this image remains standing today.

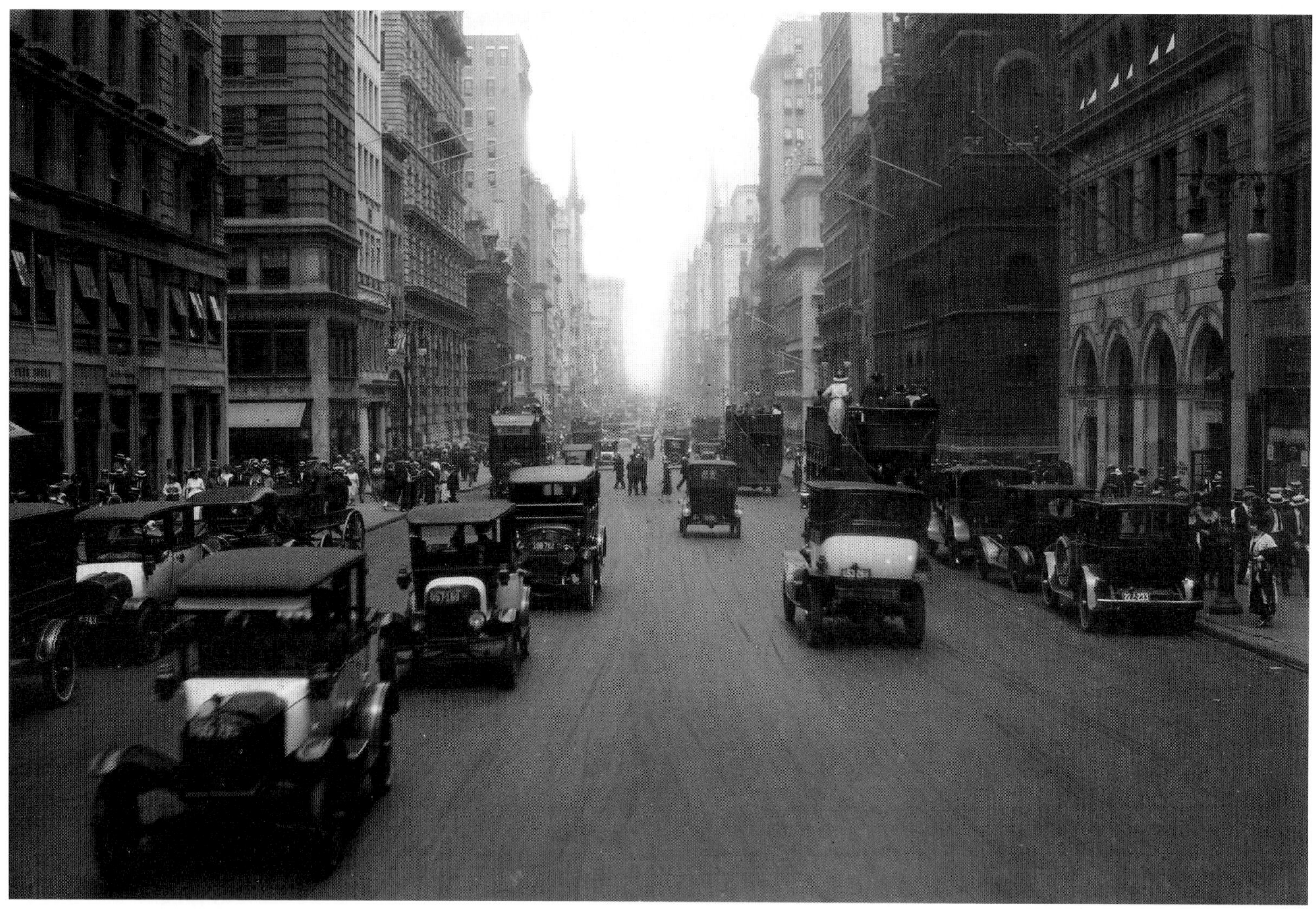

By the time this image appeared in 1921, horse-drawn carriages had nearly disappeared from New York City streets, replaced by early twentieth century automobiles. This is Fifth Avenue in Manhattan at a time when the avenue had two-way traffic. One thing that remains the same is the pedestrian-crowded sidewalk. Prominent in this image are the double-decker buses, replete with a curving staircase that leads to the open-air floor at top.

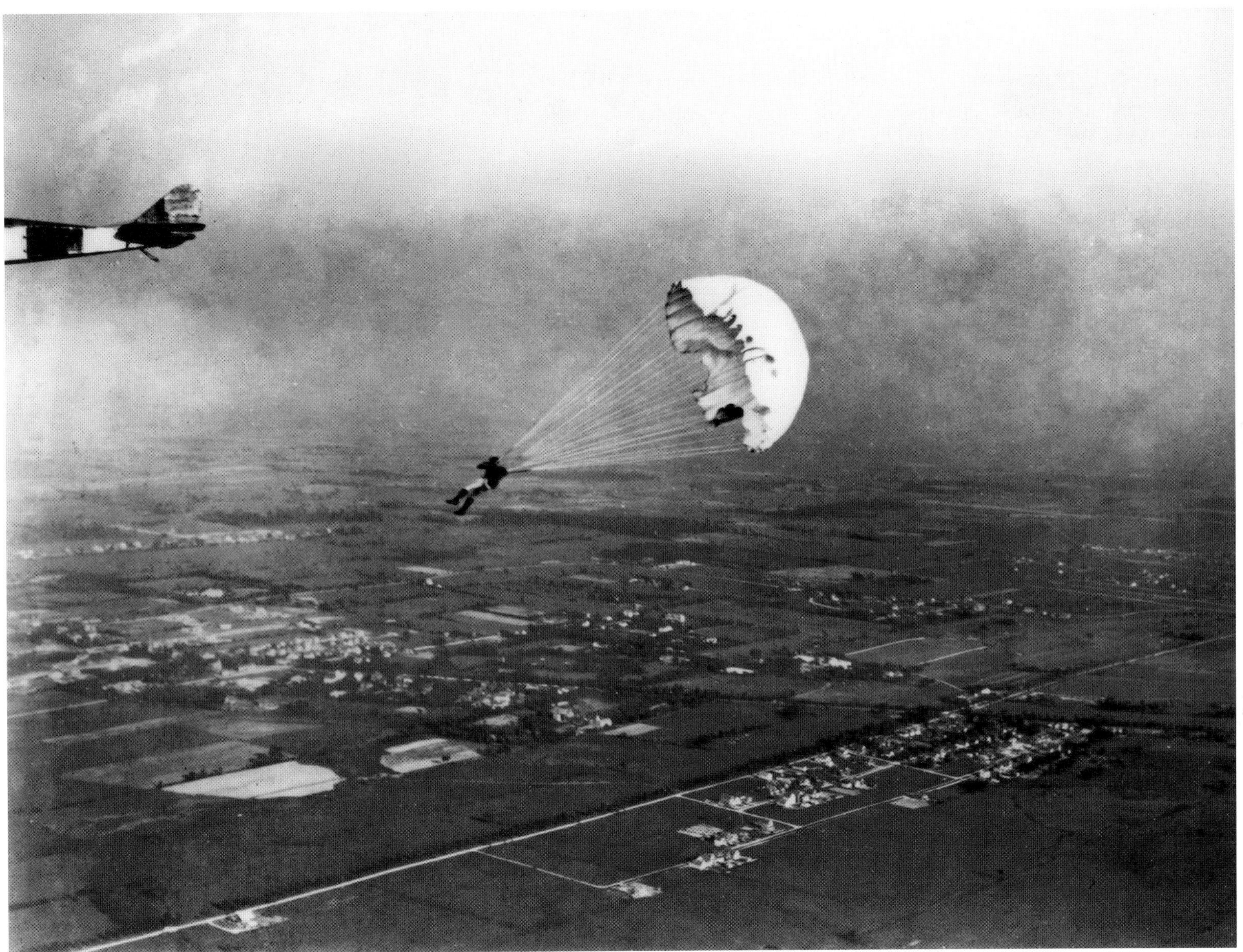

Irving Air Chute Company in Buffalo, with six other factories around the globe, became the world's largest maker of parachutes. The Buffalo factory was founded by Hollywood stuntman Leslie Irvin, who in 1919 became the first person to jump from a plane in free fall with a parachute. Early parachutes were made of cotton, but it was bulky, and Irvin (the "g" was added to the company name) persuaded silk makers to produce a superior silk for chutes. In this 1922 image, George Starr makes a practice jump near Buffalo.

Sir Arthur Conan Doyle (1859–1930), Scottish writer of detective stories and historical romances and creator of Sherlock Holmes, visited New York City with his wife and three children in 1922 during a visit to the United States to give lectures on Spiritualism. Here, on April 10, the family views the city from the observation deck of a Manhattan skyscraper. Conan Doyle was a friend of escapologist Harry Houdini, with whom he visited during his stay in New York.

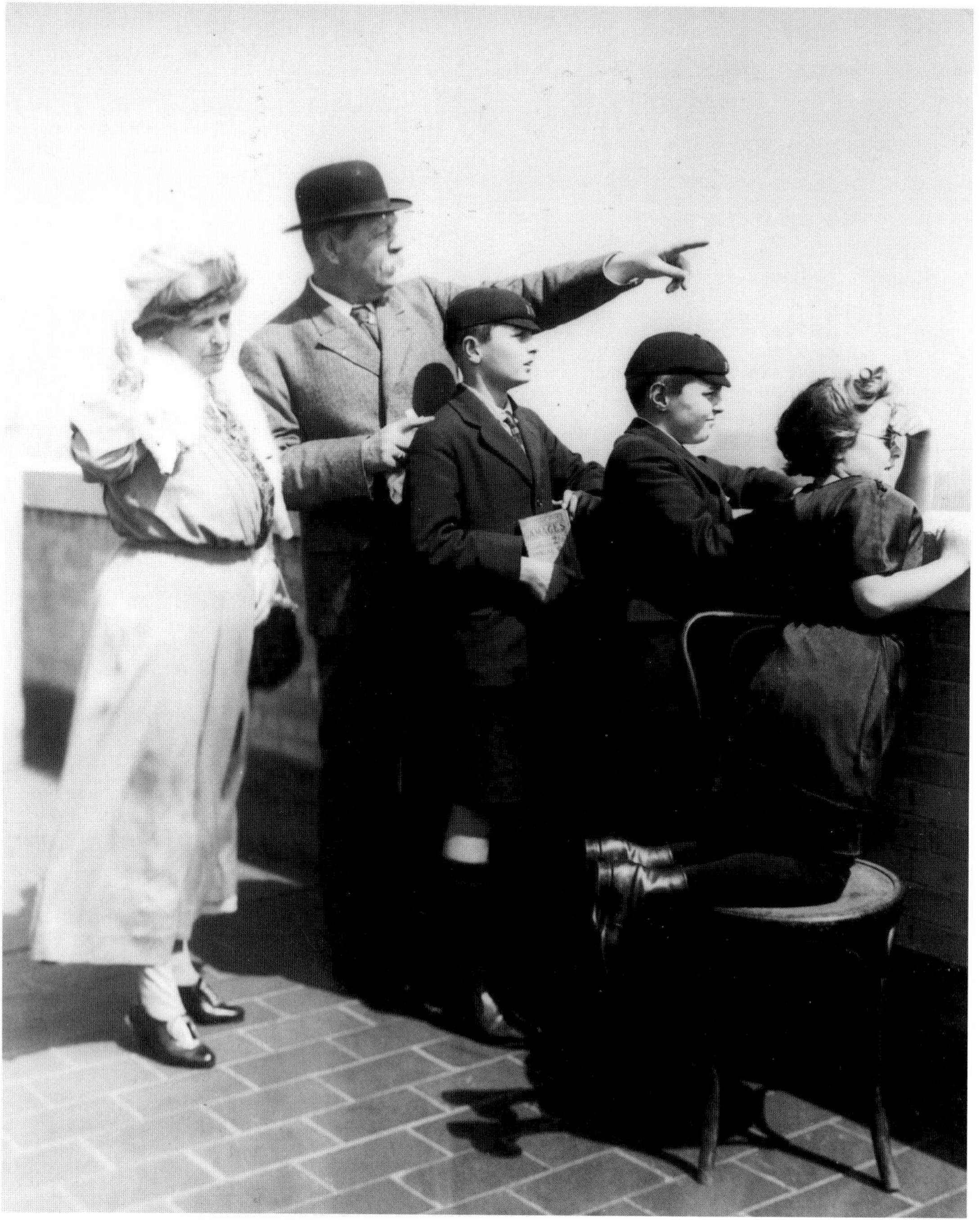

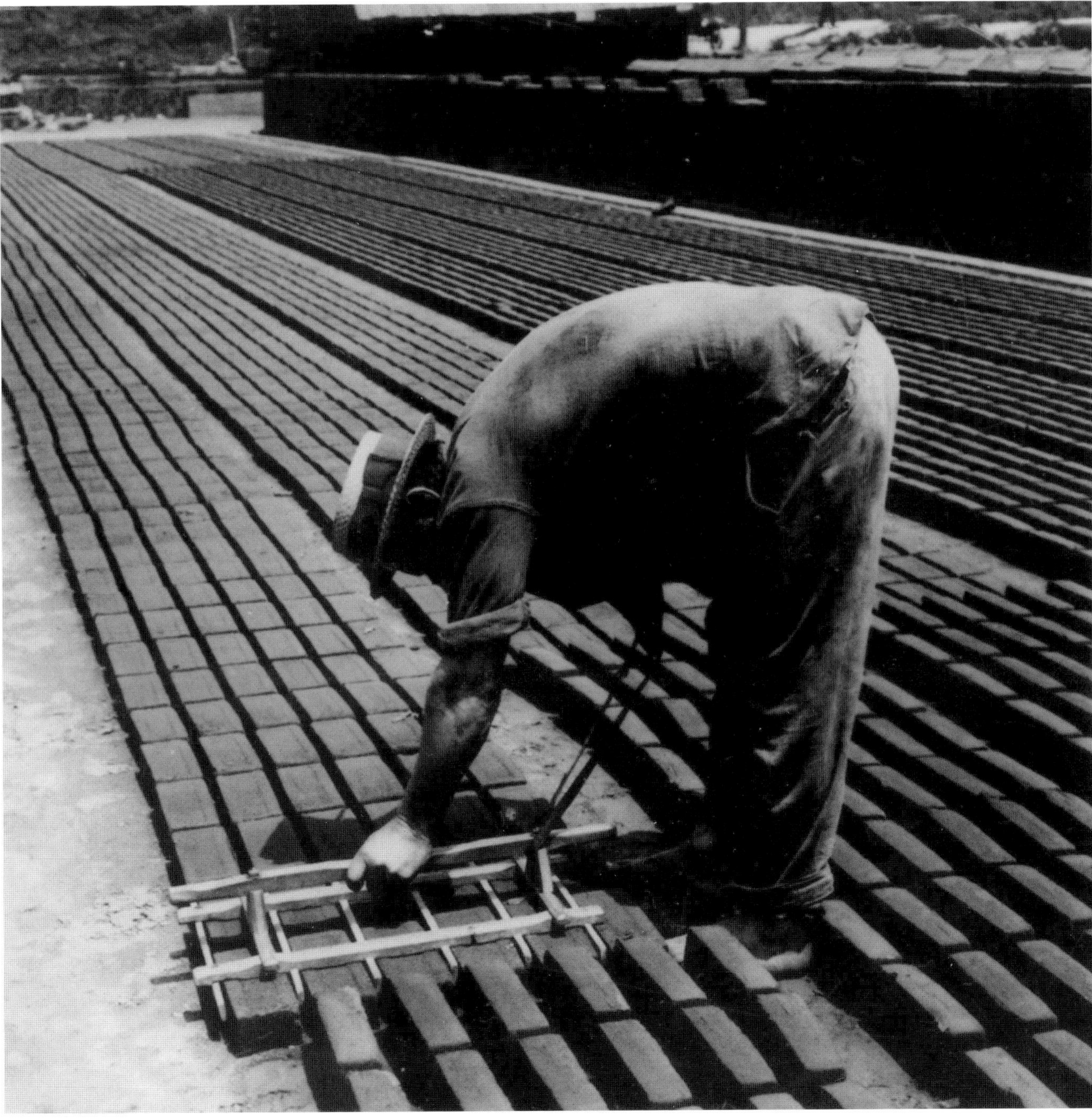

The village of Haverstraw is located on the west side of the Hudson River at its widest point. Haverstraw was once renowned for brickmaking made possible by the abundance of shoreline clay formed by the river, and at one time more than 40 brickmaking factories lined the Hudson River in the village. Many of the brownstone and brick structures constructed in New York City in the 1890s and early 1900s were built of Haverstraw brick. In this image, bricks are turned repeatedly to help them dry evenly.

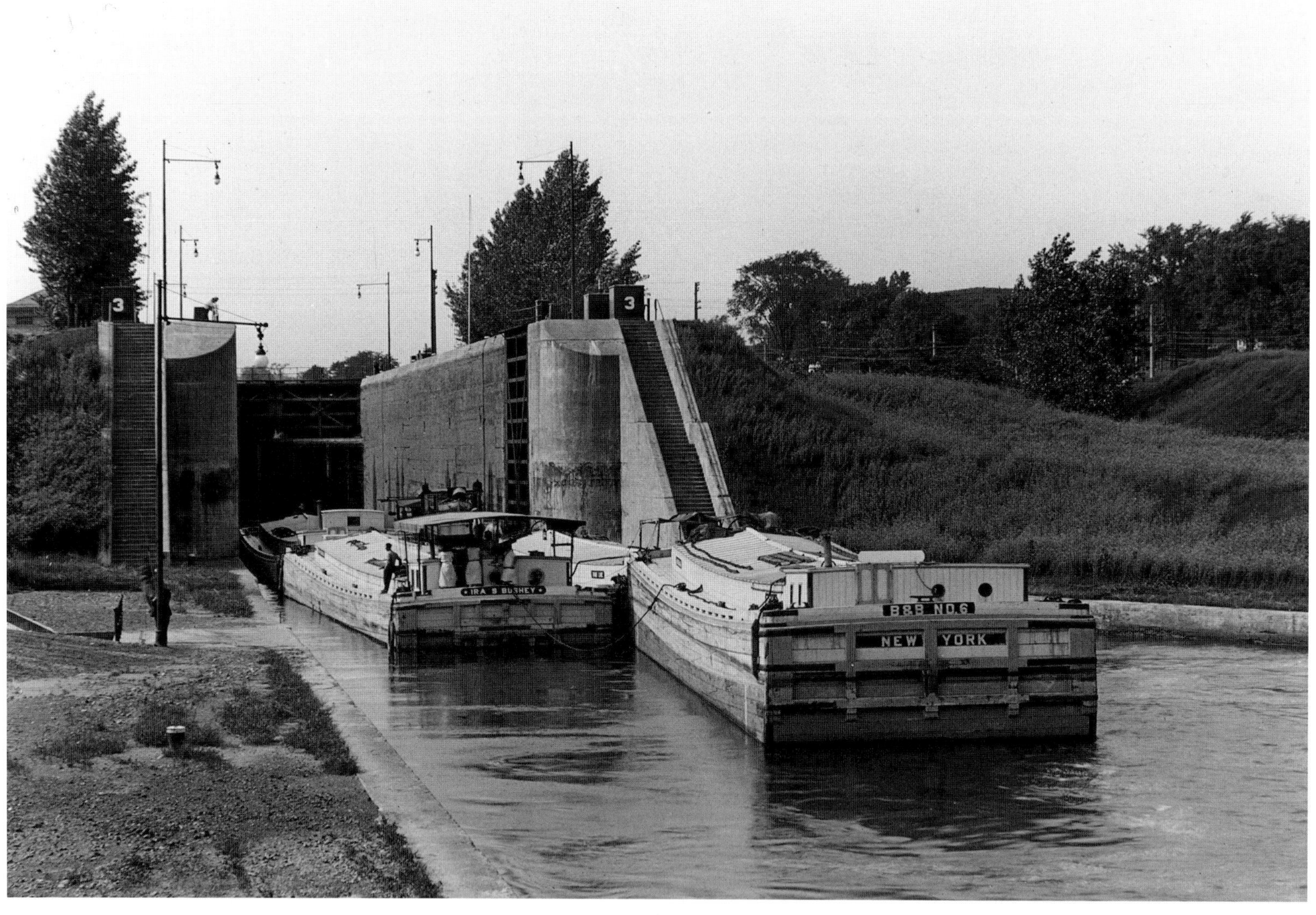

Waterford is a village at the junction of the Erie Canal, which proceeds west, and the Champlain Canal, which runs north. Here in 1925, commercial barges wait their turn to enter at the low entrance of Lock 3 to be raised to the next level of the Erie Canal as they make their way west.

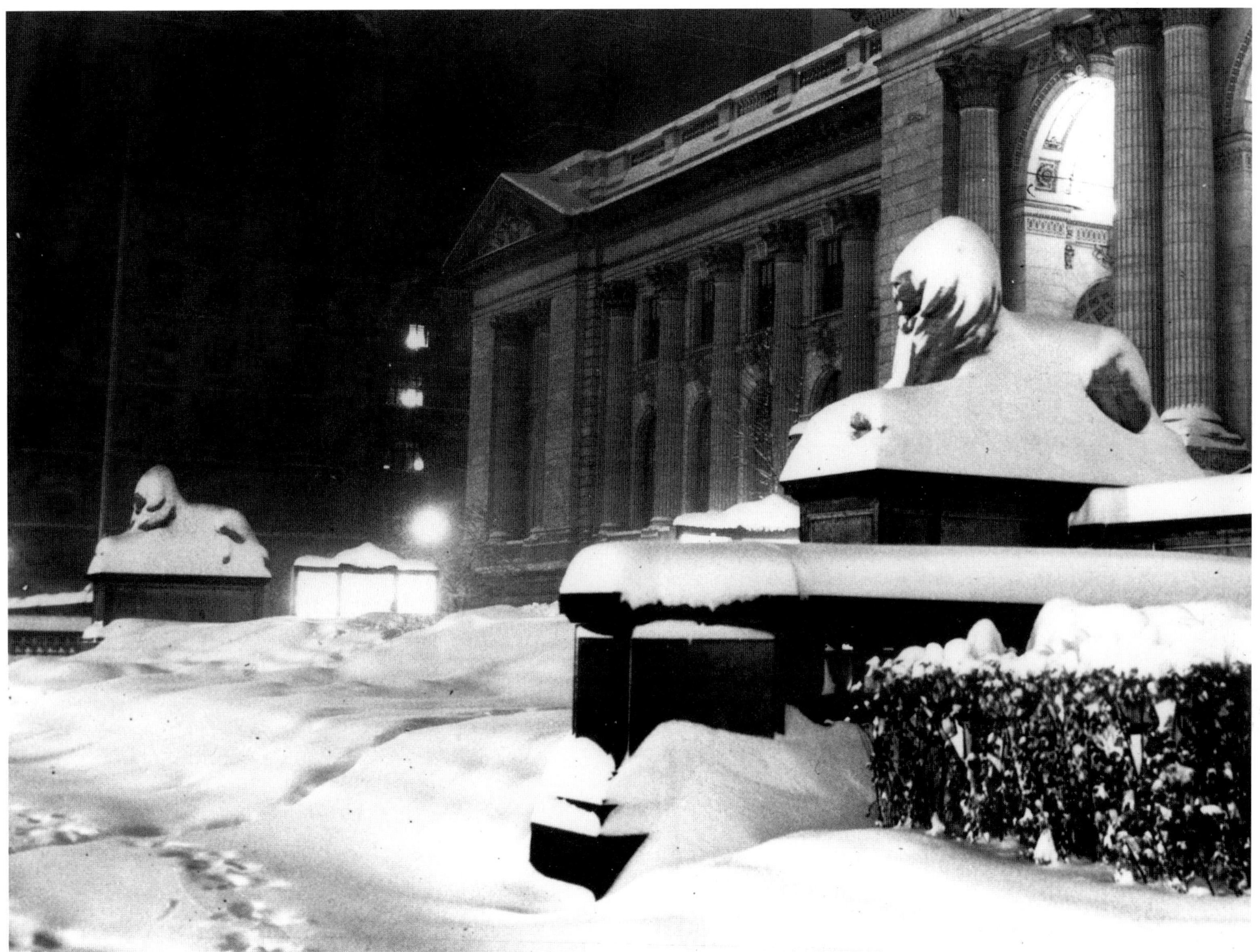

A fierce December storm has covered the stone lions flanking the entrance to the New York Public Library on Fifth Avenue in Manhattan, where the massive façade stretches two blocks (350 feet) between 40th and 42nd streets. Architects Carrère and Hastings created one of the finest examples of Beaux-Arts design in America from the finest white marble available. The chief architect, John M. Carrère, was killed in an automobile accident just before the library opened. He lay in state in the great hall at the opening in 1911.

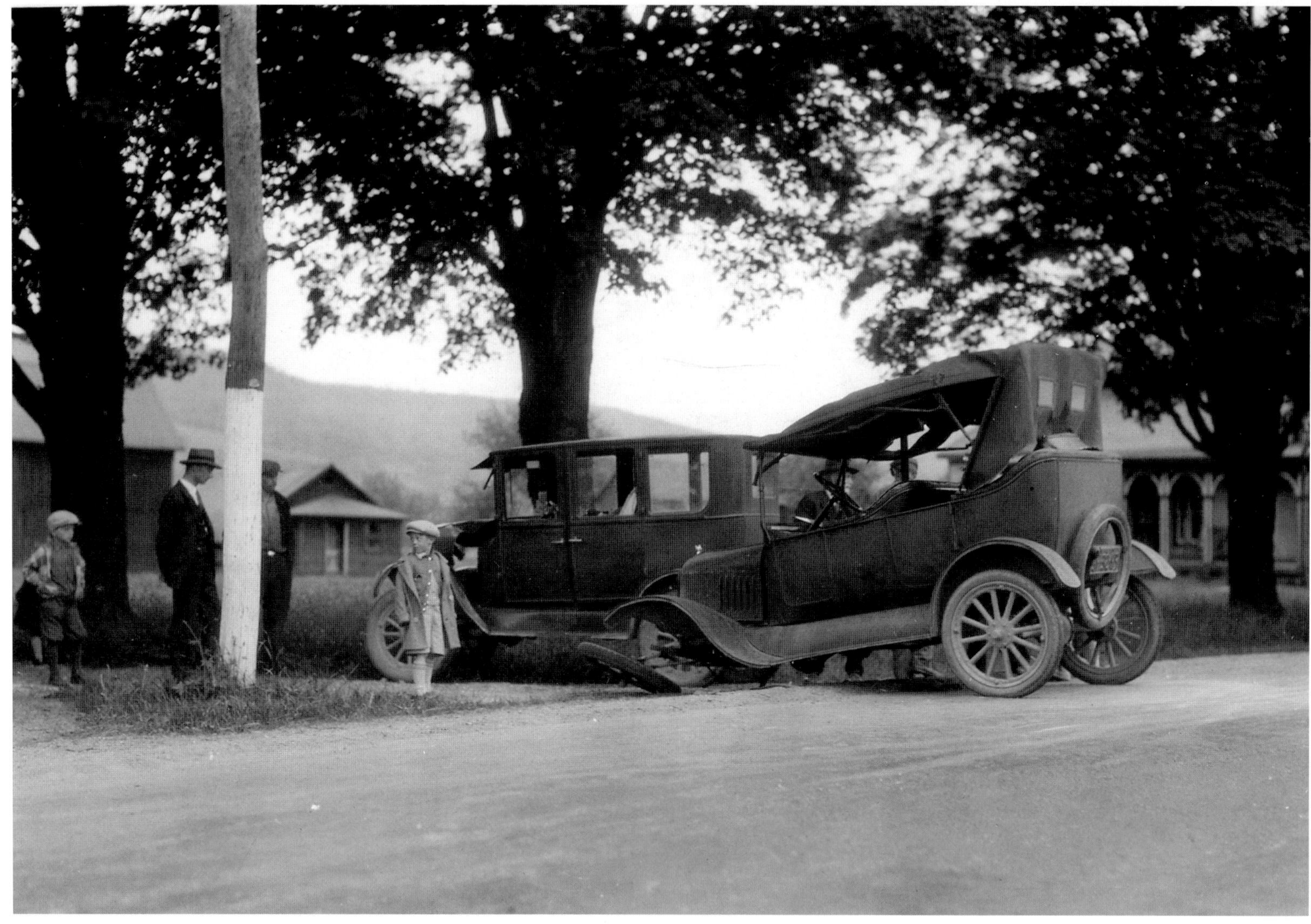

The village of Sidney is located in the foothills of the Catskill Mountains along the banks of the Susquehanna River. Here in 1928, on smooth asphalt pavement, an automobile accident has taken place, apparently a rear-end collision. The foothills are visible in the distance.

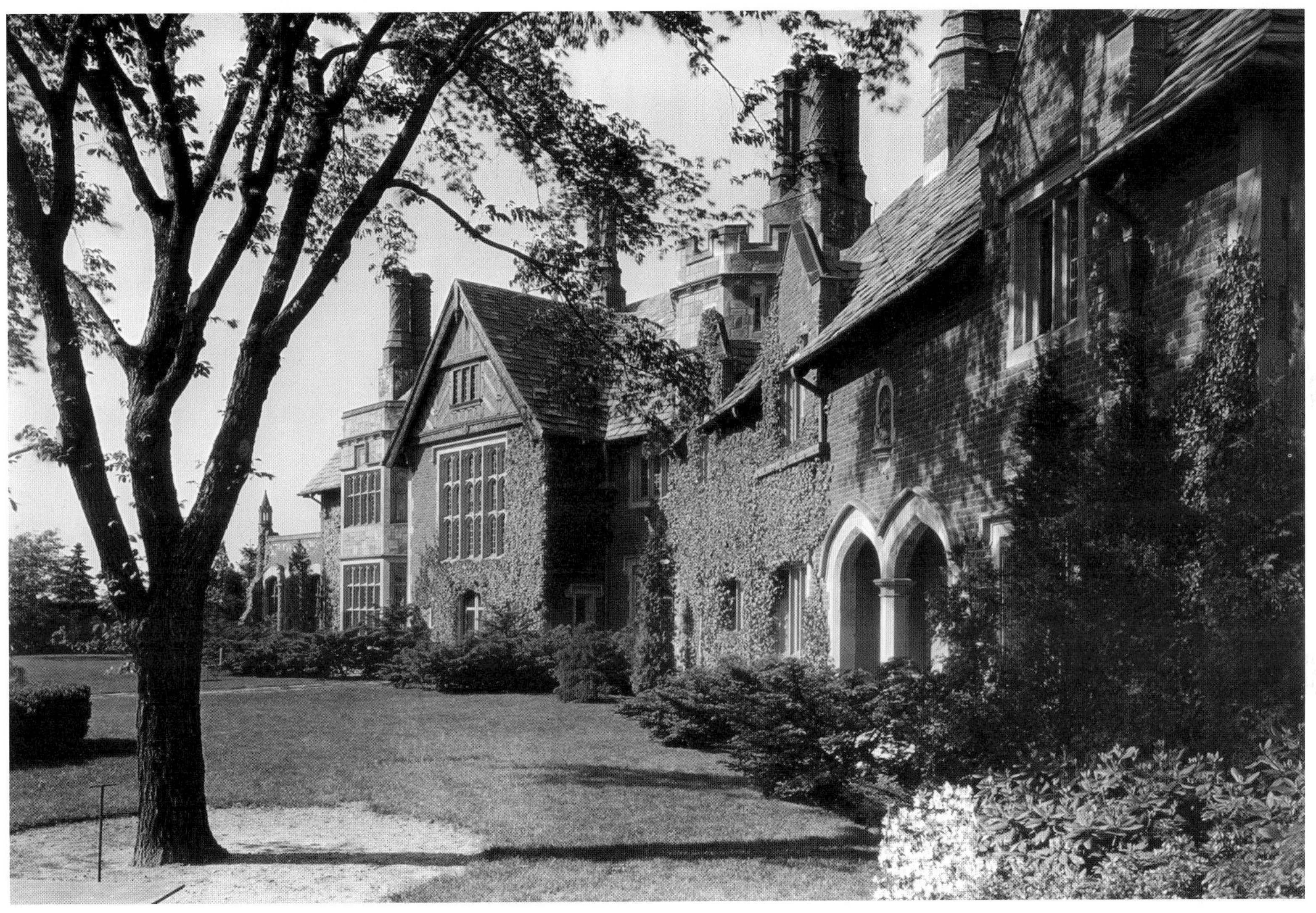

Robert Law (1852–1912), a wealthy resident of Port Chester in Westchester County on the Long Island Sound, built this impressive American Tudor–style mansion in the village. This photograph, made on June 2, 1927, depicts a large, rambling stone house with a double Gothic-arched entrance and elaborate stone chimneys.

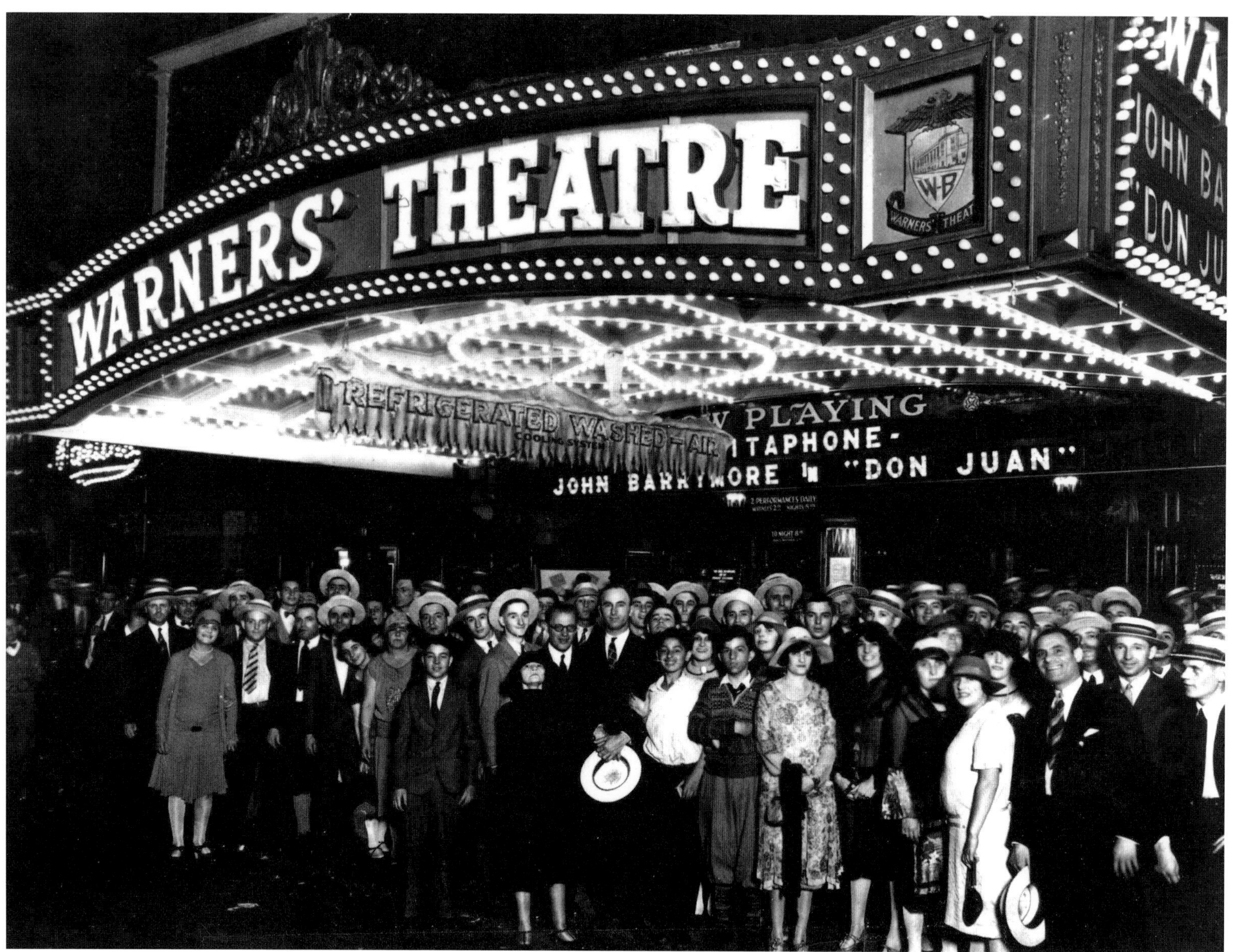

On the evening of August 6, 1926, a large crowd gathered in front of Warners' Theatre in New York City to watch the premier performance of *Don Juan* with John Barrymore in the title role. Warner Brothers owned the theater from 1926 to 1952, when it was demolished. In the silent movie, John Barrymore plays two parts: the aging father betrayed, and the indoctrinated son.

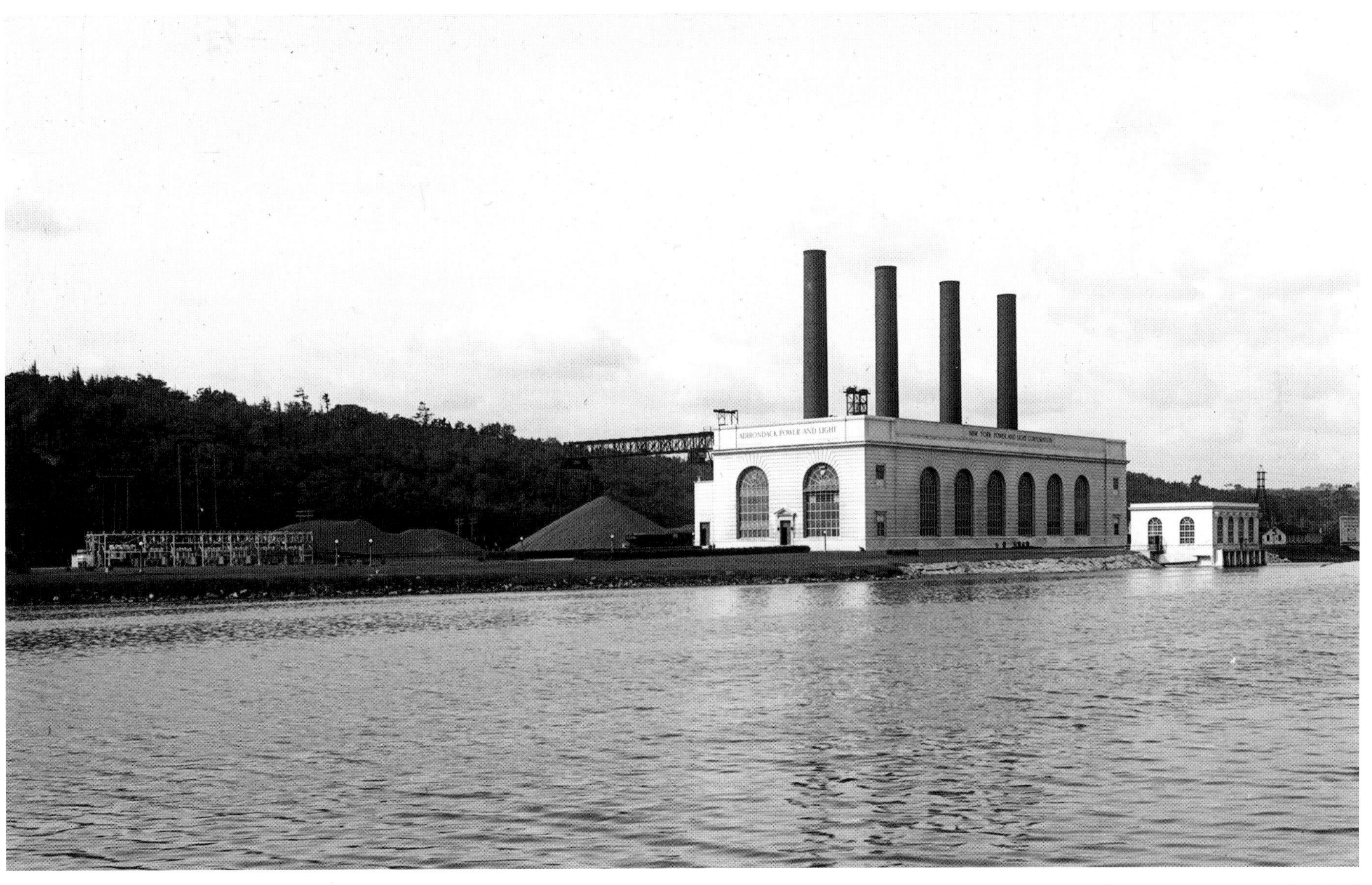

By 1928, when this photograph was made, electricity had become available for residential and industrial use. Manufacturing, which had depended on waterpower, especially in Amsterdam, now obtained electricity from this New York Power and Light Corporation steam-electric power plant on the banks of the Mohawk River east of Amsterdam. The largest carpet-manufacturing plants in the country, Bigelow-Sanford and Mohawk Carpet, were located in Amsterdam.

The German ocean liner SS *Bremen* was noteworthy for its low streamlined profile and speed, which enabled the ship to cross the Atlantic in five days. The *Bremen* made its maiden voyage to New York City in July 1929, beating all records with a total crossing time of 4 days and 18 hours. New York gave the crew a ticker-tape parade down Broadway. This image shows the motorcade drowning in white ticker tape and confetti as crowds extend greetings.

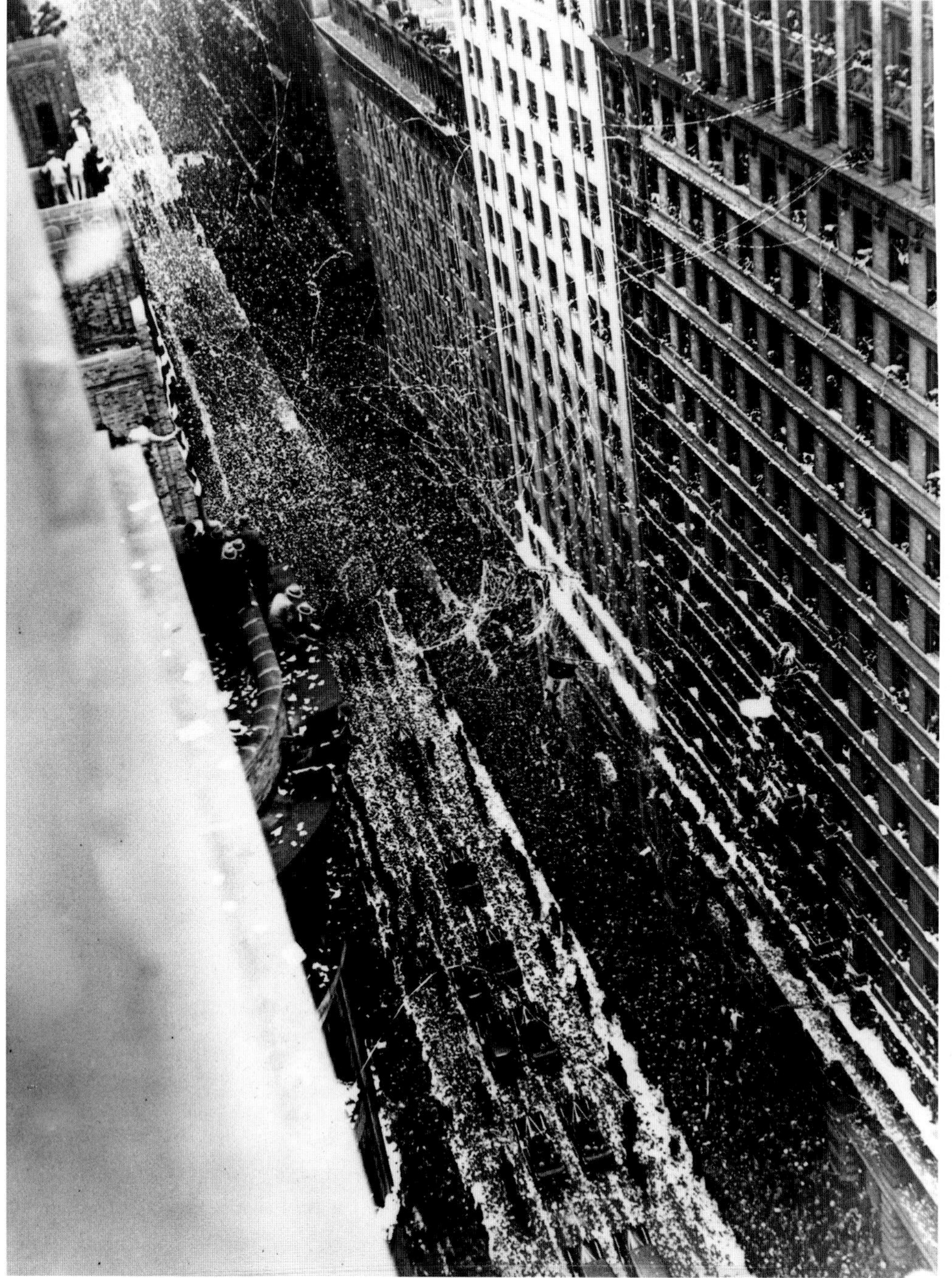

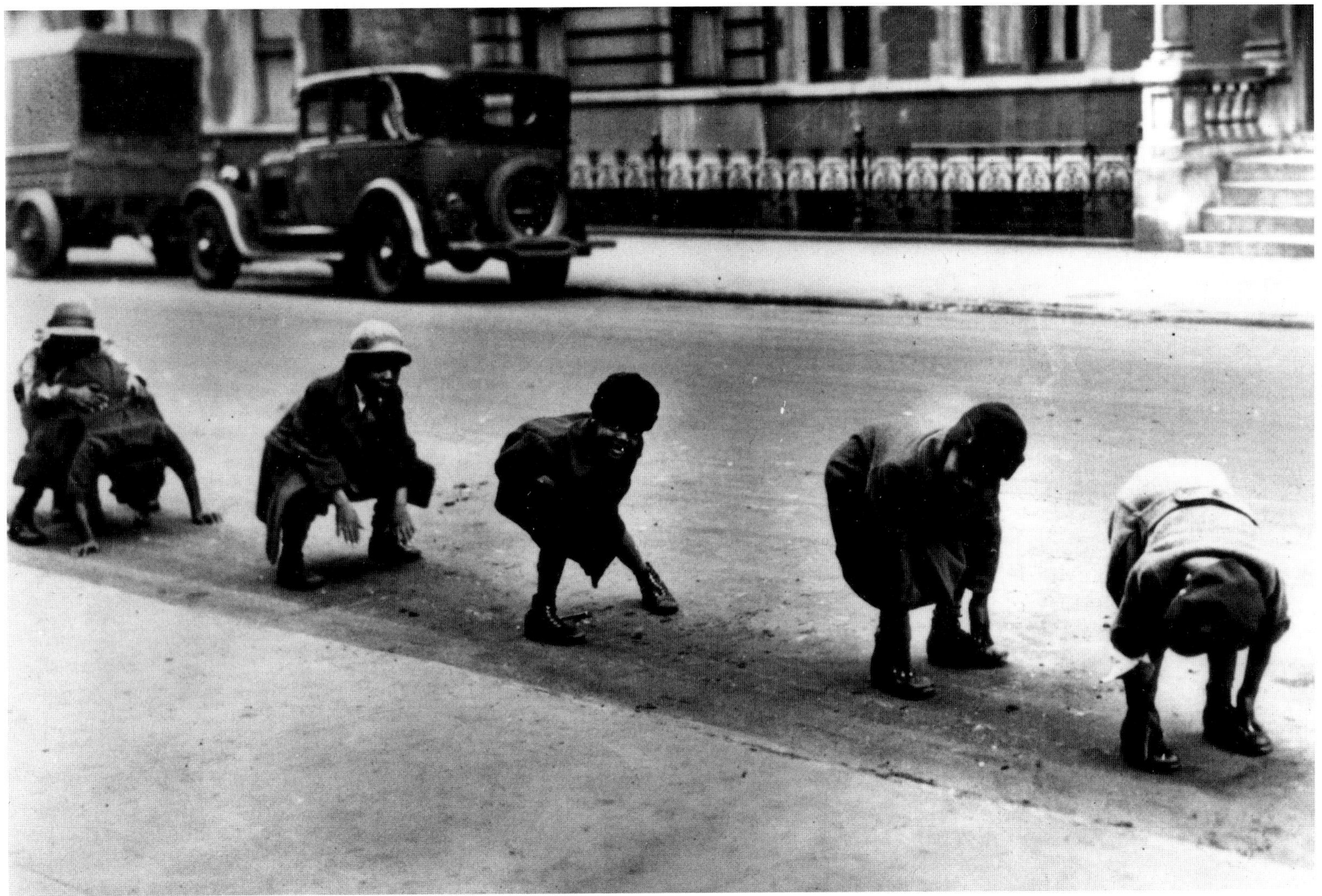

The Great Depression was hurting the American economy in 1930, but children don't worry as much about those things. One day that year, neighborhood children joined forces for a game of leapfrog on a meticulously clean street in Harlem, Manhattan.

In the 1850s, Richard Upjohn, America's foremost architect of the Gothic Revival style, designed this church, Christ Episcopal, at 187 Washington Street in Binghamton. Upjohn designed many churches in New York State, but he is most famous for Trinity Church at Wall Street and Broadway in Manhattan. Pictured here is the sanctuary of Christ Episcopal Church, with its high, pointed arches, creating the soaring space for which Gothic Revival structures are noted.

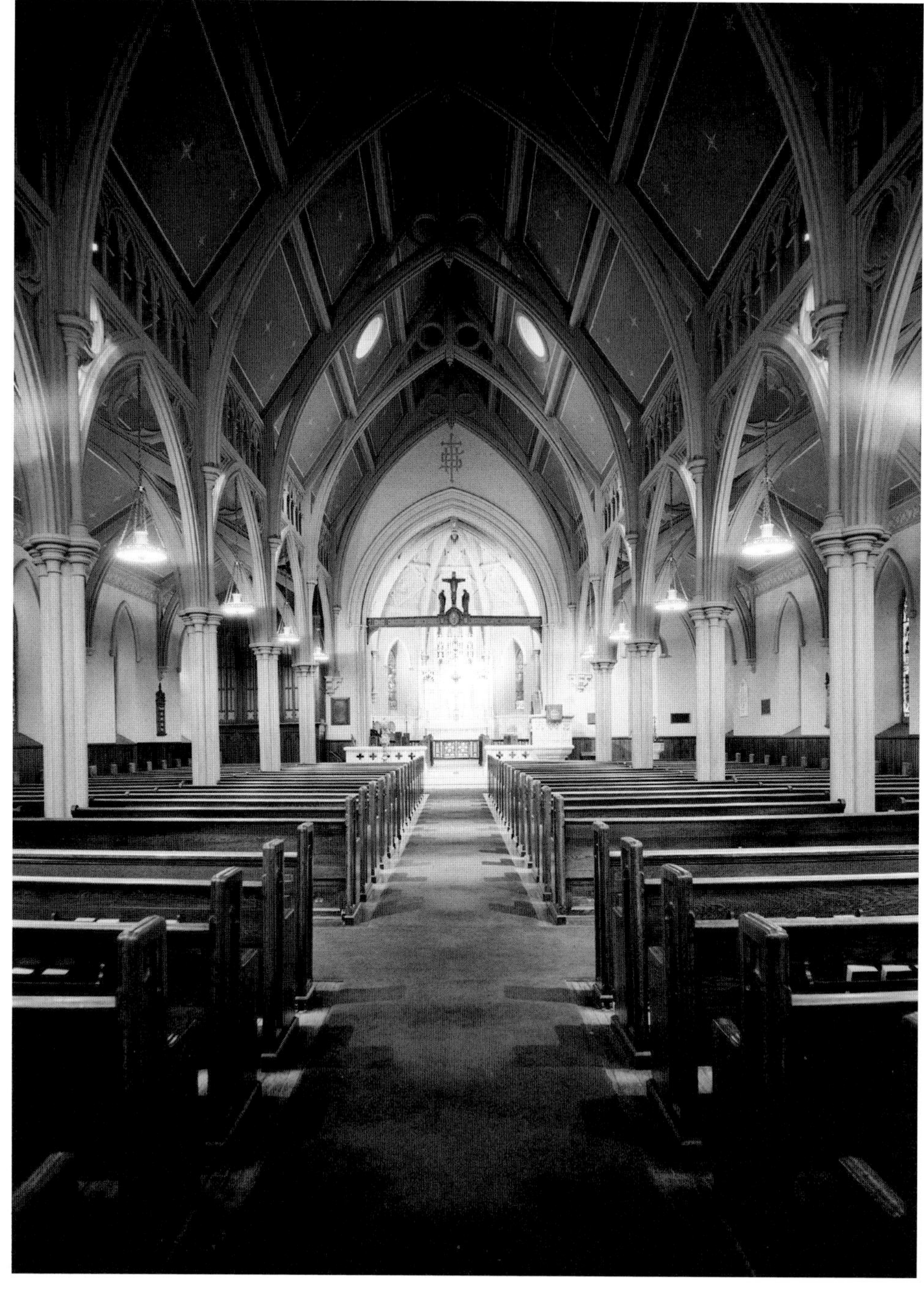

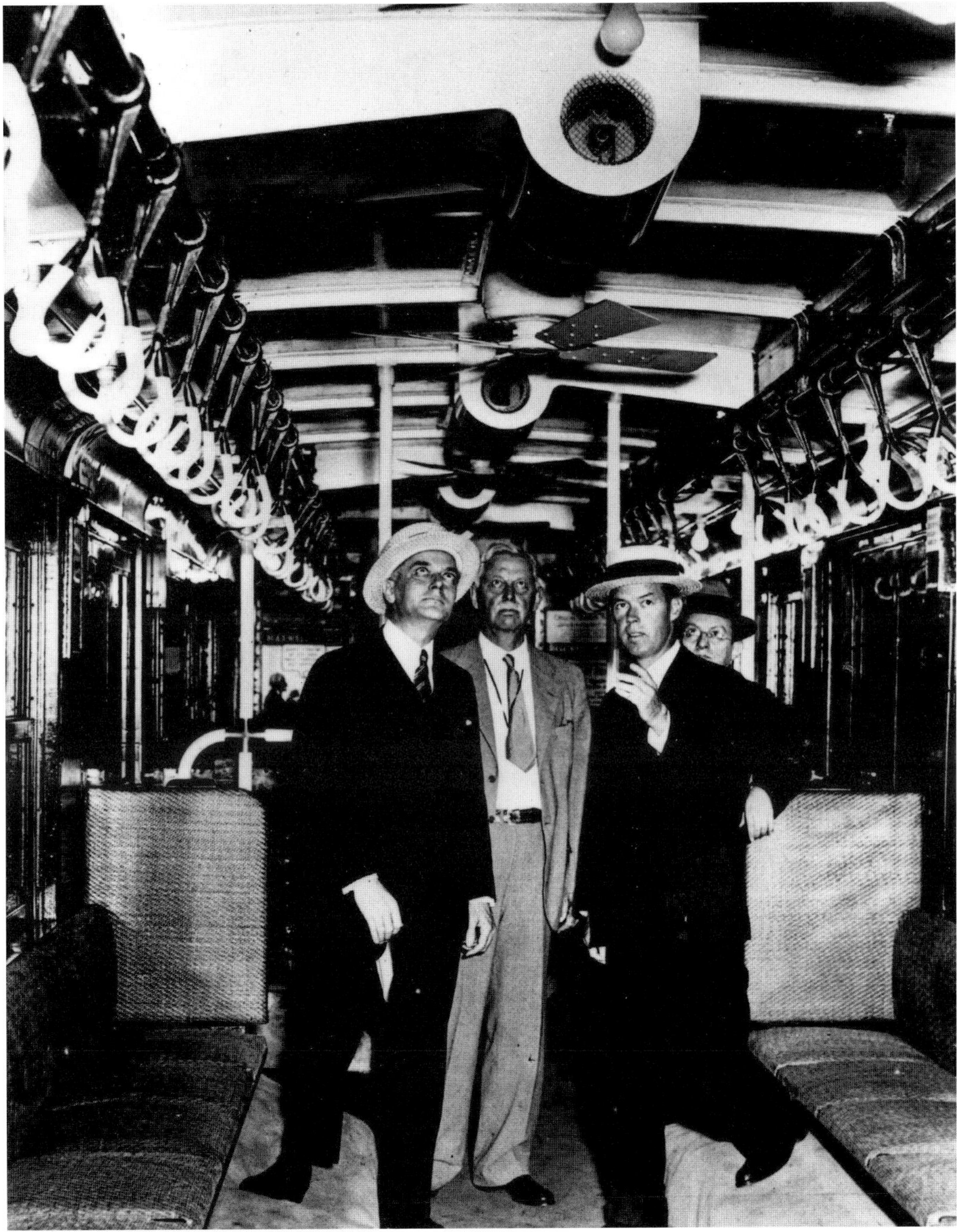

This is a New York City subway car photographed in 1933. City officials are shown inspecting the newly installed ventilating system, visible at the top. The ventilating devices introduced and circulated outside air when the subway car's windows were closed. Still in use today, the subway system dates to 1904.

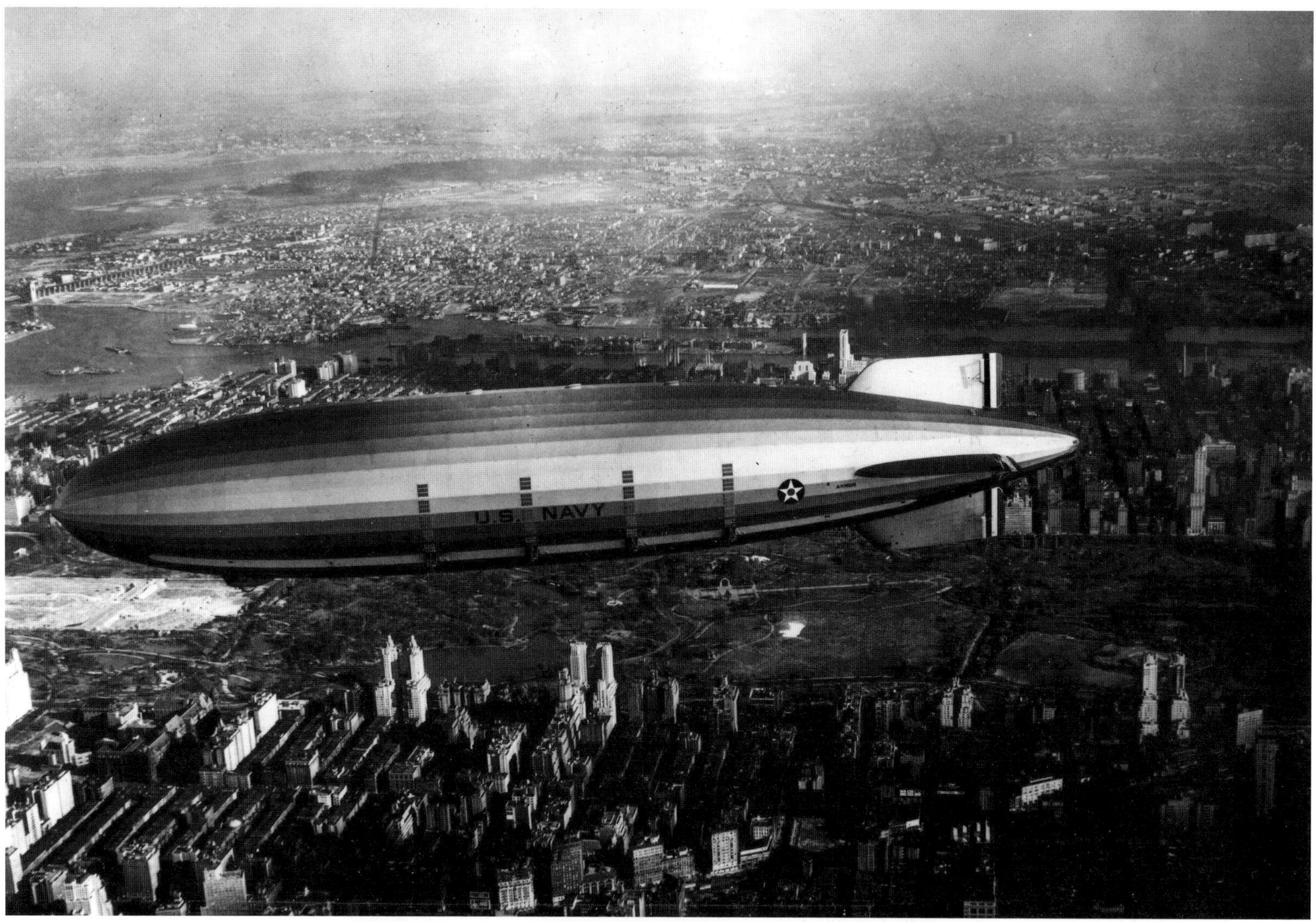

In 1931, the U.S. Navy built a giant dirigible called the *Akron.* Up to that time, a variety of materials had been used for the skin of airships, including the intestines of cattle. On the look for a better material, the Navy asked Goodyear-Zeppelin to develop a substitute. The result was a cotton fabric treated with gelatin-latex to give it superior strength. The USN *Akron* is seen here in 1932 flying over New York City. Manhattan landmarks are visible beneath the airship, including Central Park's Lake and Sheep Meadow.

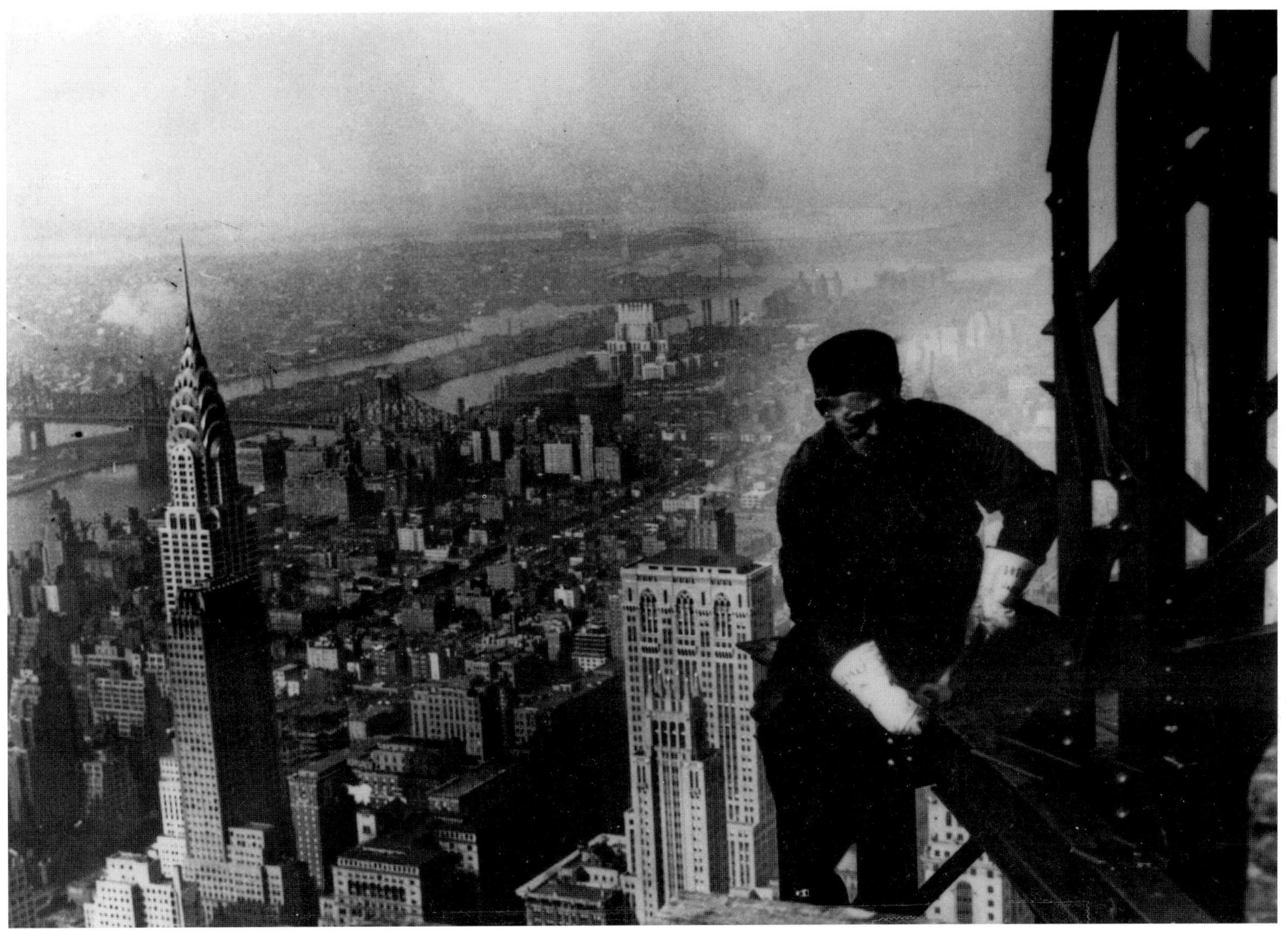

In 1930, Lewis Hine was asked to photograph the construction of the Empire State Building, named for the moniker of New York State. He spent two years following the vertical progress of the tall structure, fearlessly climbing the building along with the workers. This workman is perched on the end of a beam bolting together steel framework. At left is the Chrysler Building, which was the tallest building in the world (1,046 feet) in 1930—a claim it relinquished to the Empire State Building (1,250 feet) in 1931.

Notes on the Photographs

These notes, listed by page number, attempt to include all aspects known of the photographs. Each of the photographs is identified by the page number, a title or description, photographer and collection, archive, and call or box number when applicable. Although every attempt was made to collect all data, in some cases complete data may have been unavailable due to the age and condition of some of the photographs and records.

II **Niagara Falls, 1911**
Library of Congress
LC-USZ62-93766

VI **The Lake, Central Park, 1904**
Library of Congress
LC-USZ62-94238

X **Accident at Niagara**
Library of Congress
LC-USZC4-4771

2 **Fredricks' Photographic Temple**
National Archives
208-PR-4K-001

3 **Governors Island**
National Archives
111-B-4804

4 **Band of the Eighth, 1861**
Library of Congress
LC-B8184-4545

5 **Metropolitan Fair**
National Archives
111-B-1937

6 **Nineteenth-century Artist Studio**
National Archives
111-B-2029

7 **Early Visitors to Niagara Falls**
National Archives
111-B-2163

8 **Grand Union Hotel at Saratoga Springs**
Library of Congress
LC-DIG-stereo-1s01726

9 **Irving's Sunnyside**
Library of Congress
LC-DIG-stereo-1s01728

10 **Vassar College, at Poughkeepsie**
Library of Congress
LC-USZ62-97790

12 **Liberty Enlightening the World, 1886**
Library of Congress
LC-USZ62-19869A

13 **Winter Camp in the Adirondacks**
Library of Congress
LC-USZ62-98542

14 **Niagara Falls Frozen**
New York State Archives
NYSA_A3045-78_D47_
NiG88

15 **Glens Falls Town Square**
Library of Congress
LC-USZ62-42232

16 **Library Interior at Albany State Capitol**
Library of Congress
LC-DIG-ppmsca-15347

17 **Thomas Indian School Girls at Table**
New York State Archives
NYSA_A1913-77_B1_F1

18 **Herald Square, 1895**
Library of Congress
Library of Congress
LC-USZ62-94716

19 **Tree Planters on the New York Central**
New York State Archives
NYSA-14297-87_1657

20 **The Conference House at Staten Island**
Library of Congress
LC-USZ62-64166

21 **Tugboats at Grant's Tomb**
Library of Congress
LC-USZ62-110717

22 **Broadway, Saratoga Springs, 1890s**
New York State Archives
NYSA_A3045-78_D47_SbB

23 **At Inspiration Point, Catskill Mountains**
New York State Archives
NYSA_A3045-78_D47_CcI3

24 **Manhattan El, 1895**
Library of Congress
LC-USZ62-96201

25 **Battle of Johnstown Historical Marker**
New York State Archives
NYSA_A3045-78_D47_
JhG_full_jpg

26 **John Brown's Grave, North Elba**
Library of Congress
LC-USZ62-93540

27 **Hamburg Streetcar**
Library of Congress
LC-USZ62-90134

28 **Onondaga Street, Syracuse**
New York State Archives
NYSA_A3045-78_D47_
SyB8

29 **Ice Palace at Niagara Falls**
Library of Congress
LC-USZ62-107533

30 **Roycrofters at Work, 1900**
Library of Congress
LC-USZ62-90618

31 **Scene at Roycroft Campus, East Aurora**
Library of Congress
LC-USZ62-90617

32 **Oswego Lighthouse and Port**
Library of Congress
LC-D4-12161

33 **Lackawanna Ore Works**
Library of Congress
LC-USZ62-111697

34 **Thomas Indian School Boys at Harvest**
New York State Archives
NYSA_A1913-77_B4_103

35 **Adirondack Open-sided Cabin**
Library of Congress
LC-USZ62-135811

36 **Fishing Boat and Crew at Port**
National Archives
22-CG-269

37 **Hoffman Island Immigrants, 1901**
Library of Congress
LC-USZ62-124474

38 **Roosevelt at the Ansley Wilcox House, 1901**
Library of Congress
LC-USZ62-96529

39 **Easter Sunday on Fifth Avenue, 1900**
National Archives
30-N-18827

40 **Harlem River Regatta**
Library of Congress
LC-USZ62-124583

41 **Pan-American Exposition, Buffalo**
Library of Congress
LC-USZ62-112750

42 **Angler's Paradise**
Library of Congress
LC-USZ62-98718

43 **Smithtown Watermill**
New York State Archives
NYSA_A3045-78_D47_SmM

44 **The Dakota, New York City**
Library of Congress
LC-USZ62-101590

45 **The Palisades, 1903**
Library of Congress
LC-USZ62-119398

46 **Albany City Hall**
New York State Archives
NYSA_A3045-78_Dn_AkH

47 **Eymard Seminary Baseball, at Suffern**
Library of Congress
LC-DIG-ppmsca-18394

48 **Dreamland, Coney Island**
Library of Congress
LC-uSZ62-116412

49 **Dreamland, Coney Island, no. 2**
Library of Congress
LC-USZ62-115624

50 **Erie Canal at Syracuse**
Library of Congress
LC-DIG-det-4a12105

51 **Silver Bay at Lake George**
Library of Congress
LC-USZ62-127531

52 **Bird's-eye View of Utica**
Library of Congress
LC-USZ62-105643

53 **USS Plunger**
Library of Congress
LC-USZ62-89935

54 **Empire State Wine Company Vaults**
Library of Congress
LC-USZ62-91921

55 **Sylvan Beach at Oneida Lake, in the Finger Lakes**
Library of Congress
LC-USZ62-116331

56 **Profile Rock at Little Falls**
National Archives
208-LU-35WW-9032

57 **Trinity Church, Manhattan**
National Archives
208-LU-36B-002

58 **Port of Buffalo**
Library of Congress
LC-USZ62-111698

59 **Visitors at Goat Island, Niagara Falls**
Library of Congress
LC-USZ62-107049

60 **Stony Brook**
Library of Congress
LC-USZ62-117344

61 **Fifth Avenue, at St. Patrick's Cathedral**
National Archives
208-EX-237-001

62 **Macy's**
Library of Congress
LC-USZ62-123584

63 **Manufacturing at Troy**
Library of Congress
LC-USZ62-96094

64 **The Chautauqua Assembly**
Library of Congress
LC-USZ62-115140

65 **New York City Widow and Children**
Library of Congress
LC-DIG-nclc-05349

66 **Rochester Snow Frolics**
Library of Congress
LC-USZ62-135334

67 **New York to Paris Auto Race of 1908**
Library of Congress
LC-DIG-ggbain-00153

68 **Union Depot, Saranac Lake**
Library of Congress
LC-D4-71219

69 **Saranac Lake Midwinter Carnival**
Library of Congress
LC-D4-36985

70 **Farmhouse near Herkimer**
Library of Congress
LC-USZ62-112796

71 **Schenectady Newsies**
Library of Congress
LC-DIG-nclc-03457

72 **Greenwood Lake at Bellvale Mountain**
Library of Congress
LC-USZ62-95803

73 **Buffalo Vocational School Class**
New York State Archives
NYSA_A4199-78_B1_001

74 **Country Lane near Stone Ridge**
New York State Archives
30-N-6004

75 **Young Patient at Sea Breeze Hospital, Brooklyn**
Library of Congress
LC-USZ62-124114

76 **Remington Standard Typewriter Plant, 1911**
New York State Archives
NYSA_A3045-78_8676

77 **Crescent Athletic Club of Brooklyn**
Library of Congress
LC-USZ62-111277

78 **Shower Baths for Horses**
Library of Congress
LC-USZ62-99958

79 **Lake Champlain from Mount Defiance**
New York State Archives
NYSA_A3045-78_764

80 **Atwood Takeoff near Nyack**
Library of Congress
LC-USZ62-100393

81 **Fire at Dreamland**
Library of Congress
LC-USZ62-101974

82 **Scene at Jamaica, Queens**
National Archives
30-N-7747

83 **Hippodrome Chimp**
Library of Congress
LC-USZ62-112118

84 **Whiteface Mountain**
New York State Archives
NYSA_A3045-78_Dn_AW36

85 **Hotel Ausable Chasm near Keeseville**
New York State Archives
NYSA_A3045-78_Dn_Av2

86 **New York City Stevedores**
National Archives
69-R-1K-002

87 **Boy Scouts in the Bronx, 1912**
Library of Congress
LC-USZ62-107478

88 **At the Races, Saratoga Springs**
Library of Congress
LC-USZ62-120652

89 **Quaker Ridge Railroad Station at New Rochelle**
Library of Congress
LC-USZ62-94026

90 **Thousand Island Fishing**
New York State Archives
NYSA_A3045-78_A10097

91 **Houdini in New York Harbor**
Library of Congress
LC-USZ62-66403

92 **Manhattan Suffrage Demonstration**
Library of Congress
LC-USZ62-110997

93 **Newton's Garage, Lake Ronkonkoma**
Library of Congress
LC-USZ62-94999

94 **Brooklyn Trolley Excursion**
Library of Congress
LC-USZ61-663

95 **Toymakers at Work, 1915**
Library of Congress
LC-USZ62-113568

96 **Turtle Bay, Manhattan**
Library of Congress
LC-USZ62-137886

97 **Barroom of the Arion Society Club**
Library of Congress
LC-USZ62-75570

98 **Knitting Inmates of Sing Sing, at Ossining**
Library of Congress
LC-USZ62-98906

99 **The Jennie McGraw Tower at Cornell**
Library of Congress
LC-USZ62-116666

100 **The Senior Parlor at Vassar**
Library of Congress
LC-USZ62-100847

102 **Nyack's South Broadway**
Library of Congress
LC-USZ6-2071

103 **Officers in Training at Plattsburgh, 1917**
Library of Congress
LC-DIG-hec-07336

104 **Pageant Rehearsal at Huntington**
Library of Congress
LC-USZ62-136038

105 **First Ambulance Company of New York National Guard**
Library of Congress
pan 6a30023

106 **To Wall Street for War Bonds**
National Archives
165-WW-240F-001

107 **White Plains Rally**
Library of Congress
HAER NY-327-96

108 **The Langley Night Bomber**
Library of Congress
LC-USZ62-100390

109 **East River Battleship Escort**
National Archives
208-LU-36N-001

110 **Actors' Strike, 1919**
Library of Congress
LC-B2-4997-10

111 **Camp Ranachqua near Narrowsburg**
Library of Congress
LC-USZ62-130733

112 **Ellis Island from the Harbor**
Library of Congress
LC-DIG-npcc-00224

113 **Immigrants at Ellis Island, 1923**
National Archives
90-G-885

114 **National Park Bank, Manhattan**
Library of Congress
LC-USZ62-124927

115 **Albany Along the Hudson**
Library of Congress
LC-USZ62-113326

116 **Fifth Avenue, 1921**
National Archives
30-N-23555

117 **Parachute Jump at Buffalo, 1922**
Library of Congress
LC-USZ62-99494

118 **Conan Doyle and Family with a New York View**
Library of Congress
LC-USZ62-98125

119 **Haverstraw Brickmaker**
Library of Congress
LC-USZ62-94329

120 **Canal Junction at Waterford**
New York State Archives
NYSA_A3045-78_Dn_Bc42

121 **Snows of the New York Public Library**
National Archives
306-NT-609K-020

122 **Collision at Sidney**
National Archives
30-N-35-726

123 **Port Chester Mansion, 1927**
Library of Congress
LC-G612-T-07295

124 **Now Playing at Warners'**
National Archives
208-LU-28N-001

125 **Mohawk River Power Plant near Amsterdam**
New York State Archives
NYSA_A3045-78_Dn_M5

126 **Broadway Ticker-tape Parade, 1929**
National Archives
306-NT-958J-001

127 **Leapfrog in Harlem, 1930**
National Archives
306-NT-171611

128 **Christ Episcopal Church, Binghamton**
Library of Congress
HABS NY,4-BING,10-7

129 **New York City Subway Car, 1933**
National Archives
306-NT-671-001

130 **Zeppelin over Manhattan**
National Archives
80-G-458713

131 **Empire State Building Under Construction**
National Archives
69-RH-4K-001